SADIST IN SEQUINS

By Adrian Street

Copyright © 2012 Adrian Street. All rights reserved. No part of this publication may be used or reproduced in any manner whatsoever without written permission of the publisher, except in the case of brief quotations embodied in articles and reviews.

Contact Information:

U.S. Mailing Address:

Adrian Street
1496 Oak Drive
Gulf Breeze, FL 32563

Email: daffodil777@bellsouth.net

Website: http://www.bizarebazzar.com

ISBN-13: 978-1477695180
ISBN-10: 1477695184

Cover:
Top: Giles EX -Waterboard Boss and pneumatic Drill operator O'Bryan with Adrian.

Bottom: Adrian bridges out of trouble from Johnny Saint in The Eldorado.

DEDICATIONS:

To my Father & Arch Nemesis - Your constant opposition guaranteed my success.

To my Mother - Without you I may never have been born.

To My Sister Pamela's LOVE.

To My Brother Terence's LEFT FIST.

To Linda, the love of my life, who is and always will be the very best part of my journey of a Lifetime.

To Jean for producing such beautiful Kids.

To Adrian, Vince, Amanda, and Natasha - who are the beautiful Kids.

To Russell Plummer for your great stories in 'The Wrestler.'

To 'Wresting Heritage' & 'Wresting Furness' whose Great websites have immortalized 'THE GOLDEN AGE OF BRITISH WRESTLING'.

To Victor Rook whose advice and book 'Musings of a Dysfunctional Life' inspired me to complete my own stories.

I will be eternally grateful to those who told me I could do it. - And even more grateful to those who told me I couldn't.

I want to pay a SPECIAL tribute to every wrestler I shared the ring with. Friend or Enemy. You all taught me the lessons I needed to reach the top. I couldn't have done it without you.

INTRODUCTION

My book has been self written and self edited - there maybe mistakes - the only time I spent in Oxford or Cambridge was when I wrestled there. Throughout my life I have always done things one way - My way. - So for better or worse, This is my story.

SADIST IN SEQUINS

I'm a Sadist in sequins, I injure and grin.
A Sadist in sequins, so don't let me in,
or you're gonna find out that you'll never win,
I'm a sadist in sequins evil as sin.
A turn on for me is a scream or a howl.
When handing out violence I know every foul,
so don't take me lightly, or things could get hard,
I used to give lessons to The Marquis De Sade.

It was inevitable now that I was wrestling for all of Joint Promotions that my path would cross with my biggest enemy in the Golden Age of British professional Wrestling, the Lightweight Champion of the World, George Kidd. It was an aggravating mystery why he hated me so much. But it was no mystery why I hated him, his refusal to wrestle on the same shows as me had cost me many matches and money. I only hoped that he wouldn't exert his power to cost me more matches and money now that I was wrestling in the big time. Ah well - only time would tell.

THE WELSH WIZARDS

I wrestled in Morecambe for Relwyskow against fellow countryman Tony Charles who had beefed up tremendously, and now wrestled in the Light-heavyweight, and even in the Heavyweight division. The extra size did nothing to hamper his speed, stamina, and explosiveness. Tony was a human dynamo, he hit me with a flying tackle that was so devastatingly powerful I felt as though he had knocked my entire skeleton right out of my body, and the impact knocked me completely out of the ring. As I began to climb painfully back into the ring, I found that even though my body felt shattered my brain was working overtime, and I came up with a great idea right there and then.

"Tony," I suggested after the match was over, and we were back in the dressing room, "as we are both from Wales we should become Tag-team partners, we could call ourselves 'The Welsh Dragons'."

The tag-team craze had hit Britain and had really taken off, although all the veteran heavyweights hated it,

"Bloody tag matches are gonna kill this business!" they'd grumble, "after the fans get used to that, what else are they going to be able to show them in order to top tag-matches – feed Christians to the fuckin' Lions?!"

"Why not Heavyweight Wrestlers?!" I suggested. What the heavyweights really didn't like about tag-team wrestling was that tag-team matches would usually be Main-Event, even if they were only comprised of lesser lightweight contestants. That could drop them into the semi-main event slot, which meant a lighter payday. As a result in the belief that it would be very difficult for a single match to follow a tag-match, tag-matches were traditionally always the last matches of the night.

I had wrestled in a number of tag-team matches before, but with any odd partner that may have been available, rather than a regular partner as many other wrestlers had done. Many had become established teams, and bore fancy names like 'The Black Diamonds', 'The White Eagles', 'The Hungarian Horsemen',

'The Magyars', 'The Cadman Brothers', 'The Royal Brothers', 'The Cortez Brothers', 'The Borg Twins', 'The Flying Scotts', and so on and so forth. Mick McManus, in his wisdom, or because he had a weird sense of humor, had eventually teamed me up with 'Gentleman' Jim Lewis, better known to all wrestlers as 'The Grey Rat' when I wrestled for Dale Martins – and I was furious! I went over McManus' head and marched into Jack Dale's office,

"Jack," I demanded, "I don't want to be teamed up with 'Gentleman' Jim Lewis!"

"OH! And why not?" he wanted to know.

"Come on Jack," I told him, "I'm barely in my twenties and he's got to be a hundred and ten - I dress like a Prince and he dresses like a Tramp!"

"You've both got blond hair." Jack observed gleefully.

"I've got blond hair," I agreed, "but 'Gentleman' Jim's hair is a dirty, yellow gray - what are you going to call our team," I asked him, "Old Mother Reilly and Kitty McShane?" At that Jack laughed until he cried, but agreed that I would no longer be partnered with 'The Grey Rat' after I had partnered him in the upcoming matches that were already in print.

Tony Charles agreed that our tag-team partnership was a great idea, and so did the Northern Promoters. But instead of titling our team 'The Welsh Dragons' as I had suggested they dubbed us 'The Welsh Wizards', as they always had to have the last say. Okay – I could live with that, at least if Tony was my tag-partner he wouldn't ever be my opponent, and therefore my skeleton would once more be comparatively safe within the confines of my own body.

Whether the Heavyweights liked it or not the Tag-team craze was here and was here to stay. But another phenomenon hit Britain with the impact of 'The Norman Conquest of 1066' almost exactly 900 years later, and it was in the form of another invasion – from the same neck of the woods, when The wrestlers from France arrived in force. Just like driving on the wrong side of the road, French wrestlers worked on the opposite side of the body. When two British wrestlers came to grips, and they took a hold on an arm or a leg of their opponent, unless he took both arms or both legs, he would only take the left. The French, probably for no other reason than the fact that they were French, always worked on the right. Now, as awkward as that may have been, that was not the main cause of our concern. What did concern us was the style of the French 'CATCH LUTTES' that they employed in the ring. It was so fast, and so acrobatic, that most of it seemed to take place in a blur about 10 feet above the ring. When two French wrestlers met in British rings the audience exploded, as they had never seen anything like it before – and neither had we. We would all gather outside the dressing room, and watch in utter dismay as these French acrobats cart-wheeled, somersaulted, spun around each other. They'd leap-frog over each other, run around the ropes which they bounced off, catapulted off, somersaulted off, and did things off the corner-posts that defied both description and gravity. We were confident that the British Heavyweights would be unable to follow a match between two French acrobats, because we knew that even we British Lighter-weights couldn't follow them either. BUT, for once the British Promoter's chronic meanness worked in our favor, as in most arenas, with the exception of the big spectaculars, there would only be 4 matches on each night's card. Therefore all the matches were at least 30 to 45 minutes long, and sometimes even longer. In France there may have been 7 or more matches on a card, with the result most of the matches there, would only last about 15 to 20 minutes, or less, in which time the French wrestlers/acrobats could pull out all stops. In Britain when these same wrestlers had to wrestle 2 or 3 times longer each match, it completely threw off their timing. Even though their repertoire was extremely extensive, when they normally did so much in such a short space of time, they soon ran out of things to do. Most especially during the much longer British matches, and had to repeat their sequences. Even more to the point, they were also used to completely exhausting themselves in 15 minutes, and now they had to struggle through at least twice that length of time. So from a contest that began by blowing the roof off the building, it would gradually become more repetitious and slower and slower as the French contestants began to run out of steam, and the action would all but ground to a halt. It soon seemed to be a matter of familiarity breeds contempt. The crowd soon adjusted to the unusual speed, and the French wrestlers were so preoccupied with concentrating on what they were going to do next, they had sacrificed drama for speed. They didn't even give the British audience a space in time when they could clap, cheer and generally show their appreciation. So even though their athletic prowess and fantastic gymnastic skills were quite mind-blowing, it fortunately didn't really gel with a British audience who had been educated for decades in good Old Fashioned British style Wrestling. Then when a French wrestler was pitted against a British wrestler, as awkward as it might prove to be for the Britishers who were used to working on the left side of the body, it would prove to be equally awkward for the French who were used to working on the right. But what really brought them down to earth – literally, was in order to show off their acrobatic aerial type maneuvers to their best advantage, you needed both contestants to be versed in that style. If another wrestler either couldn't, or didn't want to engage in that sort of warfare, it couldn't possibly work. Even more so, if they were pitted against a British wrestler who firmly believed that as our sport was called 'wrestling', then wrestling is what you did in the ring rather than pirouette in space. So then the 'Flying French Aerialists' found that due to the very bad weather conditions that existed in British wrestling rings, it often kept them well and truly grounded.

So both British Heavyweights and Lightweights breathed a collective sigh of relief when the great 'French Invasion scare' turned out to be no more than a false alarm.

****

I knew full well, now that I was wrestling regularly in Scotland, that my path would eventually cross with that of the World's Lightweight Wrestling Champion George Kidd. I was sitting in the dressing room in Hamilton Town Hall, when the great Man himself walked in. A look of distaste contorted his features as our eyes locked. I don't think he really recognized me immediately, but as my identity slowly dawned on him his countenance grew darker still. He looked away from me and began talking to George De Relwyskow, and didn't even glance in my direction again for the rest of the night. He began telling jokes to all the other wrestlers, but not before making an obvious show of turning his back on me and shutting me out of his little circle of laughing wrestlers. George Kidd and I hadn't set eyes on each other since that first and only time in the Caledonian Baths more than half a decade earlier, but whatever was eating him then it seemed was gnawing at him still, whatever it was, was still a complete mystery to me, but,

"Bollocks to him!" I thought. I wrestled in the second match, George was on third, and he began telling jokes again as soon as his match was over, and he had re-entered the dressing room. Once again he made a deal out of turning his back to me, and excluding me from his circle. But I laughed, and George's circle laughed even more than they had at all his jokes when we all watched the aftermath of the last match. It was a Tag-team contest between the dastardly English 'Cadman Brothers' and Scotland's own, 'The Flying Scotts'.

Not content with merely vanquishing the Scottish team in their own back yard, The Evil Cadmans, Alf and Ken, taunted the disgruntled and disappointed crowd unmercifully. They were both standing in the middle of the ring daring anyone in the audience to enter and get a taste of what they had just dished out to the 'Flying Scotts'. Well no one accepted their challenge by stepping into the ring, but one Scottish Lady who had been booing their skullduggery from the top balcony 30 feet above the ring, became so incensed that she hurled a 4-pound Christmas pudding, which landed right on top of Alf Cadman's head and knocked him spark-out.

"How-d'yer like a taste of that," she hollered, – "Happy Christmas!"

NAUGHTY ART

The next time Mickey Muldoon came to visit, he brought with him a huge stack of photographs. Some were of drawings that were in the form of stories similar in style to comic books, but mostly they were photographs of a foursome of real people. The only person I recognized was his Wife, Sandra. There was also another Girl with blond hair and two men, Tony and Andy. Tony was married to the blond whose name was Pauline. Pauline was getting it from all directions, while Sandra merely posed on the sidelines whilst watching the other's antics. I eventually learned that although Sandra was Mickey's self proclaimed top porn Star, she was only allowed to pose and look sexy in the photos that he took, but under no circumstances was she allowed to touch or be touched. She was simply in the picture as extra decoration. I also eventually learned that Sandra resented those rules with a passion, but she was married to a very jealous Man with a very nasty temper.

Mickey left all the photographs with me, as inspiration he said, as he wanted me to illustrate short stories that comprised of 10 pictures each, which he would then photograph, reproduce by the hundreds and sell to his various customers, which included the scores of Soho Bookshops. Mickey had offered me one pound for each drawing I produced, which added up to 10 pounds a story, needless to say my pencil-sharpener was soon working overtime. I didn't want or need Mickey's photographs, so the next time I visited John Graham to get some publicity photos taken, I took them with me to give to him in trade. When I arrived, I handed him the stack of photos, he just glanced at them then immediately handed them to a friend of his who had been sitting and drinking coffee as I walked into John's studio. John introduced me to his friend whose name was Jimmy, and explained that Jimmy was an avid collector of anything and everything pornographic. He possessed a collection of photographs that probably numbered in the tens of thousands. Jimmy appreciated his new acquisition with so much enthusiasm that I promised to get him some more when ever I received any from Mickey.

****

The 'Welsh Wizards' partnership did evolve into a magical combination, although not without a certain amount of drawbacks, for myself especially. In many arenas I was slowly but surely beginning to be regarded as the 'Bad Guy'. Not that I was a rule breaker, it was more to do with my flashy ring wear, and arrogant attitude, coupled with my vicious and aggressive wrestling style. In complete contrast Tony Charles was always regarded as the 'Good Guy', crisp, precise, clever combination wrestling, but with a much more modest presentation than yours truly. Tony's Good Guy' image did tend to bathe me in a more lovable role when we were partnered together, but not without me at least retracting my horns a little, which in itself cut across my natural grain. By this time I had discovered that my best weight was 165 pounds, which was heavy enough to show plenty of muscle, and light enough for me to exercise plenty of speed, agility and flexibility. Tony also possessed most of those qualities, but he was 3 inches taller and usually hovered a little over the 200 pound mark. In those days Joint Promotions attempted to keep the bodyweight of anyone below the heavyweight division fairly evenly matched in single matches. But in tag-team matches the weight of one team might differ enormously from their opponents. One night we could be pitted against a team like the Borg Twins, who probably never weighed any more than about 150 pounds apiece during their entire wrestling career. The next night we could be wrestling against a couple of big heavyweights. When Tony and I wrestled against a very large heavyweight team, it naturally made more sense for me, being the smallest to play the fall guy, and Tony would play the Cavalry. I would get double-teamed by both big guys, which would hopefully elicit a huge amount of sympathy and concern for my welfare. I may begin the match by using my super speed and agility to avoid being crushed by our huge adversaries, and gaining a few clever advantages, until the enemy exercised some foul trap which would lay me low. Then after being beaten unmercifully for some unspecified period, which would usually lead up to me losing the first fall, I would then have to continue the match and be beaten to the very brink of defeat. Bruised and battered, I would try again and again to reach my partner's outstretched hand in order to tag myself out of the ring and my fresh partner in, where everyone knew he would begin exacting brutal revenge on his poor, partner's sadistic persecutors.

Being the fall-guy and the elicitor of sympathy may have made more sense, but that didn't make it any more palatable to someone like me. I was far more comfortable alternately showing off, and trampling all opposition into the canvas.

Outside the ring, I had always got on extremely well with the Irish 'Donleavy Brothers', Seamus and Mike, but inside the ring was a much different story. Seamus was by far the better wrestler. Mike was the smaller of the two, but still outweighed me by about 40 pounds. I liked Mike but in the ring I found him stiff, clumsy, uncoordinated and very flighty, but as long as I kept moving and kept my wits about me, I was able to manage him handily. Whenever big Seamus tagged in, I would give him 'that look', give the audience 'that look' as though to acknowledge the huge size difference between us. then I'd shrug indicating that discretion is indeed the better part of valor, and promptly tag myself out, and the much larger Tony in. Eventually, when once again I found myself sharing the ring with the mighty Seamus, I would decide to throw caution to the wind, and attack. Then in respect to a big heavyweight, when he grabbed hold of me and lifted me above his head prior to body-slamming me, I purposely made myself as light as possible, and leapt as high as I could in order to aid him, and make him look even more powerful than he really was. Normally such a gesture would be greatly appreciated by an opponent. But I should have remembered that the big, heavyweight wrestlers, had big heavyweight egos, and sharing the ring with someone who was so much smaller did nothing for an ego that needed constant fanning. Seamus slammed me so hard into the mat, that it was absolutely incredible that it didn't break every board in the ring floor, and every bone in my body! All the air whooshed out of me, I thought I was totally paralyzed. When I was able to move, I looked over at my partner, but instead of the look of horror and concern I expected to see etched on Tony's face, I saw that the only thing that prevented him falling off the ring apron with laughter, was the tight bear-hug he had on the corner post. It was only pure indignation that made it possible for me to drag my broken body close enough to Tony, and tag him in. And then crawl up the ropes that supported me while I gingerly tested the very few parts of my anatomy that still had any feelings left in them, other than extreme agony. I totally ignored a full half dozen of Tony's attempts to tag me back in, as I strove to recover from the damage inflicted by Seamus. When I did, and once again found myself facing the big Irishman, I was not so polite as I had been in our first encounter.

'We've shown the fans your power', I said to myself, 'now let's see how you cope with my speed', and I spent as much time as we had left in the contest making as big a fool out of Seamus as I possibly could.

You would imagine after a lesson had been learned, especially a lesson that had been learned so painfully, that I would have wised up somewhat, but as I may have already mentioned a score or so times, I do tend to be a slow learner. I couldn't have demonstrated that fact more proficiently than I did a short while later when 'The Welsh Wizards' were pitted against 'The Silent Ones', Harry Kendal and Mike Eagers.

They were called 'The Silent Ones' as their only gimmick was the fact that they were both Deaf. I never thought that the title suited them at all, as although they were deaf, they were certainly not dumb, and would yap as much as any wrestler that I had ever met, and that is really saying something! Harry Kendal held many amateur titles before turning professional including two Bronze Medals from the Empire Games. His partner Mike Eagers, was extremely popular with the wrestling fans, and possessed a charisma that almost equaled a pre-Blood-Boots version of Leon Fortuna.

It was an unwritten law that wrestlers didn't steal, or should I say, 'emulate to closely', a special hold or move, that had been perfected by another wrestler, and was considered that particular wrestler's speciality. I re-christened Mike 'Mick the nicker', owing to the fact, that not only did he blatantly nick every special hold or move that took his fancy, but had the audacity in most cases, to perform them better than the originator.

Mike was quite a bit taller than me, but not very much heavier and I was able to dominate him easily if I chose to. Harry on the other hand was 6 feet tall and weighed in the region of 220 pounds, so to begin with, purely for cosmetic appearances I avoided coming to grips with the much bigger man. When at last I did, the first move deaf Harry attempted was a Body-slam, and once again, in order to emphasize his size and power, I made myself as light as I could. I leapt as he lifted, which resulted in me being easily hoisted to finger tip height above Harry's head before he slammed me back down to the ring with all the force his 220 pound body could muster. Well Harry was deaf and couldn't hear what I called him, but he could lip read very well, and as a result must have deduced that he was not anywhere close to being voted first place for my most favorite person Award. I lay there in agony, and would have lay there till our team had been counted out, if not for the fact that Tony was just able to reach my hand from where he stood on the ring apron and tagged himself in to take over.

Not only had Harry slammed me down ridiculously hard, but he had also made a very sloppy job of doing so, and had landed me on one side of my hip and that caused a very severely trapped sciatic nerve. As a professional wrestler I had suffered a trapped sciatic nerve many times before, but never as bad as it was this time, I could barely stand up, let alone walk, or wrestle. Back in the dressing room, Harry looked concerned as I limped painfully out of the shower room, but then as wrestlers did, laughed his head off as he apologized. He then put on a pair of glasses that I had never seen him wearing before; the lenses must have been half an inch thick. I spitefully asked him if he was going blind in order to develop a new wrestling gimmick, as if just being deaf wasn't enough. It probably was a cruel remark, as even some of the piss-takers in the room cringed visibly and remarked,

"Shit! That was a bit strong wasn't it?!" But Harry laughed until the tears ran in torrents from under his thick goggles. When he was once able to simmer down enough to put a decipherable sentence together, he asked me if he could give me a lift back to London to make up for the pain and suffering he had caused me. I did have a return train ticket, but I knew that even after waiting for ages at the station for my train, it wouldn't arrive in London until early hours of the next morning. Then I would have to make my way from the London Station all across London to get home with an excruciatingly painful hip. So very slightly pacified, I accepted Harry's kind offer, and it was then that the real pain and suffering really began in earnest.

At that time, the Gravelly Hill Interchange, better known as 'Spaghetti Junction' which bypassed Birmingham didn't exist, and in order to reach London from the area in Lancashire where we had been wrestling that night, we had to pass right through the middle of Birmingham. It was extremely easy to get lost driving through Birmingham in those days, but after making that journey so many times, I knew the best route very well indeed. Unfortunately Harry didn't – he only thought he did!

The first time he made a wrong turn, I gave him a poke to get his attention and pointed back up the street to indicate the way he should have gone. Harry shook his head and said he knew where he was going. I thought he might know a better way, but it certainly didn't look right to me – it wasn't, very soon, I too didn't have a clue where we were. The pain in my hip had already began to stress me out long before Harry got us lost, in the cramped up confines of his car I didn't know how the Hell to sit to try to give myself some relief. If I had only used my train ticket, at least I could have stretched out the full length of one of the seats, and would have been much more comfortable, even if I did get back to London hours later. Eventually Harry would come to somewhere I recognized, and as Harry couldn't hear me, or read my lips in the dark, I would hit him to get his attention, and point the way we should go. But Harry would rarely agree with my assessment, with the result we would very soon become once again hopelessly lost. I wonder if you can possibly imagine how bloody frustrating it was, wanting to get back home after being away for a week. Traveling with someone who can't hear your directions, or complaints and won't go the way you direct him to, on the rare occasion you recognize where you are. He can't hear me cursing him for all I was worth when we pass the same point we did an hour or more before, and another hour or so before that, while being in so much pain that you don't know how to sit, or what else to do with yourself?!!!!! Even the thought of traveling in Dale Martin's dreadful transport would have been like riding in Cinderella's Coach compared with this, it seemed like a terrible nightmare that I couldn't wake up from. 'If there was a special Hell for wicked wrestlers, this was it'. I thought. Well eventually I did get back home – about a couple of hours later than I would have, if I had returned to London by train!

****

As a result of my supplying him with stacks of new photos to add to his ever growing collection, John Graham's friend Jimmy and I had also become good friends. Jimmy lived a short distance down the road from Wood Green Underground Tube Station, and had offered me the use of his premises any time I wanted to take the kind of photos he collected, when ever I began taking pictures for Mickey Muldoon.

By now Mickey and I had fallen out over the drawings I had been supplying him with. Apparently all his customers were demanding more and more, but had requested more contrast than a photographic reproduction of a pencil drawing afforded, and had suggested Indian ink as an alternative. That was bad enough, as the only time I had ever used Indian ink, was for the drawings I used to do for the History Class when I was still in school, and it was a medium I didn't much like. What really brought matters to a head was Mickey bringing all the sets of drawings around that I had already drawn for him, and asking me to ink them all in. I asked Mickey how much he was going to pay me for inking them all, and he suggested that I could do them for nothing. I explained to him that in the time it took me to ink in all the drawings that I had already drawn in pencil, I could have drawn as many pictures again, which I would be paid for. That pissed Mickey off, so I suggested that as he was also an excellent artist, and if he wanted to save money by not paying me to work on them, that he should do them himself. Mickey said I was a money grabber, and I suggested that he was too. He went in a huff, but was back within the hour with another business proposition, he wanted me to take photographs for him. For that Mickey told me he would pay me 10 pounds for each roll of 35mm film that I shot for him. Getting Girls to pose for photos was easy; all I had to do was ask. Mickey suggested that I pay my models one pound each, for each roll of film they posed for. I preferred taking photos of just one girl on her own for a number of reasons. First and foremost, if there was only one model in the photographs, there would only be one model to pay, which meant more profit for me. Secondly, it was a personal preference, as I have nothing at all against naked or scantily clad Ladies, but can't say the same about naked, or scantily clad Men.

Later the same day that I had finally arrived home after that nightmare journey back to London with Harry Kendal, I hobbled off to the nearby Brockwell Park in an attempt to fix my badly trapped sciatic nerve. Peter Rann who suffered a lot with that complaint had given me an exercise that usually worked for him. It comprised of standing on one leg, and kicking sideways from right to left for a number of repetitions with the other, then swapping legs and repeating the exercise in the opposite direction. That worked for me occasionally, but what I found more effective, even if it was also more painful, was to run in Brockwell Park. Although Brockwell Park wasn't huge, it was big enough, and had great pathways that had steep grades and lots of bends, some hairpin. Once I got going I would be running up, down, straight, and flying around corners. I would have to force myself to begin with; biting my lip and pushing the pain to some hidden corner of my mind, and eventually the pain in my hip would ease considerably. The cure for the majority of our wrestling injuries was, if you got something knocked out of place one night, you'd get back in the ring the next night, and hopefully knock it back in again. After much pain, gasping and sweating, I began walking back home in a much more sprightly manner than the way I had limped to the Park an hour or so earlier. Then as I was passing the Grocery Shop that was just around the corner from where I lived, a Girl staggered out of the Shop, under the weight of a small mountain of grocery bags. At first I didn't recognize her, or she me, but suddenly the penny dropped for both of us,

"Hello Adrian." She said.

"Hello Sandra." I replied. I had less excuse than she did for not recognizing her immediately, as Mickey Muldoon's Wife Sandra, was a very dominant figure in most of the photographs that I had received off Mickey. I offered to carry her very extensive array of heavy grocery bags and as I took them I said,

"Damn somebody must be hungry!"

"Its Mick," she told me, "he wants to bulk up to 15 stone."

"Why would he want to do that?" I asked her, "He looks fine as he is."

I didn't get an immediate reply, as Sandra's attention was elsewhere – and when she did answer she said,

"Fuckin' Bollocks, - look at the fuckin' prick on that Dog!"

"Er – ah – what?!" I spluttered. I wouldn't have been more shocked if someone had jumped out of one of the doorways we had been passing, and hit me in the chops with a plank. My first impression of Sandra had been that she was a very quiet and shy girl. I looked in the direction that she was staring in, and there indeed was a huge Dog attempting to mount a Bitch about one third its own size.

"Go and get it!" Sandra demanded, "We'll take it home with us!"

I was so astounded by Sandra's behavior that for once I was unable to respond with a witty retort that I was famous for,

"Why would you want to do that? – The fucking thing is filthy." I replied lamely, as nothing more appropriate came to mind.

"We can put it in the bath first," she insisted, "Mickey won't know, - he won't be home for ages!"

"I won't have time," I lied, "I've got to leave for a wrestling show in about 15 minutes." I added, actually I was wrestling in Brighton that night, and had a few hours before I had to be at the office. I didn't know if Sandra had been serious about kidnapping the Hound or not, the fact that she'd even thought about it shocked me, but that was just the beginning. I was soon to discover that I had more than met my match when it came to someone who would say – or do most anything to attract attention. Unfortunately where Sandra was concerned this included stirring the crap, and causing as much trouble for friend and foe alike, as long as it made her the centre of attraction.

As a member of the Wrestling Fraternity, I was used to World Class 'Shit Stirrers', but when it came to stirring shit Sandra could have given the most tainted and talented in my profession advanced lessons.

POUR MOI

Having refused to learn any languages other than English, when I had attended Grammar School, I wouldn't have even known what 'Pour Moi' meant, but that wouldn't last, especially if your opponent happened to be French. The moment you stepped inside the dressing room, your French opponent would be right in your face, telling you what he wanted to do to you during our contest. He would explain exactly what you were supposed to do, in order to aid him execute as much of his extensive aerial acrobatic repertoire as he could possibly squeeze into the allotted time you were to spend with him in the ring. His role was Superstar; your role was to make him look as fantastic as you possibly could, even if you make yourself look a total twat in the process – yeah, right, - not in my backyard mate!

"Pour moi ---" he would begin.

"What?!" I'd reply.

"Pour moi --- er – ah, 'for me' – first I headmare you in the middle of the ring – we? – An' then as you get up, I catch you with the flying head-scissors – we? An' then – pour moi – pour moi – pour moi" – and so on and so forth. Eventually I would point a finger at myself and ask politely,

"Oh we! – And what about POUR MOI, POUR MOI, MON AMI?!"

For that I'd get – how can I say? – Not exactly a blank look, more an expression that said,

'Do you REALLY think we'll be able to do everything that I want to do to look marvelous, and still have time for a little 'pour moi' for you?!" – HO-HUM!

Although I am not in the least bit superstitious, there were many in my business that were, it was the 13th of December and 'The Welsh Wizards' were going up against the French duo of Billy Catanzaro and Vassilious Mantopolous in Leeds Town Hall.

Billy Catanzaro was quite a bit bigger than me, and looked a bit dozy, Vassilious Mantopolous was a bit smaller, but looked great, he had been both Middleweight European Champion and Mid-Middleweight European Champion, which was a new one on me. I entered the dressing room, and had no sooner put my kit bag down and said,

"Hello." To Tony Charles, when both Catanzaro and Mantopolous descended on us, but a few 'pour mois' later Tony just sighed and walked out of the dressing room without agreeing with one of them. That left me standing in semi bewilderment between the two overly eager Frenchmen getting 'pour moi' loud and clear in stereo. It was obvious that Tony had already decided that he wasn't going to co-operate, but I thought I might give the French style a try. When Tony walked back into the dressing room and observed that I was now getting 'pour moi' in stereo on steroids, he just gave me that look, shook his head and chuckled. I took that gesture as a challenge, and became determined to show Tony that I was up to emulating anything the French team threw at me, and then some. I did have a few more reasons for playing their game other than merely showing off for Tony's benefit, and they were that I was always on the lookout to learn something new. My own variation of some of their moves might make a flashy addition to my own wrestling arsenal, and last but not least, if I were ever to wrestle in France, being proficient in their style in advance could prove to be very advantageous.

By now the French team seemed to have lost sight of the fact that they were competing against the Welsh team, as they were now in hot competition with each other as to who was going to get the most and best 'pour mois' into the match, with me playing the foil for both of them. As bewildering as it was fast becoming, I was determined to jump in with both feet, and graduate in the French style with flying tri-colors.

"Pour moi – I take you in a head-lock – we?! – An' then you throw me into the ropes – we?! – I then bounce off the ropes – we?! – I jump over you – an' run across the ring – we?! I charge you – an' you leap-frog over me – we?! – then we crisscross an' pour moi – I catch you with two flying head scissors – we?!" and on and on and pour moi and on! No sooner had I absorbed a long sequence of future events from one of my opponents, than the other would run through yet another sequence that he wanted to perform that was longer, more elaborate, and much cleverer than the one I was still attempting to get my head around. Well there was going to be leapfrogs by the dozen, crisscrosses by the score, flavored with somersaults, back-flips, front-flips, nip-ups, dropkicks, flying head-scissors, and aerial gliding galore, with hardly a 'pour moi', pour moi. 'Nevertheless, it would be good experience pour moi.' I thought. Well that WAS what I thought!

Both our teams entered the ring to a fanfare befitting our international Main-event status, the Leeds audience was beside themselves with pent up excitement and anticipation. Everyone, especially me, was anxious to get the match started as soon as possible – especially as I had an awful lot to remember. At last the bell rang to begin the action – and action there was, by the truckload. We must have resembled Gibbons on speed, all the acrobatics I alluded to and more had the Lancashire fans screaming to full lung capacity, and I was there matching the French aerial experts somersault for somersault, back-flip for back-flip, leap-frog for leap-frog and crisscross for crisscross.

After a particularly prolonged sequence of acrobatics, seldom witnessed outside a World Class Circus, I took advantage of the resulting uproar of approval from the fans to give my partner Tony Charles a smug look of triumph. The second that look took, was a second too long, Vassilious Mantopolous had entered the ring, and was determined to top the climax that his partner and I had just achieved, and was already charging like a mad Rhino in my direction. Ha! But I recovered, and was ready - a split second before he crashed into me, and with the aid of the most powerful legs, pound for pound in the whole World of wrestling I exploded skywards. I expected my opponent to charge straight between my legs – BUT – one of us - probably me, had got the sequences mixed up. Vassilious had also leapt high into the air before me – and to cut a very short story even shorter, he was on his way down, as I WAS VERY MUCH ON MY WAY UP!

SMASH! The top of my head EXPLODED right under the Frenchman's chin with all the force of a nuclear rocket. With the result he did an unscheduled backward somersault with all the grace and co-ordination of a double-jointed marionette with seven broken strings.

'SHIT – THAT WAS A POUR MOI' I thought, but not one that Mantopolous would be happy with, my intuition proved to be correct. Vassilious was not pleased, in fact he was so distressed that he began to display a complete lack of judgment. After dragging himself out of the corner where he had landed with an uncharacteristic lack of grace and coordination, he grabbed hold of me in a choke-hold and attempted to strangle me. I countered by grabbing hold of one of his fingers and almost pried it off his hand; he countered by smartly tagging himself out of the ring and his eager, action starved partner in. Billy Catanzaro was primed up and ready to go, he grabbed me, bounced me off the ropes as he whispered,

"Crisscross." But I had other things on my mind, I ran across the ring, bounced off the opposite ropes, ran between Billy's legs as he leapt high into the air, then instead of continuing the sequence I continued straight into the Frenchmen's corner and punched Vassilious right in the jaw – and that was the end of that!

Tony and I entered the dressing room from our side of the arena, as the French team entered the dressing room from the opposite side. As soon as he spied me, Vassilious began to scream all the obscenities he could think of, as he marched straight into my face whilst nursing his jaw with both hands. That was a mistake, he made another mistake by leaving the left side of his face unguarded when he began waving his left hand about in order to add emphasis to his complaints, and my right fist exploded right into the large hole in his face that was making all the noise. The Frenchman hit the deck as though he had head butted a Blacksmith's anvil. His jaw was smashed, whether I had broken it accidentally when I jumped into the air, instead of running between his legs. Or when I punched him to end the match, or after we entered the dressing room I don't know. But it was only Tony Charles' timely intervention when he hurled himself between me and the prone Frenchman that prevented me from stomping on Mantopolous' upturned face. Well that and the Tarzan like yodel from George De Relwyskow as he screamed across the dressing room,

"Noooooooooooooooo!!!"

What I soon learned was that George De Relwyskow was anything but pleased that he had paid the fares from France, and had Vassilious Mantopolous billed in Main Events all over his territory only to have him demolished first night out – OOH LA-BLEED'N-LA! I'm pretty sure that if I hadn't been Relwyskow's tenant he would have probably fired me on the spot.

****

I had been taking photos for Mickey for a while, mostly at Jimmy's house in Wood Green, which soon resulted in a number of adjustments. At first I was using my own female models and Mickey's male models, Tony and Andy, but after a very few sessions I was told by Mickey that I would need to recruit my own male models. This surprised me, as it was Mickey himself who had offered their services in the first place, in order for them to make some extra money, and at the same time put a dent in my preference to only use Ladies in the photos I took.

I never did learn whether Jimmy was queer or straight, but at this time there was a guy named Danny living in Jimmy's house who openly claimed to be bi-sexual. Danny was a Submarine Sailor, but was presently AWOL, and basically in hiding. Danny introduced me to a 'friend' named Eric, who had a house next to Streatham Common, which he told me was available any time I wanted to use it for taking photos. As Streatham Common was only a couple of miles away from where I lived, I then began taking photos there instead of at Jimmy's house.

Eric's hair was really very blond, and I was as jealous as Hell, as my own hair was bleached, but I had never managed to get it that shade. Eric offered to do it for me and soon became my hairdresser, it was then thanks to Eric that my hair went from 'just barely blond' to brilliant platinum.

Danny also introduced me to another friend, Brian Epstein who was apparently a frequent visitor to Jimmy's home. Danny told me that Brian had a fondness for men in uniform, and he claimed to be Brian's number one procurer. I told Brian that I had often seen 'The Beatles', who were huge wrestling fans, at Liverpool Stadium. Although, I was too polite to tell him that in those days, I didn't like the Beatles, and had chased them out of the dressing rooms on a number of occasions, when they were there endeavoring to have their photographs taken with some of the good guy wrestlers, which in those days they thought would be good publicity. I was a bad guy in Liverpool and didn't need to be polite,

"Get out of the wrestler's dressing rooms, you long haired Liverpudlian tarts!" I'd shout at them, "I know why you're hanging around here – you're hoping to see Vic Faulkner and his Brother Bert Royal taking a shower!" In fact they did get their photos taken with Vic and Bert, the ultimate good guys. But, it was Jack Pye, one of the dirtiest old time grapplers in the business who was John Lennon's all time personal favorite. I also wondered if the American Wrestling Ballet Dancer, Ricky Star may have had any influence in The Beatles' drummer changing his name from Richard Starkey.

Brian told me that he would get all the Beatles albums for me next time he visited Jimmy, I only accepted them out of politeness, and the fact that Jean liked them. I had already predicted on a number of occasions that the Beatles were no more than a flash in the pan, and that within a very short spell they would be gone and forgotten. I must admit that I got that one wrong, in fact after listening to the albums at home over a period, I soon began to appreciate just how talented and special they were, and as a result became a huge fan myself.

****

Although Mickey Muldoon had two very able and proficient Male Models in Andy and Tony, he was always on the lookout for the All Time Super-stud of the Century. When I told him that Ernie Bishop, who was Britain's answer to the American porn star Big John Holmes, was rumored to frequent 'The Locarno Ballroom' in Streatham, he was intrigued – but not anywhere nearly as intrigued as Sandra was! I don't know whether 'The Locarno' was one of Sandra's favorite haunts before I mentioned Ernie 'Mr. Big-Dick' Bishop, but both she and Tony's Wife Pauline, certainly haunted The Locarno afterwards.

Strangely enough, Mickey's own model Andy could have passed as a younger Ernie Bishop, facially, also with the same blondish hair color, both were very pale skinned, muscular, but almost painfully skinny – except where it mattered most if you happened to be a Pornographic Male Model. Obviously as co-model, Sandra would have been well aware of Andy's outstanding physical endowments. It must have driven her to the very brink of insanity with Mickey's iron rule of you can look, but not touch, whenever they posed together. But, when Mickey wasn't present, Sandra certainly did everything she could to satisfy the hunger that 'a look but don't touch' rule had generated.

As Mickey only lived a couple of minutes walk from me, it was not unusual for me to pop around to his house when I had the time, and help him print the photographs, and then sort them into sets of 5 photos per transparent cellophane envelope, ready for delivery to the various Soho Bookshops. I often found myself alone with Sandra, sorting out Mickey's photos while Mickey was out making his deliveries. In contrast to my first impression of a quiet, shy Girl that I had originally thought her to be, Sandra hardly shut her gob long enough to draw a breath. I felt as though I was her confessor, as tale after lurid tale of her sordid extramarital indiscretions spilled out of her scarlet painted mouth faster than my brain could absorb them.

"Andy comes creeping into my bed every morning as soon as he hears Mickey leaving". She told me, and then goes on to describe a blow by blow of what occurred as a result,

"Every time Mickey turns his back he's right on top of me!" she gloated. I remember asking Andy to confirm Sandra's claim, and after he recovered from the shock that Sandra would confide in someone who was as close to Mickey as I was, he admitted that what she claimed was almost true. The only difference being, that it was Sandra who always crept into his bed every morning, not the other way around as Sandra told it.

Sandra's most outrageous boast was one that I found almost too difficult to believe, and was that during her pornographic posing sessions, when Mickey would be changing the film in his camera, he would go into a corner of the room in order to shield the film from the light. While his back was turned Sandra told me that she would impale herself on anything erect, with any orifice she had available, and only disengage herself a split second before she saw that Mickey was about to turn around. All I can say is that if there was any credence to Sandra's claim, and with everyone being well aware of Mickey's rules and terrible temper, that her antics must have done very little to aid the libidos of Mickey's Male Models.

"That fuckin' Mickey won't buy me a Dog!" she was telling me one afternoon as I was busy sorting out photos and popping them into cellophane envelopes.

"I'm really not surprised!" I replied, remembering the time I had helped her with her groceries.

"The silly fucker had me bent over the back of this chair last night," she continued, while she demonstrated the position she had adopted by all but sticking her buttocks in my face "he tried to make up for it by scratching my back and growling and barking all the time." I thought it was funny, even more so, because she seemed to be so indignant.

"Look at this!" she said suddenly, "the Baby has pissed all over the front of my trousers, it's made my pants transparent, and you can see my cunt right through them!"

She stood right in front of me with her legs spread wide, I looked – and indeed the white pants she was wearing were wet and very transparent,

"Yes, you're quite correct," I agreed, "You can see the lot." Then I looked back at the photos and continued sorting them. I was well aware of what Sandra was attempting to do, but in spite of the fact that she was a very attractive Girl, she held no attraction for me at all. As far as I was concerned she possessed about as much sexual appeal to me as Lon of London would have had. Her Husband Mickey was my friend, and although I would have never have told him what Sandra had told me, I would never have betrayed him myself with the crude and Horney trollop he called his Wife.

****

For the very first time in both our lives, The Lightweight Wrestling Champion of the World, George Kidd spoke to me.

I had been wrestling all over Scotland more and more frequently, and as a result my path had crossed more and more frequently with the Great 'King of Scotland'. On this occasion I was sitting on a table in the middle of the dressing room in Kirkaldy Ice Rink lacing up my boots. While George Kidd with his back turned towards me was telling the rest of the dressing-room's occupants a string of his latest jokes. Even though I was out of his line of vision, as was usual for me when George Kidd was being funny, I wore a sullen mask of bored indifference. Suddenly The World Champion whirled around, and as he stuck his face within a yard of my own, his cold blue-grey eyes bored into mine as he growled,

"Don't YOU laugh at my jokes!"

"I don't think there's much fear of that," I replied, "I haven't heard you tell one yet that's worth laughing at!" I'll admit that, that was a lie, George's jokes could be very funny indeed, but it was easy to appear not amused when you hated the comic as much as I hated George Kidd. George turned back around, and continued entertaining all the other wrestlers; I just continued lacing up my boots, while ignoring the resident entertainer as best I could.

As I confess to my chagrin, George could be extremely funny, but as with so many others in our business, it was only funny to George when he was telling the jokes, and it was not funny at all when he became the brunt of one. As a result there was a wrestler who George Kidd held in even less regard than he did yours truly. The Wrestler who reigned supreme on the very zenith of George Kidd's hate list, was the self anointed 'King of the Highlands' the Scottish Strongman, Andy Robins.

My earliest memory of Andy Robbins was in Winchester, just after I had began wrestling for Dale Martin's Promotions, and Andy was on the same card, making what was for him a very rare appearance south of the Scottish border. The reason I remembered him, was due to the fact that on that night he barred my path as I was about to leave the dressing room for the ring, and demanded to know who had given me permission to wear a white jacket, white boots and white trunks, which he claimed were his exclusive colors. I told him most politely to go and attempt to commit an impossible sexual act on himself, and further explained that although he was older than I, I had been wrestling professionally longer than he had – and that I had been wearing white ring-wear since day one.

"So," I added, "if anyone is stealing anyone's color scheme it's you, not me, who's doing the nicking!"

I estimated at that time that Andy Robbins was only slightly taller than I, and weighed about 170 pounds. But shortly after this encounter, Andy who was also a top Highland Games contestant, left Britain to compete in Canada. By the time he returned to Britain, just a short time later he had transformed himself from a Middleweight, to about 220 pounds of muscle. Speculation was, that while he was in Canada he had discovered the same brand of medicine that had doubled the bodyweight of the 'Gillette-Man' 'Dangerous' Danny Lynch. He also suddenly became much taller, but that was due to his new habit of wearing some very thick padding under his heels inside his wrestling boots rather than a sudden spurt of growth.

The very fact that Andy Robbins was insanely popular with the Scottish wrestling fans, in itself would have banished him from any chance of ever being invited to celebrate Hogmanay at George Kidd's home, but his practice of observing the 12 daft days of Christmas all the year round, definitely put the holly on the Haggis. Not content with all the attention showered on him by all his country's adoring fans, Andy began openly competing with George for attention dominance in the dressing room, Bad mistake. Andy was as strong as an Ox, and almost as smart, and his attempt to match wits with George Kidd, was like a Neanderthal Village idiot armed with a heavy club battling against a Champion Sword-Master armed with a Rapier. Nevertheless, Andy's stupidity and Rhino thick skin, served as a much better defense than his much more intelligent, but thinner-skinned adversary possessed. George Kidd would verbally shred Andy Robbins to Ribbons, Andy would simply respond by chuckling, puffing up his 50 inch chest, flexing his 18 inch biceps and then going into his George Kidd wrestling impersonation.

"Go on take my arm - go on take my leg – HA-Ha – GOTCHA!!!" He'd grunt at his imaginary opponent, as he leapt about the dressing room while he comically aped the Master Grappler's wrestling skills. I must admit that the first few times I had watched his insulting antics, I had found him quite funny. Especially when I observed the discomfort his nonsense caused George Kidd, but after witnessing the very same act over and over for more than a year, even I found it mind numbingly irritating. But, even though the muscle-bound Scotsman's brand of humor lacked even the slightest rudiment of sophistication it still seemed to penetrate very deeply into the tender flesh of the World's Lightweight Champion. Even though Andy's behavior branded him as a total buffoon, it still got him what he wanted - to wrest the dressing room attention from the World's Lightweight King, and onto himself, I repeat - a bad mistake.

Just a couple of weeks later I was wrestling in Paisley Ice Rink, and once again sitting in the dressing room, lacing up my boots. The dressing room door suddenly burst open, and in marched the Lightweight Wrestling Champion of the World, a vicious scowl decorating his face in contrast to his usual smiling countenance. His icy grey eyes scoured the dressing room, and when he found who he was looking for, he growled like a Lion,

"HEY – YOU, COME WITH ME!" In spite of the fact that the Celtic Hercules outweighed the slightly built Lightweight Champ by about 70 pounds of solid muscle, his jaw dropped, and as ordered he almost ran across the dressing room to comply with George Kidd's command. Andy followed George into a small room adjoining the dressing room, the door slammed behind them, and a loud undecipherable commotion arose. Only a few minutes past before a white faced, and very subdued 'King of the Highlands' slunk back into the dressing room. He walked quietly back to his place, and continued to prepare himself for his match in an uncharacteristic silence. George walked back in, and with his usual jovial smile addressed the rest of the wrestlers with,

"Have you heard this one - ?" and carried on with his usual recital of funny stories as though the disturbing, and puzzling incident between him and Andy Robbins had never occurred. No one was foolhardy enough to questioned George on the subject, but after he had wrestled, showered, and left the building, everyone descended on a much quieter than normal Andy Robbins and asked him what had transpired in the small adjoining room. According to Andy, the moment the door had slammed behind them, George had stuck a handgun halfway up Andy's snout and threatened to blow his brains out if he ever saw him aping the Champion's repertoire again.

"He must be one Hell of a marksman, if he could manage that, even at that range," I observed and added, "If Andy had another brain, he'd still only have one!"

Did I ever have to sit through another of Andy Robbins' comic impersonations of the World Lightweight Champion's wrestling matches? Unfortunately, yes I did – hundreds of times, - BUT, never, ever in the presence of George Kidd.

****

It was late Monday morning and it had been exactly a week since I had last seen Mickey Muldoon, since then I had been wrestling up north in the Manchester area. I had arrived back home the early hours of Sunday morning, grabbed a few hours sleep before rushing out, and making my way to a number of different train stations in order to pick up various models. They had come to spend the day posing for photographs at Blond Eric's home. I had taken 7 rolls of film, 2 rolls more than I had the Sunday before. Mickey had come around last Monday before I left for Manchester in order to pick up the rolls of film and pay me 50 pounds for the 5 rolls I had taken the week before, prior to going back home to develop and print them. I looked at the clock, if Mickey didn't hurry he would have to wait for the new batch of film, as I had to be at Dale Martin's office within the hour. I was eager to give him the film, and on this occasion, receive a hefty 70 pounds in return. 'Good!' I thought, as I heard a knock on the door, 'I didn't think Mickey would disappoint me by being late.' It was Mickey, but he did disappoint me very much, when he said in way of greeting,

"You owe me 10 quid!"

"Do I - what for?" I asked.

"One of the 5 rolls of film you sold me last week didn't come out," he replied, "look at this, the negative is completely blank!" He held up a length of film for me to examine in order to prove his claim.

"Well whose fault is that?" I asked him.

"Yours," he answered, "there must have been something wrong with your camera."

"Did all the others come out okay?" I inquired; he told me that they did. I gave Mickey the 7 new rolls of film I had taken the day before, and he paid me 60 pounds instead of the 70 I had expected, in order to make up for the roll that Mickey claimed was blank. Ten pounds right off the top was a bitter pill to swallow, especially after buying all the film myself, and paying all the models for posing.

A week later when Mickey came to collect yet another batch of film, he told me that 3 rolls of film out of the last batch had not come out.

"That's 30 quid to come out of this next lot!" he told me and he gave me 3 blank rolls of film as evidence.

"How many rolls did you take yesterday?" Mickey asked.

"Seven." I replied.

"Well, you owe me 3 of those, so that'll be 40 quid instead of 70." He told me as he counted a number of bank notes onto the table, and then held out his hand for the 7 latest rolls of film. Instead, I handed him my camera,

"Just let me slip my wrestling cape on," I told him, "I want you to take some publicity photos for me."

Obligingly, Mickey snapped away,

"I hope these turn out okay," he said when he'd finished; "I think they'll look great - I'll do them the same time I do the photos you took yesterday." He added.

"That's okay Mickey," I told him, "I'm going to take them all to John Graham's Studio and do them all myself."

"But I need the film now!" he demanded.

"Too bad, Mickey," I told him, "you're just going to have to wait!"

There was no way of proving whether Mickey was telling the truth or not, so I had no choice other than to take his word for it, but I was not going to take any more chances ever again. I was desperate to save enough money for a deposit on my own house, and after that Mickey and all his pornographic friends could go and fuck themselves for all I cared. I decided that unfortunately under these circumstances I would have to invest some of my house deposit savings into purchasing my own photographic equipment. I had a lot of experience printing photographs from negatives, first for John Graham, and then when I had the time, for Mickey, but not so much at processing the negatives, my next quest would be to get John Graham to teach me how it was done properly. I had never liked processing the negatives as much as I enjoyed printing photographs, but nevertheless I became quite good at it. I was also gratified to find that every one of the 7 rolls of film I had taken the last Sunday came out great – makes one think doesn't it? Also the publicity photos that I had got Mickey to take of me were really good, many of which eventually found themselves gracing the pages of many wrestling magazines, programs and posters.

While John Graham had been teaching me how to process photographic film, I had asked his advice about what kind of equipment would be best to suit my needs, at a reasonable cost, John was happy to supply me with a complete list. Rather than rush to the first photography supplier, I began to ask around to see if I could get a better deal from another source, and struck pay-dirt almost immediately.

Graham Guthrie, better known as Gus to his better friends, was a M C for Devereaux Promotions, he was also my self-appointed procurer-in-chief, as soon as he learned of my second job he had began recruiting models for me. Amongst his best discoveries was a Lady named Anne who lived in a High-rise apartment in Battersea, and the Big Busted, Blond, Anne very soon became an even better procurer than Gus. Not only did she recruit a number of her female friends as models, but she would also pose herself with her Husband and any number of his male friends – and last, but certainly not least, I could take the photos in her apartment. That meant that instead of having to rush all around London meeting models and taking them to Eric's house, all I had to do was to take my camera to Anne's apartment and start snapping away at Anne, and whoever else she had brought to the party.

The phone rang; it was Anne's husband,

"I heard you're looking to buy some photography equipment." He said.

"I certainly am," I agreed, "what have you got to sell?"

"What do you want?" he asked. I ran through my list, and he told me that he could get me everything with the exception of the chemicals and dishes used for developing.

"Is everything legitimate?" I wanted to know, "I'm not in the market for anything that's been stolen." He assured me that everything would be legal and above board.

"The remnants of a big liquidation sale, I got in on the ground floor, I'll give you a call when I get the stuff," he told me, "should be within a couple of weeks."

"I want first pick." I told him. He agreed that I would. It was well over two weeks before I got the call, and by then I was chomping at the bit. I was wrestling at Oxford, Town Hall that night, but as I had more than a couple of hours before I had to be at Dale Martin's Office to catch a ride, I decided to go and purchase the equipment immediately, before anyone else got a look at it.

Well, I thought I had given myself time to get to Battersea, check out the merchandize, make my purchases, and get to the office in plenty of time to catch my ride to Oxford, but the traffic was terrible. The bus just crawled and stopped for the entire journey. By the time I reached my destination I knew I stood no chance at all of getting to Dale Martins before the transportation left, so I decided to call the office and tell them that I would be making my own way to Oxford by train. Finding a public phone in Battersea that actually worked proved to be a quest in vain, so I thought that if I hurried to Anne's abode I could use her phone instead.

It was turning out to be a bad day - BUT, it could have been so much worse, and would have been, if I had left earlier and got to Anne's home in plenty of time. When I arrived, there were cars parked higgledy-piggledy all around the High-rises. Mostly Police cars! So instead of walking towards the High-rise where Anne lived, I walked to another that faced it, and climbed the stairs until I was level with her apartment. I reached it just in time to look down to ground level and get a Bird's-eye view of Anne's Husband and a few of his friends, all wearing handcuffs, being loaded into the Police cars. Meantime more Police carrying boxes of photography equipment were busy stacking them into their vehicles also.

To say I fell victim of highly mixed emotions would be an understatement, I was so disappointed that I wasn't going to get my photography equipment. So happy that I wasn't in Anne's Husband and his friends present company, as I most positively would have been if I had been just a few minutes earlier. I was annoyed that I had been lied to concerning the legitimacy of the equipment, and Royally pissed off that I was going to have to go to Oxford by train, instead of getting a free ride from the office.

The next morning I got up early, ate breakfast and then went directly to the photography store where I had originally decided to make my purchases. When I arrived back home I had all the equipment I needed to start my own processing and printing setup.

****

Almost as far back as I can remember I have had trouble dealing with 'figures of authority', from my school teachers, especially the Headmasters, my Brother, my Father, and a list of bosses at various jobs I've held, from Summers in Beynon's Colliery, to Morris in Wembley Stadium, to Giles when I worked for the Water-board.

Now I am not entirely stupid, and I do realize that there has to be bosses whose job it is to tell workers what to do, and I didn't mind being told what to do as long as I was told what to do politely, and without attitude. Put on that air of superiority and you've lost me mate, hence my problem with some of Joint Promotion's Masters of Ceremonies and Referees. I say some, some were great, some were okay, and some were the screaming shits.

Traditionally, the M.C.s or Referees were given the orders by the promoters, telling them who was to win, who drew, who lost, and it was their job to pass the orders on to the wrestlers concerned. Which to my mind made them no more than messengers, but in their minds they were imparting the orders, which made them the boss.

"Street, you are on second with Brian Maxine," they might say, then give the impression that they, themselves were deciding what the result would be, "Ah, I think you'll be doing a draw." They'd muse.

Lou Marco was the undisputed Prima Donna of referees, and was firmly convinced that he was the star and main attraction of every show that he appeared on, he would stand in the middle of the dressing room, read out who would be wrestling on that night's card, and then groan dramatically,

"Oh no, just look at the material they've given me to work

with tonight!" as he'd shake his head in utter dismay and sigh, "I'll really have my work cut out for me if I can pull this one off!"

Lou and I did not get on; neither did anyone else if Lou thought that the perpetrator might be attempting to attract the attention of the wrestling fans that he truly believed was meant solely for him. Amongst his other endearing qualities was that Lou was a rabid alcoholic who would do anything to avoid paying for his own booze. A classic example occurred one Sunday night in Folkstone.

Two wrestlers were partway through their match, and were in the process of bouncing off the ropes in order to body-check each other. It was the force and weight of two heavy bodies hurtling into them that caused the top rope to snap with a resounding twang, which sent one of the wrestlers spinning out of the ring and landing in a heap on the hardwood Ballroom floor. Although such a tumble could cause a career ending injury, the wrestler lucked out, badly shaken, but not badly hurt, he was in the act of attempting to raise himself off the deck when Lou Marco leapt out of the ring, knelt beside him, and whispered to the wrestler as he cradled his head on his lap,

"Stay there, don't move." Then as a crowd of fans all gathered around, he ordered, "Quick somebody go and get a double Brandy!" and then again to the prone wrestler, "Stay there, don't move." A member of the audience rushed to the Bar at the back of the hall, and was back in seconds with the Brandy for the supposedly injured wrestler. Lou snatched the glass and swallowed the contents in one gulp, then handed the glass back, pointed to the wrestler, and ordered the fan,

"Okay, now go and get one for him!"

Lou had a weakness for anything that contained alcohol but favored Scotch, and although I was not fond of it myself in those days, it was Lou's preference that prompted me to buy a bottle of it for our trip home from a show one night. I didn't buy it to share with Lou; I bought it to tease him with it,

"Damn, this is great Scotch," I'd tell the other wrestlers in the van, "what do you think Peter?" I'd ask as I'd pass the bottle to Peter Rann in order for him to sample it.

"MMMM! Excellent Ada." He'd reply, smacking his lips

after he'd taken a swig.

"Gimme some o' that!" ordered Lou Marco.

"No way Lou," I'd tell him, "if we give you any you'll drink the lot."

"Na, I won't," he'd promise, "just give me a swig!"

"Na, I don't think so Lou, I don't trust you - what do you think Boys?" I'd ask the rest of the van.

"Na, don't trust him," they'd tell me,

"Give me a swig Ada." Says Tony Scarlo, "mmm, delicious." He'd gasp.

"Gimme some!" Lou would plead, getting frantic as the bottle was passed around the van. Half an hour later Peter Rann relented, or at least pretended to,

"Just give Lou a little swig of Scotch, Ada" he told me, "just look at the poor sod, he's gasping for one!"

"No, I don't think so, Peter," I replied, "the greedy git will drink the lot!"

"Gimme a swig!" Lou demanded.

Eventually I'd concede to Peter's plea on Lou's behalf and hand the bottle to Lou,

"Just one swig Lou, then you give it back, okay?!" I'd demand.

"Na, - I'm keepin' it! He replied after snatching it and guzzling greedily, and there was no way he would have given up that bottle without a fight. Mind you – there was no way I would have accepted the bottle off him if he had given it back, as Peter, myself, and all the rest of the wrestlers who had been pretending to drink the Whiskey had instead been pissing in the bottle from the time it was half empty.

"Give me my Scotch back Lou," I asked for the dozenth time, "you promised!"

"Na, fuck off, I'm keepin' it!" he growled.

"It's really good Scotch though, isn't it Lou?" I asked, pretending to have come to terms with the fact that he was not going to keep his promise - we all laughed our heads off when he replied,

"Na, it tastes like fuckin' piss!"

ADRIAN STREET

THE MYSTERY OF THE INCREDIBLE SHRINKING WALKING STICK

Famous for his vicious, cruel, but imaginative pranks, it was not at all surprising that Peter Rann was the prime suspect in 'The mysterious case of the incredible shrinking walking stick'. Peter denied the accusation, but the fact that his denial was punctuated by that sinister hissing chuckle, cast serious doubt on his claim of complete innocence. Another suspect was Johnny Black, one of Dale Martin's ring-crew, who had began to double as a van driver about the time the walking stick began to shrink. At first Johnny also denied any involvement with said walking apparatus, but later 'feigned' a reluctant admission of guilt, which seemed to clear up the entire mystery. I say 'feigned', as I know for a fact that Johnny was also completely innocent, and had only claimed guilt because of the huge amount of amusement and notoriety the incident had generated. Now I will clear up the mystery once and for all.

In 1967 Lou Marco's career as a referee came to an abrupt and violent end when as inebriated as a Butterfly he skipped headlong into an oncoming car which smashed one of his legs, and sent him somersaulting gracefully into the tarmac. Then after a period of convalescing he returned to wrestling as an equally obnoxious and officious Master of Ceremonies, as he was now far too lame to referee, and could only limp with the aid of a wooden walking stick. On route to a wrestling show one afternoon, I was sawing and filing the flash off a boxful of my Napoleonic metal soldiers, when I spied Marco's walking stick hanging on the edge of the van's seat in front of me, while Lou was snoozing soundly. I took the stick and examined the rubber tip at the bottom, and found that it could easily be removed. I used my hacksaw to cut a couple of inches off the bottom of the cane before replacing the rubber tip, and then re-hanging the walking stick back on Lou's seat. When we stopped at a café for refreshments, as usual I opened my healthy packed lunch as I watched through the van window, the wrestlers including hop-along Marco file into the greasy-spoon. I was certain that Lou was bent over a little more than before I had shortened his walking stick, but neither he, nor anyone else seemed to notice. After the wrestlers had eaten, returned to the van, and we were once again on the move Lou slid back into to arms of Morpheus, so I took his walking stick and cut a couple more inches off it. When we arrived at that evening's venue I watched Lou hobble into the hall with a definite extra stoop, but once again he seemed to be unaware that his walking stick was shrinking. On our way home that night the stick mysteriously lost a couple more inches, and again Lou didn't notice the difference. But on this occasion, considering how much booze he had consumed I wasn't really surprised, in fact the much shorter stick may have been better suited to his condition. Over the next few weeks, whenever Lou and I were on the same card, and I was able to gain undetected access to his stick, out came my hacksaw. Once again I would circumcise an inch or two off the end before replacing the rubber tip. By this time everyone had noticed that the walking stick had shrunk to less than half it's original length, and that Lou was bent over like a humpty-backed Troll - everyone that is, except Lou himself.

Tiny Carr was a Lou Marco wannabe, just without the gravel voice and the all black referee garb. He too was star struck, the same diminutive size as Lou, and had the same craving for very large quantities of firewater. I had always got on with Tiny very well when I had first began to wrestle for Dale Martins, but that was I suppose, due to the fact that I used to buy my suit fabric from him. The very fact that I now had my own private tailor, and no longer needed to buy fabric from him anymore tended to stir more than a little resentment. But not as much as an incident that occurred one very cold February night after the show had ended in Norwich Corn Hall. My Baby Son Vincent was no more than a few weeks old at that time, and I was very anxious to get home and re-count his fingers, toes, eyes etcetera. I along with most of the other wrestlers was sitting in the big navy blue coffin that was Dale Martin's transport, freezing our arses off, and waiting for Tiny who was busily getting blotto on other people's money in a pub on the opposite side of the road. It was well past closing time, but the pub owner was only too happy to extend his closing time when any of the wrestling fraternity was in there drinking. Tiny would always be treated as a major celebrity, and the booze that flowed in his direction would always be plentiful and free, and Tiny being of the Lou Marco ilk could not have been induced to leave, even if a ticking atom bomb had been placed on the bar in front of him. Needless to say that after loosing patience as well as the feeling in my legs, hands and nose, and marching into the pub to ask Tiny if he was ready to leave, and receiving a very abusive and negative reply, I was not a very happy camper.

"We are leaving with you, or without you!" I informed him as I left the pub, and marched back to Dale Martin's mobile icebox. Unfortunately our driver truly believed that Tiny Carr was the boss that night, and wasn't prepared to leave him behind as I suggested, even after another hour had past without the slightest sign of Tiny.

I'd had enough! I marched back into the pub and shouted,

"OI SHITHEAD – THE DRIVER SAID, IF YOU DON'T COME IMEDIATELY WE'RE LEAVING WITHOUT YOU – COME NOW, OR STAY THE NIGHT!"

Tiny was livid - no worse than that, drunk and livid. No one, especially a young snot nosed wrestler spoke like that to the all important, self acclaimed boss and celebrity darling of his Norwich wrestling fans – especially in the presence of his fans.

"FUCK OFF!!!" He screamed at me, and then in spite of his inebriated condition, realized what he had just screamed, and clumsily attempted to apologize for his bad language to his shocked fans before glaring daggers, and staggering towards me with a speed that suggested that he meant to do me harm. Considering the mood I was in, I would have liked nothing better than to have let him try. But for the first time in hours I had him moving in the direction of the transport van, and was unwilling to risk a confrontation that may delay our departure by another single second more than was necessary. I tailored my speed to lure him right back to the van, and then leapt inside and back into my seat by the time that the furious Tiny scrambled through the van door. Immediately he was in my face, screaming obscenities for all he was worth – which wasn't much in my books.

"Sit down and shut up, Tiny, you stupid twat." I told him in a matter of fact manner. Well he sat down in the seat right behind mine, but he must have missed the shut up part, because he began to rant and rave in a way that would have done credit to Dad at his worst,

"HUH – ADRIAN STREET SEEMS TO THINK HE'S SOME BIG WRESTLING STAR, BUT HE DOESN'T MEAN SHIT IN THIS BUSINESS!" He'd rant, "HE'LL NEVER MAKE IT – HE ISN'T SHIT! He'd rave.

"Well I may not be shit Tiny," I told him, "but you certainly are!" and with that he retaliated by slapping me across the back of my head and renewing his verbal assault with a vengeance. I felt both of my hands ball tightly into fists, but decided that ignoring him would belittle him more than gently ripping his ugly face off his balding skull.

"He thinks all the fuckin' Birds fancy him," he told the rest of the van, "huh! I could still pull more Birds than him and I'm twice his fuckin' age!" he added.

"Yeah, and the fucking rest!" I replied. Tiny's attempted ridicule of me for the benefit of the other wrestlers wasn't going as well as he hoped, firstly they were all pissed off at him for being made to wait in the freezing van, and now they would prefer to sleep than to listen to a drunken idiot trying to be funny. Tiny suddenly changed his tactics when he punched the back of my head, and then tried to impale my eye on one of his forefingers as I turned around in protest. His finger missed my eye, and instead almost went up my nose, but my right fist didn't miss, when I spun around and smashed it right into Tiny's face which tore him right out of his seat and onto the floor of the van.

"HOORAY – WELL DONE!" Everyone shouted.

"Now that's what I call a Carr crash!" I replied.

****

"I HOPE THE FUCKIN' BITCH CATCHES THE FUCKIN' POX!" Snarled Sandra, she was so pissed off with her best friend Pauline that she didn't know what to do with herself, and I was getting the full brunt of it as I was busy sorting out

Mickey's photos. Apparently, a couple of nights earlier Sandra and Pauline had been cruising the Locarno Ballroom and had hit pay-dirt, when suddenly out of nowhere Mick had appeared to take Sandra home. That left poor carnivorous Pauline all alone to deal with a small army of male prey. The next day Pauline had given Sandra a blow by blow of what had happened next. She had accompanied the whole gang to a nearby flat where all night long the action had been hot, heavy and nonstop with Pauline taking on all 'comers' single-handedly,

"They were even phoning up their friends to come and join the party!" Pauline boasted, "I lost count!" she added gleefully. – Sandra was livid.

"That could have been me," she groaned, "if only that fuckin' Mick hadn't turned up when he had!"

"Well you can hardly blame Pauline for that." I replied as I popped another set of five photographs into their see through envelope.

"FUCKIN' BITCH!" She snarled, "I HOPE SHE CATCHES THE FUCKIN' POX!"

If Sandra was on her own she could be quite amiable, funny, even friendly, although sometimes a little too friendly for my liking. She was very talkative, but there was only three subjects that I ever heard her discuss - herself - sex – and herself having sex. In company she would only be happy if she were the main, if not only topic. If she couldn't get enough attention by fair means she would get them by foul, and in Sandra's case there was no limit to how foul she was prepared to go. A prime example always occurred when Mick and some of his associates would come to the matches to watch me wrestle, and then give me a ride back home in his car after the show. Mick and many of his friends were huge wrestling fans, and great admirers of my style of wrestling. That tended to make me the centre of attention on our ride home, but if Sandra was with him too, their comments and questions would be loudly and rudely interrupted all the way back to London, with Sandra yelling at the top of her voice,

"FUCKIN' WRESTLIN' IS FUCKIN' FAKE – WHAT A LOAD OF FUCKIN' SHIT – IT'S ALL A LOAD OF FUCKIN' FAKE RUBBISH!"

I'll admit that, that would piss me off, but not as much as she did when Mick brought her to my home. Mickey might be picking up my latest batch of negatives,

"Will you be taking any more photos next week, Ade?" he'd ask.

"No, not next week Mick," I might reply, "I'll be going to Bradford on Monday and wrestling in Yorkshire for the whole week."

"Oh – and what will you be doing while Adrian is away for the week?" Sandra would ask Jean suggestively, then she'd give me a sly sideways glance, and continue with a smirk, "You ought to come to the Locarno with me 'n' Pauline I'll bet you'll really enjoy yourself!" and add, "I can get someone to mind your kids while your having fun with me 'n' Pauline."

I really could not understand the girl. She was purposely baiting me, and all I would have had to do to get back at her, was to spill the beans to Mickey about the very things that Sandra had told me that she and Pauline got up to when they went to the Locarno. The more I learned about Sandra, the more I marveled at the razor sharp edge on which she constantly craved to dance. Finally I had had enough, I didn't tell Mickey about Sandra's continuous carnal escapades, but I did tell him,

"Mick, you are welcome in my home anytime, but your Wife isn't, don't ever bring her around here again – if you do she can wait for you in your car or on the fucking sidewalk!" – 'Where she belongs!' I thought.

I was amazed that Mickey seemed to be totally unaware of Sandra's bizarre extramarital extracurricular activities, but was shocked one day when he told me he was going to pick Sandra and Pauline up and I'd asked him,

"Where are they?"

"Up at the Locarno getting their oats." He replied with a chuckle - well his mouth chuckled, and made the appropriate chuckling sound, but there was a flint hard, inquiring look in his eyes that totally belied his flippancy. I realized that he knew nothing for certain, and didn't really believe that Sandra was cuckolding him. But was attempting to save face by making a joke out of it, on the off chance that she was, whilst monitoring my reaction to see if it suggested that I knew something that he didn't. I also realized that if Mickey had known just a small fraction of what I did know about Sandra, that he would have ripped her up into very many small pieces.

****

Tony Charles had been a great tag-team partner, but my increasingly outlandish ring-wear and outrageous behavior was causing a wider and wider contrast to both our formally compatible styles. Added to that was the fact that although Tony and I were regarded as one of the top tag-teams for most of the northern promoters, we had never, ever wrestled as a tag-team in the south, and my very numerous requests to do so always seemed to fall on deaf ears. When I wrestled in tag-matches for Dale Martins I would be teamed up with any number of different partners, amongst them were Sid Cooper, Brian Maxine, Zoltan Boscik, and of course the 'Grey Rat' Gentleman Jim Lewis, who I had very strongly objected against. Mostly the matches I'd had with the aforementioned partners cast us as the villains, and we would be matched against one of the Blue-eye, or hero teams. I decided it was time that I had a regular partner with more edge, a villain whose style was more compatible with my own, and after scrutinizing just a very few, I found one who I thought would be a perfect candidate, 'Bad-Boy' Bobby Barnes.

When I first broached the subject with Bobby, I was disappointed to find that he seemed to be very much less enthusiastic than I. I remember him sniffing and replying,

"I've never seen you wrestle as a villain - next time we're on the same card wrestle villain, remind me to watch you, and I'll let you know what I think."

Well he did watch, and agreed to give me a trial period to see how I shaped up, we approached Dale Martins requested that we wanted to be a team, and they also agreed to give it a whirl. At first we would, as often as not, find ourselves as adversaries rather than tag-team partners, and then on the very next show instead of wrestling against each other we would be teamed up against a team of Baby-faces. It was not a great way to establish a great team. Another obstacle was the fact that I was still tagging with Tony Charles up north as a 'Welsh-Wizard'. But little by little 'Bad-Boy' Bobby Barnes and I began to register, and after I had spoken to the northern promoters Bobby began tagging with me for them too, and 'The Welsh Wizards' eventually faded into history.

Many of the established Tag-teams used to wear matching ring-wear, and had catchy titles like good-guys Terry Jowett and Johnny Eagles, who were 'The White Eagles' and wore all white from Jackets to trunks, and both had Eagles tattooed on their chests. In contrast the evil 'Black Diamonds', John Foley and Abe Ginsburg wore all black, from their black leather helmets, to their leotards, trunks, long tights and boots.

To begin with Bob and I simply wore the same ring-wear that we would normally wear in single matches, and when asked what we were going to call our team, we replied that we were not going to call it anything. We were a tag-team comprising of 'Bad-Boy' Bobby Barnes and 'Nature-Boy' Adrian Street, and that our gimmick was not having a gimmick other than being the best. That, apart from being the best was soon to change.

An article written for 'THE WRESTLER' by Russell Plummer tells it best. –

TAG-TEAM SPECIAL
STREET and BARNES
Have the best of both Worlds.

It is strange how two wrestlers of completely different personality can so often strike up a successful tag team combination, and in doing so still retain all their own individuality and style. This has happened on the continent several times with French heavyweight teams, and one of the best examples here has been the long run of Bobby Barnes and Adrian Street in recent times. Certainly the often supercilious Londoner, Barnes and his sometimes arrogant Welsh partner are opposites in many respects, but they do have one thing in common, in tag bouts at any rate. Barnes and Street both want to win and they have little concern about the methods adopted, as long as the ultimate objective is achieved. This, of course, can be said of most successful teams, especially the more rugged outfits, but Street and Barnes bring their own brand of subtlety to the old and these days almost honorable art of ring villainy. Of similar wrestling experience, they have not followed the example of most teams, of wearing identical trunks or dressing gowns, and have also stuck to their own styles of wrestling.

Barnes, Lewisham born and bred, had his first professional contest at the age of 17 and it did not take him long to realize that the quickest way to get to the top was to forget about some of the more orthodox approaches he had learned from his amateur days. With a good background and natural speed and height he would almost certainly have come to the fore in due course anyway. But Barnes was, and still is, an impatient young man and this, and a general dislike for authority ended with him being branded as a tearaway before his first full year as a professional. In many respects his style and attitude to opponents is not unlike that of Jackie Pallo, and is with 'Mr. Television' that the South Londoner has had some of his most exciting solo matches.

Pallo also figures in the record of partner Street, and in his first 6 months as a professional, after joining Dale Martin's, Street's baptism of fire included matches with more than half a dozen of the men who still rate as the top middleweights and welterweights in the land, if not Europe. Street came from a background of weight and strength training, but also had some amateur experience with London clubs before he decided to try and break into a professional career.

Barnes got his break with Dale-Martin Promotions from the onset, Street had to gain experience with independent promoters before his chance with Joint Promotions members came along.

After about a year the young Welshman from Brynmawr, near Cardiff, decided that the time had come for a more flamboyant approach and he became noted for his smart ring attire, at one time having more than a dozen different dressing gowns with boots and trunks in matching colors.

At the same time he was encouraged to inject a little fire into his bouts and from that time on his career and that of Barnes have followed generally parallel paths.

Despite having to fulfill numerous tag team engagements in the past 12 months, Street has always had the great ambition to win a Welsh Championship, and when Tony Charles moved up out of the welter and middleweights he hoped to get a crack at one of these titles. However, the chance never came, but more recently at Bristol, Street got his chance to tackle Cardiff's

Johnny Williams for the Welsh Lightweight Championship. Not only did Street have the problem of beating the speedy Williams, he had also to shed quite a bit of weight to make the Lightweight limit. He won his battle without losing any strength or speed, and the Colston Hall crowd saw Street emerge victorious after a cracking contest, in which most of the support went, not unnaturally to Williams.

Barnes also had his title chance recently in the tournament to decide the new Southern area Lightweight Champion, and he reached the final only to be beaten by Alan Miquet. In tag contests Barnes and Street – they have no fancy title – have confined their activities mainly to the South, but have had a pretty busy winter, and can claim the distinction of being one of the few teams to appear in a tag contest at the Royal Albert Hall. Notable Battles have been against the Cortez Brothers, Borge Twins, Ignatius and Tony, while lively encounters have resulted from matches with the White Eagles and visiting foreign combinations.

On occasion when one or the other of the team have been unavailable due to prior commitment, such as Street's trips to the North from time to time, then Hungarian Zoltan Boscik has deputized. Usually mild mannered in his solo contests, even 'Zolly' has become rather worked up when encouraged by Adrian or Bobby, which ever the case may be. Perhaps at a disadvantage against some teams when it comes to weight and experience, I like the look of this well balanced combination, for lets face it, they are never in a dull contest.

-Russell Plummer.

I began introducing Bobby to many of the Northern Promoters which turned out to be a fantastic career move for both of us. Bob and I were wrestling one week for Relwyskow at Leeds on Monday, Hull on Tuesday, and Sheffield on Wednesday. We had arrived at Sheffield very early in the afternoon, and had a few hours to kill before the show began in The City Hall. Whilst window shopping we noticed that 'The Blue Max' was showing in one of the movie theaters. I had already seen the film recently, and told Bob what a great movie I thought it to be, and as Bob hadn't seen it yet we decided to kill a couple of hours by doing so. Bob liked the movie very much, and I enjoyed watching it again as much as I had the first time. We were discussing the movie as we once again began walking around the City, and I told Bob that I wished that they would make a movie of the same period and subject about the short but illustrious career of Manfred Von Richthofen, 'The Bloody Red Baron'.

"I wonder why they haven't made more movies about the World War 1 fighter Aces?" Bob replied.

"I wonder the same thing." I told him, "the only other movie I remember, was an old 1930's movie starring Jean Harlow and Ben Lyons called 'The Hell's Angels'. That stopped me in my tracks, "Shit, Bob – what do you think about that as a name for our Tag-team – 'The Hell's Angels?!" Immediately an image of our 'Hell's Angel' ring-wear appeared in my mind's eye - White capes to suggest a pair of innocent 'Choir Boys', but white capes with a blood red satin lining, and worn underneath, blood red trunks and blood red boots.

The thing that had first attracted my attention to Bobby and had made him stand out was the red trunks he wore one night. In those days I only wore various pastel colors, blue, pink, yellow, or gold or silver metallic. But bright red, with his dark blond hair under the ring-lights I thought was really very showy.

I asked Jack Robinson if he would make a white satin cape each for Bob and myself. They had lines of pearl studs down the front, bright red satin linings, a silver sequined 'B' with a sequined Halo over it, on the left breast of Bob's cape and a matching 'A' with a halo on the left breast of mine. Bob's dark blond hair began to get lighter each match, until it matched my platinum shade. When we made our ring entrances we would walk slowly to the ring looking totally Angelic in virginal white. We would stand in our corner as though we were about to pray or sing a hymn, but then when we were introduced we would both throw open our pure white capes and suddenly turn Satanic Scarlet. After establishing our new look, I asked Jack Robinson to make us a cape each made of metallic silver leather, again with red satin linings but with large red sequins that really blazed the reflected light when we threw open our capes. Later after the new capes had completed the rounds, I jazzed them up by painting a large, muscular green Demon, armed with a trident leaping out of the flames of Hell on the front, in place of the halos. Then on the backs of the capes I painted a huge snarling, Bat-winged Skull wearing the halo.

At that time neither Bob or I had ever heard of the American 'Hell's Angels' motorbike gangs, but after we did I designed yet another 'contrasting look' of 'Bat-winged Skull' paintings decorating the backs of sleeveless, metallic studded black leather jackets. With this ensemble, we wore metal studded, black leather arm-bands, black leather trunks with the winged Skull, and halos in white and black boots that matched the jackets and trunks, with white winged Skulls on the front and zip fasteners on the backs instead of having laces on the front. After adopting the metallic studded, shiny black leather look, we were often asked if we had 'borrowed' our title 'The Hell's Angels' from the American Hell's Angels Motorbike gangs – the answer to that question is definitely not. It came from watching the movie 'Blue Max' which reminded me of the old 30's movie 'The Hell's Angels.'

****

His usual jovial countenance, and highly animated gestures were totally absent as Scotland's Lightweight King of the wrestling World, George Kidd burst into the dressing-room in Hamilton Town Hall – he had obviously seen the posters outside the venue.

"George," he shouted angrily across the dressing room, addressing Promoter, George De Relwyskow, "who have you got me billed against?!" he demanded, although judging from his ferocious demeanor he must have already known the answer to his question.

"Frank Dhondt, from Belgium." Relwyskow replied.

"Who the fuck is Frank FUCKING Dhondt?!" George demanded with a total disregard for diplomacy. I sympathized with the bewildered Belgian, whose welcoming smile at the first sight of his illustrious opponent vanished in a flash. George Kidd had never ever met Frank Dhondt, and had already made his mind up that he was never going to, especially in a wrestling ring within the borders of his native Scotland.

"He's your opponent tonight George," Relwyskow answered, "Champion of Belgium." He added in an unsuccessful attempt to pacify the angry Scot.

"He is not my opponent tonight," Kidd corrected, "tonight, or any other fuckin' night! – Who else have you got on the bill? – you are going to have to change the matches around!" he told the promoter.

"The only other wrestlers your weight is Jimmy or Adrian," Relwyskow replied, indicating 'Wee' Jimmy McKenzie and me.

"NO FUCKING CHANCE!!!" Roared the World's Lightweight Wrestling Champion furiously.

"Well the other four wrestlers on the bill are all very big heavyweights George," Relwyskow told him, "you can't wrestle any of them, they're all much too big!"

George was beside himself with fury, he glared at Frank Dhondt, whose sheepish attempt at a disarming smile almost brought a tear of sympathy to my eye. Although I can't say that I wasted any sympathy on 'The World Champ', on the contrary I was enjoying his frustrating predicament immensely.

"Well, it's up to you George," Relwyskow told him, "You can wrestle the Belgian Champion, Wee Jimmy, or Adrian Street."

In spite of his diminutive size of 5' 6" and rarely weighing more than 150 pounds, George Kidd was nevertheless a force to be reckoned with. He possessed a filthy temper with a very short fuse, probably the result of beginning his early schooldays as an undersized runt who seemed to be top of every school ground bully's hit list. But it was not a part of George Kidd's nature to remain a victim or to run; instead he bought a book on Jujitsu which became his Bible, and then began to use each and every would-be bully as a practice dummy, honing his skills and getting forever more proficient with each violent confrontation. The former prey gradually became the predator, and now the bullies were in full flight with vindictive Georgie in hot pursuit.

During the war at the tender age of 18, George enlisted in the Royal Navy where he learned to wrestle, and competed in the sport until leaving the Navy in 1946 with the idea of turning pro. At the age of 21 he approached George de Relwyskow who was promoting in George's hometown of Dundee, Relwyskow told

Kidd he was too small to become a professional wrestler. – where have I heard that one before?! Nevertheless, George's persistence eventually paid off, and he was given a chance to prove himself in Dundee. In the spring of 1947 Kidd defeated Scottish Lightweight Champion, Tony Lawrence in Edinburgh, and later that year took a trip to meet promoter Norman Morrell in Bradford with the idea of advancing his career. Once again George was told he was too small, which prompted him to challenge the ex-Olympic wrestler to a match in Morrell's infamous gym. George held his own for no more than a few minutes before making a dive for Norman Morrell's legs and found himself well and truly trapped in one of Morrell's favorite face-locks. Poor George all but had his head torn off his shoulders, but refused to give in until the cracking sound from his neck caused the ex-Olympian to drop the savage Scot in a heap of pain onto the canvas. George Kidd had been beaten fair and square. But even in defeat he impressed Morrell to such an extent that he immediately offered to take Kidd under his wing, and coach him to become the best. Kidd spent a year and a half with Morrell before taking a trip to Billy Riley's 'Snake-Pit' in Wigan, where he claimed he learned more in a few weeks than he had learned so far in his life. From Wigan George traveled south and trained with expert leg-submission wrestler Dave Armstrong, who, after teaching George all he knew advised him that it was time for him to go to college with Mike Dimitri. So intent on learning more and more about his chosen profession, Kidd even followed Dimitri to France in order to learn from the Master. I thought it strange that my most hated enemy had learned so much of his submission wrestling from my own teacher and former manager. But I had learned from Mike when he was an old beaten up cripple - in contrast George Kidd leaned from Dimitre when the Master was in his prime.

It was with the advice of Bert Assirati that George began the practice of visiting the slaughter-house every day to get himself a pint of Bull's blood, which Bert believed enhanced his strength, stamina and aggression.

But in Hamilton on that fateful night poor George Kidd was up 'Shit Creek without a paddle'; his dilemma was that he knew that the Continental high-flying, acrobatic style of his scheduled

Belgian opponent was not compatible with his own highly technical, and skillful repertoire. His opponent was a great performer, but was not only totally unfamiliar with George's style, but also would be insanely intent in making a big name for himself, especially against such a huge star. It wasn't that George Kidd wouldn't have been more than capable of demolishing the Belgian if push came to shove, but it would have probably resulted in a horrible, brutal massacre of a match, instead of the World's best technical wrestler demonstrating what he did better than anyone else in wrestling. Proving once again to his Scottish worshipers just why George Kidd was the undisputed Lightweight Wrestling Champion of the World.

For Kidd to wrestle my scheduled opponent 'Wee' Jimmy McKenzie was also completely out of the question. 'Wee' Jimmy was not only a very popular local hero, he was also the Scottish Lightweight Champion, and George Kidd realized that he would derive very little glory by wrestling and demolishing a fellow Scot and lesser Champion in front of a Scottish audience. Not that it would have been a bad match anywhere outside Scotland, 'Wee' Jimmy was an excellent wrestler, and I for one would have really enjoyed watching two such great wrestlers in action against each other. But, for George to beat the beloved 'Wee' Jimmy in Scotland would be like Roy Rogers gunning down his own faithful sidekick, Gabby Hayes, or Tarzan, Mighty Lord of the Jungle, beating the crap out of his diminutive Mate, Cheetah the Chimp.

Never before had I witnessed George Kidd at such a complete loss, and I'd made up my mind that I for one was not going to make his frustrating dilemma any easier for him if I could help it. He stood all forlorn on the other side of the dressing room, looking beseechingly at the promoter, and then with a frown at the Belgian, and then with a deeper frown at me. I turned from him and pretended to ignore his existence as I laced up my boots, and readied myself for my match, whoever my opponent would turn out to be. If it was going to be me who the champion chose, then George Kidd would have to come to me, I was loving it, I didn't like him and that was that. Finally with a huge World Championship sized sigh of resignation The Lightweight King of the World made his decision – and his way in my direction.

"Well it looks as though it's going to be you and me." And he sighed again with even more resignation.

"Yup, - looks that way." I answered.

"Well this is going to be a dubious pleasure." He retorted.

"Yes, - a dubious pleasure indeed, - for both of us." I agreed. George Kidd's icy grey eyes narrowed, and he just stood there and seemed to be analyzing me for one long minute,

"Have you seen me wrestle," he asked at last, "do you know my style?"

It did cross my mind to tell him,

'No I haven't, - why the fuck would I want to watch you?!'

A medley of possible scenarios passed through my mind, but I quickly made my choice. It would be very easy indeed to go into the ring with George Kidd and purposely have a lousy match designed to diminish my opponent's image. I was a villain in Scotland and would be booed and jeered whatever I did, so I had nothing to prove to the fans. It would be simple to be a spoiler, any mug could do that. Although I knew that George Kidd already had a very poor opinion of me, I also knew I would derive much more satisfaction by proving to him that I was not a mug and could, if I chose to be, every bit as professional as him, even if I did lack his technical skill. I intended going into the ring with the Champion of the World and giving him a first class World Championship quality Match, so instead I replied,

"Yes, I've watched you wrestle for over 10 years – and I'm very familiar with your style." I had never ceased being a student of my profession, and I never would. Throughout my entire career I've studied the styles of everyone who I thought merited my attention.

There was a particular throw that I had only seen performed by George Kidd where he leapt at his opponent, grabbed his head in what looked like an attempted 'head-mare', but would step across with his right leg at the last second, blocking his opponent's legs. This resulted in the opponent being forced into a fast spinning pirouette before taking off into a very high and spectacular somersault, and landing with a resounding bump on the opposite side of the ring. It looked like it was not only a very complicated maneuver to perform, but also a very complicated maneuver to respond to, so I asked the World Champion for his advice on the best way to achieve the best results. George complied and we were soon both engaged in what must have looked like a very weird dance, but with very precise dance steps. Warmed, I assume by my apparent knowledge of his technique, and by my apparent willingness to cooperate, Kidd began showing me other little secret tricks that would cosmetically enhance his own patented method of annihilating yet one more Sassenach challenger. There seemed to be a lot to remember, and the memory of the results of my attempting to get my head around another untried style in the 'Vassilious Mantopolous Disaster' was obviously foremost in my thoughts as I entered the ring that night. Especially as my Boss on this evening, George De Relwyskow was also the promoter on that unfortunate occasion.

George Kidd would always act as his own matchmaker, no promoter would presume to give orders, or even advice to the World Champion. Whatever Kidd wanted to do would be done, and tonight in Hamilton Town Hall, George Kidd, World Lightweight Wrestling Champion would be beating his hated non-Scottish opponent by two falls to none. Originally if I had been given the choice, I would not have exchanged my preliminary win over the Scottish champion in order to suffer a main event defeat against the World Champion. I consoled myself with the fact that I would be demanding main event wages from Relwyskow as soon as the match was concluded. But, even more importantly, this alternative match that I was about to undertake had suddenly become an irresistible challenge, and I was determined to prove my worth to my biggest enemy so far in the World of professional wrestling. I had also decided that in spite of having to lose by two straight falls, I was not going to go down without getting my fair share of the match – and then some!

The Scottish crowd roared their approval the moment the change in the night's matches was announced, as they knew from my past encounters with their Lightweight Champion, 'Wee' Jimmy McKenzie that I had his measure. Even though he was very capable of giving a very good account of himself, they also knew that the final outcome would be a very decisive victory for the much despised and cocky Sassenach. But, now with the foreign villain pitted against their own great World Lightweight

Champion George Kidd instead, it seemed like they might enjoy a reprieve, and it put a fresh and real hope for yet another Scottish victory. They were more confident that instead of watching their own champion 'Wee Jimmy' soundly and savagely beaten whilst the evil Sassenach gloated sadistically at their expense, that now their own Scottish Saint George could and would slay the much hated Welsh Dragon.

The Scottish audience screamed their approval as only the Scottish fans could, I had never been booed so loudly or more sincerely, and I doubt if George Kidd had ever been cheered louder or more enthusiastically in Hamilton Town Hall in his career so far. I began to fear the roof would be blasted right off the building. Introductions were made amid much more deafening booing and cheering, then a hush fell over the scene as the bell rang to herald the action. I walked tall and proudly around the ring, regarding the diminutive Scot with the utmost contempt as I flexed the strong and powerful muscles that I was about to unleash upon my hapless opponent as I crushed and ground him into the canvas. I moved slowly and powerfully relishing the anticipation of coming to grips and displaying my vast physical superiority as I soundly and savagely vanquished my enemy. Then as fast as a hungry Cheetah I pounced on my helpless prey – but the prey was gone – all I grasped was empty air. I tore after him, but he was a ghost, nothing grab-able, graspable, or tangible! Then I had him cornered, he seemed to concede that I had him trapped, and as though to confirm that fact he offered up his left arm as a sacrifice. I grabbed viciously at the proffered limb, and in a flash found myself completely enveloped helplessly in a cocoon of arms and legs, some were my opponents, the rest were my own – The Scottish fans EXPLODED!

"KILL THE JESSIE, GEORGIE!!!" They roared. I struggled, I fought for all I was worth but the more I struggled the more entangled I became. The more I fought the greater my humiliation, as each of my counter moves were re-countered almost before I was able to employ them to any degree of effectiveness. Eventually I exploded back to my feet, only to be re-entangled in yet another ball of muscle and bone, arms and legs. The whole of the round continued in the same vain, with one new humiliation being piled neatly upon the last. The next round began where the first left off, my flaring temper only succeeded in further inflaming the raging fans into louder and louder support for their homeland Hero. In desperation I flung myself at the Champion's legs in a fit of fury in an attempt to upend him, but was caught in the act, spun around, turned upside down, dropped onto the back of my head and pinned for the three-count, giving my opponent the first fall - I was livid! The crowd was ecstatic!

As the bell sounded to begin round 3 the crowd roared even louder, urging the World Champion to go in for the kill, while I seemed to stagger out of my corner and into harms way, bewitched, bothered and bewildered. I slowly circled my opponent as the Scottish fans chanted for their Hero as he readied himself for the big finish – when SNAP! – My right foot shot out in one blinding flash, exploding with bone crushing force just above the Champion's left knee, and he dropped like a stone into a pain ridden heap onto the canvas. Then I was on him with all the fury of the Valkyries on steroids, and I twisted his left ankle viciously as I stamped, kicked and drove my knee into his leg with all the force I could muster. The World Champion screamed in agony, while I turned up the pressure, the remainder of round 3 was mine. I could hardly contain my impatience while I waited for the sound of the bell to begin the fourth round. My opponent had only been able to reach his own corner with the aid of his second, and now seemed as reluctant to leave the sanctuary of it as much I was bursting to explode out of my own, and into his face. CLANG!-CLANG!-CLANG! Was as far as they got before I was on him, kicking, stomping and smashing! I paid the World Champion back for all the pain and humiliation he had piled on my head so far in the match with double the interest. The crowd screamed and booed like never before in their lives, but it sounded like music to my ears, and re-enforced the power of the blows that I rained on their Champion – again and again and again. Round 4 was all mine, I punished their Hero, I taunted and goaded the crowed whilst I mocked and ridiculed my opponent. I was all powerful, invincible, round 5 would be mine too, poor George Kidd, his Scottish fans couldn't believe what was happening to him, and I was loving every precious moment of it.

Little by little the crowd was becoming more and more silent as they watched me methodically dismantle their Hero; I had torn their God down from Mount Olympus, and was systematically destroying him right before their very eyes. an almost whispered plea of,

"Come on Georgie." Would periodically break the silence but would be drowned out by the monotonous thump of my continued stomps into Kidd's thigh, my grunts as I exerted ever more force behind them, which in turn served as a duet to George Kidd's screams of agony – It was lovely. I smiled broadly, almost affectionately at the hostile horde that surrounded the ring as they watched the spectacle before them in utter dismay and disbelief, and I walked almost casually up to their beloved Champion and unleashed a kick to his thigh that would have done credit to a rabid Stallion. He grunted in pain and dropped like a stone, I was enjoying this; I waited patiently for Kidd to stagger back to his feet as I slowly sauntered over measured him then lashed out viciously with my right boot once more,

"Damn it!" I missed; - I lashed out again, - DAMN IT – I MISSED AGAIN!"

With renewed vigor I charged, and this time as I lashed out I was neatly caught by the head, the Champion hopped around in his little dance step, which spun me right around where I got blocked by his right leg causing the impetus to spin me into orbit right across the ring. I took one horrendous bump, but was up and at my opponent only to be caught again in the same maneuver which sent me spinning high above the ring in a repeat flight – The crowd went insane!

As mad as Hell, I found my feet and dove at the Champ, who dove sideways, entangling his legs with mine as we both hovered in mid air. We both crashed to the mat, with me laying flat on my face, Kidd leapt behind me grapevining both my legs with his own, then like a flash, he leaned forward caught both of my wrists in both of his hands, and threw himself backwards as he heaved me bodily off the mat, and thrust me aloft into the full glare of the ring-lights in his own patented, and excruciatingly painful 'Surfboard' submission hold, and once again the King of Scotland was victorious.

THE CROWD WENT BERZERK!!!

Once again Scotland's World Champion had triumphed they were ecstatic! But, little did they know that I was ecstatic too. Not only had I had an incredible match, but in spite of the Scottish crowd's joy concerning my downfall, I was nevertheless extremely gratified to detect a huge amount of relief and reprieve flavoring their triumph. My triumph was the fact that I had succeeded in convincing the Scottish fans of the very real possibility that tonight they might witness their beloved Champion sadistically slaughtered right before their very eyes.

The second that George Kidd entered the dressing room, he almost startled me when he rushed right into my face, grabbed my hand, and as his pale, blue grey eyes bored into mine he told me,

"That was terrific – that was great," he told me as he pumped my paw, "will you wrestle for me in Dundee? – I'll pay you 30 pounds when you wrestle anyone else – 50 when you wrestle me! If you have to come up from London, I'll fly you both ways, or if you'd prefer to come by train I'll pay for a sleeper on your trip back. What do you say?!" He demanded.

"Yes I will." I replied without a second's hesitation. I was more than gratified to receive such praise from such an illustrious opponent, especially in the presence of my promoter that night. George de Relwyskow, was standing right in front of me and beaming smugly all over his face. In complete contrast, I noticed the Champion's scheduled opponent, Belgian's Frank Dhondt who seemed to be snarling at me with so much jealous hate, I could almost see the poisoned daggers flying from his hostile eyes straight at my throat.

It was strange that such an awful faux-par by George de Relwyskow turned out to be the best thing that had happened to me in my wrestling career so far. That night was the start of more than a decade long feud between the World Lightweight Champion and I which catapulted me right up amongst the top stars of British wrestling, and added so much credibility to me as a wrestler, just when I needed it most. For more than 10 years George Kidd and I would do battle, and as often as not, I would defeat the champion in non title matches, when I might outweigh him by as much as 20 pounds. But, with the title at stake, and I had to make his weight he always triumphed and retained his title. Nevertheless, in time I would be recognized by wrestling historians as the greatest challenger to ever to step into the ring with the World's Lightweight Wrestling Champion.

STREET DREAMS

I had a very strange, but vivid dream; it was made even stranger by the fact that during the dream I knew that I must be dreaming. And I knew that I must be dreaming because I knew that I had never ridden a Horse before, and here I was galloping amongst a number of other riders at a speed that seemed to force all my blood to the very back of my body. The Sun flickered and flashed through a very tall hedge on my left making me want to sneeze, and I became vaguely aware of hundreds of white stones scattered all over the green, grassy hill we were all charging down. Even in a dream I realized that there had to be a lot more to knowing how to ride a Horse than just getting on one and being able to gallop at such a breakneck speed.

In real life the closest I had ever come to really riding a real Horse went all the way back to the time when I was a very young kid in Wales, and at the very zenith of my fanatical desire to become the greatest Red-Indian War-chief in History. Following an imaginary spoor of an imaginary Grizzly Bear one day, I happened upon a beautiful, and very real Pinto Pony. It was rubbing an itch on it's side against one of the posts of a barbed wire fence that surrounded the field it was in. A picture flashed through my mind's eye of myself mounted on that majestic black and white War-Horse, my feathered War-bonnet flying behind me, whilst charging down on Custer, determined to relieve him of his long yellow scalp. Stealthily I approached my quarry so's not to spook him, so far so good, I climbed onto the lowest strand of wire on my side of the fence, stretched up and stroked the neck and shoulder of my mount. It accepted my caress, I climbed higher with the idea of using the fence as a ladder, which I could use to hop aboard my new found equine wonder. Slowly but surely I reached the top of the fence, but as I readied myself to mount, the fence began to wobble with me on it to such an extent that it startled the Horse who began to move away.

'It's now or never', I thought, and attempted to throw my left leg over the Horse which spooked it even more. It leapt away into a gallop with me clinging to it for about 5 seconds before landing headfirst in a prickly gorse bush, after leaving the arse of my trousers on top of the barbed-wire fence. The scratches all over my hands and face would have added much credence to a tall tale of my life and death struggle with the Grizzly I had been tracking before I saw the Horse. But, with the arse of my trousers missing, and the scratches decorating the very same area, might have suggested that I had been running from the vicious beast when it wounded me, rather than facing it like a brave Brave. What might have been even worse was if my adventure gave me a Red Indian title like 'Little Chief' Bare-Cheeks. But getting back to the strange dream, a very real incident was about to make it seem a lot stranger still. There was a knock on the door, which when opened admitted Joe Quesek, who was a fairly new addition to the ever swelling ranks of Dale-Martin's wrestling fraternity.

"Have the Borge Twins arrived here yet?" he inquired in lieu of greeting.

"No," I replied, "and why would they? – I'm wrestling in London tonight."

It was not at all unusual for wrestlers who had their own vehicles, which included both of the Borge Twins, to call and pick me up from home and take me to a show where we were all competing. We would share the price of the petrol and forego the pleasure of Dale's free, but much dreaded transport for the day, but if the venue was in London I always made my own way by public transport.

"You're wrestling in Croydon tonight - right?!" he asked.

"Yes, I am." I confirmed, and then asked, "So, why would the Borges be coming here today?"

"We are all going Horse riding," He told me, "and we agreed to meet here."

"Why here?" I inquired.

"We are all going," he stated, "you, me and the Borges."

"Not me Mate!" I informed him, "I was just going out to get my hair cut."

"How long will that take you?" He inquired, "We'll wait for you."

"I love Horses," I told him, "but I'm not interested in riding one!"

"You'll love riding them too." He assured me.

"Okay, I'll come with you," I agreed with a sigh, "but I may ride, or I may just watch the rest of you." After the Borges arrived we all bundled into Joe's car and he drove us to his friend's stable in a beautiful Surrey suburb. By the time we arrived I had agreed to ride, but had insisted that was only if I could choose the very smallest Horse they had in the stable. His name was Pancho, a Chestnut Pony of about 14 hands, and immediately everyone attempted to dissuade me in favor of a much larger model. But I was adamant, "The closer my feet are to the ground, the happier I'll be." I told them.

About a half dozen or so, more friends of Joe had been waiting for our arrival at the stables, three guys accompanied by their girlfriends. We were all soon mounted up, and filed out to begin our ride with me bringing up the rear. At first we proceeded slowly along a country road, and my only concern being the occasional vehicle that past us. Just sitting astride my diminutive Steed as it followed in line, was so much easier than I could ever have imagined it to be. When we left the road and turned into a narrow country lane I relaxed even more and really began to enjoy my first real Horse ridding experience. The lane led us through a small Farmyard, and then continued beyond a Farmyard-gate. The first rider opened the gate and held it open as the rest filed through. Just as I was approaching the gateway we rode past an old rusted out Farm tractor, that for some strange reason seemed to spook Pancho, who after leaping away sideways with a start from the rotting vehicle did it's very best to emulate a frantic French wrestler on a cocktail of speed and Angel-dust. Pancho leapt high into the air, spinning, crashing back to earth, rearing. Joe came galloping back intent on my rescue, but was almost kicked in the face by Pancho's hind hooves, even though he towered over us as he sat astride the majestic 16.5 hand 'Diablo'. Joe had to retreat and give Pancho all the room it desired to go completely insane, by performing twists, turns, and acrobatics designed to throw me off, antics that even 'Horseman Joe' had never witnessed before. BUT – try as it may, and HELL DID IT TRY?!!! It could not unseat me. I had shortened the reigns by twisting it around and around my left fist, and I had stuffed my right hand as far as I could under the front of the saddle. The only way that Pony could have unhorsed me would have been to throw all four legs into the air and fall flat on its back, and thank goodness it didn't as I'm sure that that must have been the one and only tactic that Pancho didn't employ. Finally the bucking, rearing and twisting came to an abrupt end, as exhausted, Pancho just stood and wheezed. All the other riders gathered around, shook my hand and patted my back, and asked over and over,

"How the Hell did you manage to stay on?! – I've been riding for years and I would have been thrown in seconds!" they all told me. My fury at my furious mount, dissipated in record time, as my ego grew and grew to replace it as the compliments from my fellow riders continued unabated to be heaped upon me. Joe once again offered to swap mounts, and this time I agreed,

"But, only after I had ridden Pancho to our destination in order to show him who was the boss." I gratefully gave charge of Pancho over to Joe's tender loving care, and mounted the huge Black and White Charger, 'Diablo' as soon as we reached the 'Flint Field'. The Flint Field comprised of a green, grassy hill, scattered with white stones, white stones everywhere. We began to gallop down the slope at a speed that seemed to force all the blood to the back of my body, and I immediately became aware of the sunlight flickering and flashing through a high Hawthorne hedge on my left hand side, making me want to sneeze - this was the same dream I had had just nights ago, except that this time it was not a dream?!

ADRIAN STREET

THE BALLAD OF SPOTTY MULDOON

Spotty Muldoon – Spotty Muldoon, he's got spots all over his face,
Spotty Muldoon – Spotty Muldoon, he's got spots all over the place.

Comedian Peter Cook had invented a character he named E. L. Wisty for 'The Dudley Moore Show.' E. L. Wisty sat on a park bench and told hilarious stories about his eccentric fictional friends. The funniest and most successful being Spotty Muldoon, who went on to become the hero in an equally funny and successful recorded ballad.

Mickey Muldoon was so furious when he heard it that he threatened to put a hit out on Peter Cook,

"If anyone EVER calls me Spotty Muldoon," he warned, "I'll kill the fucker myself!" In Mickey's line of work as in my own, toughness ruled, respect was paramount and nothing dented a tough reputation more thoroughly than ridicule.

A story he told that was obviously designed to color himself as a dangerous and ruthless character that was not to be messed with, was during the time he was on the run from the law, and driving away from the scene of a crime when he found the road blocked by a Policeman. Not only did Mickey run him down, but backed over him and then ran over him again for good measure – don't ask me if that was the truth, I only have Mickey's word. Another claim concerned a violent confrontation with Boxer, Tough-Guy, Stuntman, Actor, Bouncer, Doorman and Minder, Nosher Powell.

During his Boxing career Nosher had 78 fights, only losing 9 of them and claimed that he had never been knocked out in his life, inside the ring or out of it. When he worked for the legendary Boxing Promoter Jack Solomon as a sparing partner, he sparred with very many Boxing greats, including 'The Brown-Bomber' Joe Louis, 'Sugar' Ray Robinson, Archie Moore, Jersey

Joe Walcott, Joe Erskine, Freddie Mills, Ingmar Johansson, Joe Bygraves, Bruce Woodcock, Nino Valdez and last but certainly not least, The Greatest, Muhammad Ali.

As a Doorman at Jack Isow's nightclub one night he even barred entrance to the notorious Kray Twins for not being properly dressed, and lived to tell the tale.

According to Mickey's story he walked into a Soho bookshop that didn't purchase any of his merchandize from him, and found that the store was pirating his product. After tearing everything he could find to shreds he threatened the terrified owner, who claimed he had bought it all in good faith from another bookstore that was also not dealing with Mickey.

"We'll soon see about that!" snarled Mickey, and rushed out of one bookshop in the direction of the other. Before Mickey arrived the owner of the first shop telephoned the one that Mickey was bound for, and warned them that a furious Mickey was on his way there. When he arrived at the other store his path was blocked by one of the owners, who told Mickey to,

"Fuck off!" Instead of doing what the owner suggested, Mickey knocked him out and entered the store where he began wrecking havoc on everything he could find that had been ripped off of his own merchandize. The terrified son of the unconscious shop owner phoned for aid from their Minder, who quickly appeared like the 7th Cavalry in the form of big Nosher Powell. Nosher was massive, 6 feet 4 inches tall and weighed around 250 pounds, he towered a half a foot above Mickey, and outweighed him by at least 50 pounds, and threw the first punch. According to Mickey's story, he ducked under Nosher's huge fist, threw one right hook of his own which lifted the giant Nosher an extra foot in the air before depositing him flat on his back and out cold!

Now that's Mickey's story, and very impressive it is too, if it was true??? I never heard anyone else confirming his claim, but in fairness to Mickey, I never heard anyone refute his claim either. True or not, Mickey was beginning to make his presence felt as he strove to develop and nurture the image of a Soho Hardman and villain who was not one to mess about with.

As a successful villain in my business it was just as important to be taken seriously, and to allow public ridicule to go unchallenged I believed was professional suicide.

Former R.A.F. and E.N.S.A. man George Lawson-Peake, was one of Dale Martin's top Master of Ceremonies and very much an egotistical company boss. George had been a Master of Ceremonies for over two decades, and before that he was a variety artist, appearing on stage as one of the '8 Lancashire Lads' and also as one of the '5 Bombays'. He was also another alcoholic who could even give the Piss-headed Lou Marco a run for his money – and talking of piss! Whenever inebriated, which was almost every night, George could not hold his water as many a rookie wrestler found out the hard way. It was standard practice to get the newly recruited grapplers to share George Lawson-Peake's seat in one of Dale's dreadful vans, and then laugh the rest of the way back to London after the newcomer leapt out of the seat soaked in hot, smelly piss.

Many are the times I've watched 'Pissy-Peake as he was affectionately known in the business, stagger out of the arena at the end of a wrestling tournament where he would immediately be surrounded by wrestling's autograph hunters. With a look of extreme strain on his reddened face George would begin signing the fan's books; suddenly relief would flood his features as he flooded his trousers. The panic stricken fans would then leap away in all directions, leaving a smiling and smelling George swaying happily as he stood in an ever expanding pool of his own steaming piss.

The Hell's Angels, both Bobby Barnes and myself were always very careful to remain outside the range of George Lawson-Peake's urinary stream, nevertheless 'Pissy-Peake' found another method of pissing on us.

Without fail, the very second The Hell's Angels stepped outside the dressing-room door each night and into the spotlight as we strutted towards the ring, the crowd would erupt. Then the intensity would grow to a crescendo with each and every arrogant step that brought us closer to our battleground. The screamed abuse and booing would be deafening as we entered the ring to await the introductions. First Master of Ceremonies, George Lawson-Peake would introduce the good guy's team, the response would be immense, and the cheering would go on and on. Then one could actually feel the whole audience draw in a collective breath in readiness to vent their rage and disapproval as

The Master of Ceremonies readied himself to introduce the villains. Both Bob and I would then prepare ourselves to throw our pose and receive the screams of hatred and abuse at the climax of our introduction as George Lawson-Peake began his spiel –

"AND – Ladies and Gentlemen – in this corner we have the World Famous – DOLLY SISTERS!!!" Well, the crowd erupted alright, but not with the booing, hate and abuse we were used to, but instead with hysterical laughter. Okay, it was funny, but totally inappropriate, we were there to be feared and hated not laughed at. Pissy Peake's amusing quip not only robbed us of much of our credibility, but also made our night's work much more difficult. In order to be once more taken seriously Bob and I would often have resort to all the dirty tricks and foul tactics imaginable, and dirty wrestling was not our style. Bob and I were very capable of stirring up ultimate hostility by using nothing but our patented aloofness, conceit and arrogance which is very hard to maintain if one is conceived to be a figure of fun. I asked Pissy-Peake again and again to do his job properly and introduce the Hell's Angels in a more fitting and professional manner. But not only was he an ex singer-dancer and comedian, who was determined to display his talent to the fans. He also fancied himself the boss, and a mere wrestler, even of main event caliber should know his place and simply put up with anything that the great ex variety star threw at him. In total exasperation, as I had threatened to do many times, I went to complain to the real boss, Jack Dale. As I expected, Jack came very close to emulating George Lawson-Peake by almost pissing his pants with laughter when I told him of my complaint. I did manage to sober him up when I asked him what he thought of the initial impact the old horror movies, starring Boris Karloff, Bela Lugosi and Lon Chaney jr. had on movie fans,

"Incredible, they were great!" he responded.

"Yes, they were, weren't they? – movie goers were terrified of them" I agreed, but then added, "But Jack, how much did Frankenstein, Dracula and The Wolfman mean after they met Bud Abbot and Lou Costello?"

That really sobered Jack Dale, and I could see that he had fully absorbed my point, but I added, "Don't you agree Jack, that meeting Bud Abbot and Lou Costello put the final nail in Count Dracula's coffin?" and concluded, "Nothing robs a villain of his credibility more thoroughly than ridicule."

"Yes, you're quite right," agreed a very much more serious Jack Dale, "I'll have a word with George Lawson-Peake."

I was gratified that Jack Dale agreed, but for good measure I added,

"If the people representing your business don't take wrestling seriously, how do you expect the fans who buy the tickets to? – If you allow them to turn it into a joke that's all it is. What are you promoting Jack, a rough tough, serious professional sport, or Sunday fucking night at the London Palladium?" From that time on we never heard another word concerning the Dolly Sisters, even from George Lawson-Peake. Bob and I were always introduced as 'The Hell's Angels' as we ought to be, but once again I had made myself yet another very serious enemy.

POLITICS.

As if it wasn't enough to worry about protecting one's own image and reputation in the Wrestling Business as a wrestler, the powers that be, namely all of Joint Promotion's Bosses were constantly jealously jostling for the upper hand amongst themselves. The trickle-down effects of many of their foul schemes and dastardly deeds against each other could also result in very frustrating consequences for their own meal tickets, namely us wrestlers.

Here is just one example of a scheme hatched by Norman Morrell against Dale Martin's Promotion that had a personal effect on me.

By now, without a doubt Mick McManus was the biggest name in British Professional wrestling, much to do with his own skill and personality, also much to do with the fact that he was Dale-Martin's matchmaker, with the power to decide which wrestler would win and which would loose. Obviously as a result Mick never ever, EVER lost a match. He also never had to overly worry about a close rival stealing his thunder as a series of loses to lesser contestants could cut the biggest of them down to size. He would regularly book himself on TV and on every one of the biggest best paying venues in the Dale Martin territory. He would only travel to the Northern Shows if the show he was to appear on was a top big paying spectacular, and that was the very cause of Norman Morrell's disgruntlement. Why should Dale Martin's Promotion have a virtual exclusive of Mick McManus' services for any and every venue in their territory, while he, Norman Morrell could only lure McManus into his own parlor with the promise of spectacular shows which included spectacular pay days for Mick?

Norman Morrell came up with what he thought was the perfect solution. As afore mentioned, as well as his Northern and Scottish venues Norman Morrell also promoted Portsmouth on the South coast and Lime Grove Baths. As Lime Grove Baths was in London, he knew that he would have no problem at all in booking Londoner, Mick McManus to top the bill on his next TV show there.

Originally Mick was billed to wrestle against Mike Eagers, an opponent he had wrestled against many times before, and with whom he had a great match. Mike Eagers was an excellent performer who had great matches with most opponents, especially villains. So lulled into a sense of false security, McManus arrived at Lime Grove Baths confident that he was going to have his consistently great match against a consistently great opponent, and score his consistently great victory, only to find out, too late, that there had been a last minute switch. He was now told that instead he would be opposing Peter Preston, from Norman Morrell's home town of Bradford in Yorkshire, and what he didn't know, but was soon to discover was that Preston had been groomed as Morrell's 'ringer'. Preston had been called to Norman Morrell's home, informed of the last minute switch, and then told by Morrell that he was being offered the chance of a lifetime, by pretending to go along with Mick McManus' usual patented performance. But once in the ring he was to pull an almighty double-cross, by instead beating the formally unbeatable 'Superstar' right there on TV. Then, explained Morrell, Dale Martin's Promotions might still have their exclusive services of The Great Mick McManus, but he Norman Morrell would then have the exclusive services of 'The Only Man to Beat Mick McManus on Television'. "Now is your big chance," he had told Preston, "take it!"

Before both contestants entered the ring it had been agreed

that McManus was going to win by scoring two falls to Preston's one, but Preston was to take the first fall early in the match with Mick scoring the last two. That was not an unusual scenario, as Mick was a master at giving the fans false hope. Hope that tonight was going to be the night that he would finally meet his Waterloo, and towards the end of a match he would often seem to take a terrible hiding and just seconds away from being beaten. Only to suddenly snatch an unexpected victory right out of the very jaws of defeat. Then as hundreds of times before, the fans would leave saying,

"Damn, he almost got beaten tonight - but next time - he'll get it next time – and I'm going to be there to see it!" Unfortunately for Mick, tonight was going to be different, as soon as Preston had taken his scheduled fall he just stopped cooperating, and the match just went to shit. McManus was unable to do anything about it, so instead of trying to beat the younger heavier man, he chose instead to get himself disqualified. Now in my opinion if you are disqualified you have not been beaten. True, you may have lost the verdict, but in my books I regarded a disqualification to be almost as good as a win. A second class win if you like, but not a loss. If I was disqualified, it was usually awarded to me as a reward for my extremely spiteful, sadistic and overly aggressive tactics. By the conclusion of the match it left my opponent laying in a heap of helpless pain, and me boasting and strutting victoriously back to the dressing room, whilst exuding the image of an ultimate winner. This would often aggravate the audience even more than if I had won, as if any of them attempted to insinuate that I had lost the match, I would just laugh and point at what was left of my opponent. I also believed that there was no glory at all in winning a match via disqualification, as you haven't actually beaten anyone. If anything your opponent has beaten himself thanks to his own over exuberance, or by resorting to foul tactics. Either way, he usually ends up walking back to the dressing room uninjured and you don't.

So, even though 'Porky' Peter Preston may have been dubbed as 'The only man to beat Mick McManus on Television', he had made an extremely bad job of it. And if Norman Morrell had imagined that he was going to create a 'Superstar' with Preston he had definitely laid his pennies down on the wrong Pony. I couldn't decide what was more pathetic Preston's method of execution, or Morrell's choice of executioner. Its said 'that you can't make a silk purse out of a Sows ear,' and this was a case in point, even though Morrell had in Preston the whole damned Pig to work with. Peter Preston was not the stuff of a Superstar Wrestler, he had none of the necessary ingredients, his wrestling skills at best were mediocre, his performance skills poor to average. For charisma he'd score nil, and last but certainly not least he had the appearance of the family Butcher rather than a professional athlete. A family Butcher who would become invisible on days when whole carcasses of Pork were delivered to his Butcher shop. His Porcine features would actually quiver, as he waddled his fat physique towards the ring on his little Piggy trotters. He claimed to have had received wrestling tuition from some of the best in the business, why then was he unable to dispatch Mick McManus in a more decisive manner? Mick McManus was a great performer – one of the very best, BUT if it ever came to a real fight my little Sister Pamela could have beaten him in a much more decisive manner than Porky-Preston.

Why, I have often asked myself would an intelligent Man like Norman Morrell make such a terrible mistake in his choice to use Preston, when he had truly great Northern wrestlers like Jimmy Breaks, Johnny Saint, or Alan Miquet at his disposal? If he had really wanted to do a job on McManus, I can't think of anyone better to commit the crime than Bolton's Keith 'Blood-Boots' Martinelli, but why, oh why, use Preston?!

The one and only explanation that makes any sense to me at all, is that in Preston, Morrell was not really interested in creating a bigger star than Mick McManus, but in creating a burr with which he could eternally torment the Southern Superstar. It was no secret that Norman Morrell didn't like Mick McManus, and I believe that his actions were mostly personal. By really scraping the very bottom of the barrel in his choice he was adding the ultimate insult to injury. Not to mention his satisfaction of feeding McManus a tasty dish out of Mick's own kitchen when it came to using a looser to cut a Star down to size. AND – can you imagine the impact felt by McManus for years to come, every time he saw a sorry specimen like Peter Preston on TV, or on wrestling posters, or magazines described as 'The Man who beat Mick McManus on Television'?

Now if you think for one tiny second that Mick McManus would not try to retaliate, and avenge this gross insult with any and every, sly, devious, slimy and petty little trick that he had in his arsenal then you have obviously not been paying attention!

I don't know of any of the many tricks and schemes that he may have hatched except for one that involved me.

Next week I would be leaving home and going up North to work for 3 solid weeks in a row, but this week I was wrestling down South, which included a match on TV at The Fairfield Hall, in Croydon. 'Great,' I thought, 'not only an excellent pay day, but an excellent opportunity to really showboat myself on TV which will add considerably to my drawing power during my upcoming Northern tour. Especially as that would include a few encounters with World Lightweight Champion, George Kidd.' I was also very pleased when I discovered who my opponent on TV was going to be, as I knew that I could have a very exciting contest when matched against Idris Musa the Turk. Now, I wouldn't go so far as to say that Musa the Turk possessed star quality, or even star potential, but he was a very good, solid wrestler, and was very capable of having a great match. Especially if he was wrestling a top wrestler - which I considered he would be on this occasion. When I entered the dressing room I noticed with a little surprise that Johnny Dale, the white haired oldest Brother of the Dale clan was present. Not that his presence at arenas was unheard of, but just unusual enough to attract my attention. He further provoked my curiosity by hovering close by, and seemed to be regarding me speculatively as he sucked on the end of his ever present pipe. Joe D'Orazio the referee called Musa and myself together in order to issue instructions concerning the results of our contest,

"You are in the second televised match," he told us, "it's two falls to one, Musa gets two falls, Street gets the one."

"Great!" I replied, turned and quickly walked away, but still noticed Johnny Dale's eyes narrowing, as my brain was in turmoil, and my former exuberance came screeching to a crashing halt!

'WHAT THE FUCK ARE THESE IDIOTS DOING?!!!!' I

thought.

"You've got that?!" D'Orazio called to my retreating back.

"Loud and clear!" I replied. I walked out of the dressing room and stayed out until after Joe D'Orazio had entered the ring to referee the first televised match. I knew that he would not return until all the televised matches had ended. When I did reenter the dressing room I was extremely relieved to find that Johnny Dale was also absent, and had gone out to watch the matches. I changed quickly into my wrestling wear but waited until the very last moment before speaking to my opponent,

"What are you going to do for your fall?" I asked Musa.

"For my first fall ---," he began.

"What do you mean, for your first fall?!" I interrupted, "you're only getting one!"

"The referee said I get two falls and you get one." Argued Musa.

"Don't be fucking stupid," I told him, "you've never beaten me before – and you won't be beating me today! I'll take my first fall in the second round," I told him firmly, "I'll take a submission in the sixth! I suggest you get an equalizer in the 4th" I told him.

"We should ask the referee." Musa pleaded, "I'm sure he said I get two falls."

"We can't, he's in the ring, and he won't be out until after our match," I replied, "so how do you want to play this?!" I asked threateningly as I stepped closer to his face.

Musa's argument just crumbled, I was certain that he could clearly recall the very rough reception I had given him years earlier when I was preparing myself for the 1,000 pound fight I had hoped to have against 'The King of the Gypsies' Uriah Burton. On that occasion I had all but crippled Idris Musa the Turk.

As we both entered the ring I wondered whose stomach contained the most Butterflies, mine for what I was about to attempt, or Musa's for his inability to prevent the inevitable. If I had been rough with Musa in preparation for The Gypsy King, imagine what he would have to endure now, especially as I was buzzing with bottled up anticipation of firstly would I get away with it, and secondly what would Dale Martin's reaction be if I do?! Well I battered poor Idris from the sound of the very first bell, there was no way that my opponent could get any kind of message to the referee as 'no talking to each other' was strictly observed on TV as paranoid promoters number one rule. I knew that D'Orazio would not suspect what I intended until it was too late. I would get one fall, Musa would get the equalizer, and then the referee would expect Musa to take the third and winning fall in the 6th round. Well, there was nothing he could do about it, I took a submission hold in the 6th and really cranked it up. There was no way that Joe D'Orazio could ignore the fact that my opponent was screaming loud and clear - THAT HE SUBMITTED. If the referee had even attempted to break us up, I was fully prepared to break Musa the Turk's bones. So I won – and very decisively too I might add. I left the ring in triumph. BUT! The second I entered the dressing room all Hell broke loose, D'Orazio and Johnny Dale literally collided with each other in an attempt to be the first one in my face.

"WHAT WAS THAT?!!! They wanted to know, "YOU WERE SUPPOSED TO LOSE NOT WIN!!! They screamed in unison.

"Oh really," I replied, as calmly as I was able, "I obviously must have misunderstood."

"MISUNDERSTOOD!!! They both screamed, "HOW COULD YOU POSSIBLY MISUNDERSTAND YOU WERE TOLD TO LOSE!!!"

"Well I've never lost to Musa before, so why would I be asked to lose to him now – especially on television?" I inquired.

"I DON'T KNOW!" Lied D'Orazio, "They must have had some big plans for Musa and now you've gone and fucked them all up!" he blasted.

"Damn, - that's a shame," I replied sympathetically, "Ho-hum."

Straight away the real reason for this annoying episode was clear to me.

I was going up North to wrestle the very next week, for 3 full weeks, mostly for Norman Morrell's Promotions, and this was just a small part of their pathetic attempt to get back at Norman Morrell by devaluing me as a box-office draw before I left the South to work for him. It would have not only hurt Morrell's promotions, but would have damaged me too. How much would I mean as a challenger for George Kidd's World Lightweight Title, after everyone in Britain had just seen me beaten on Television by a no name, preliminary wrestler who had probably never had a TV win before in his life?!

THE S.S. MAN

Jimmy and his teenage children, Son Jamie and Daughter Janie numbered amongst my best friends north of the Scottish Border almost from the very first time we met. All 3 were great wrestling fans, and amongst the very few Scots who refused to hold both my villain and Sassenach status against me. If I ever needed a ride to or from Airport or railway station, or to a good restaurant, or to my hotel after the matches, this friendly trio were always happy to oblige. They even came to my home in London where Janie fell in love with both my young sons Adrian and Vincent. During a visit to Brockwell Park with my kids, I filmed Janie dressed in the full Scottish regalia dancing on two crossed Scottish Claymores.

One night in Edinburgh after the matches were over, we must have walked right by each other outside 'The Eldorado Stadium' where we had planned to meet, and so I crossed the road and into a large pub looking for them. The noise generated by its customers coming from the main Bar was almost deafening until I opened the door and stepped in. Then almost instantly I could have heard a pin drop in the furthest corner of the large room. Every eye in the crowded Bar was fixed on me, every jaw hung on the chest of the owner of each hanging jaw. I moved further into the room in search of my friends, followed by the only other moving objects in the Pub, namely the eyeballs of every single patron present. Everything else was as still and as silent as a graveyard at midnight. Satisfied that my friends were not present, I left – but as I closed the door behind me the noise erupted again to a much higher level than before I had entered. I quickly reopened the door and the noise abated as quickly and as suddenly as though I had flipped a switch and turned it off.

'Strange,' I thought and was still puzzling when I walked back towards the Stadium and spotted my friends. I related to them what I thought was a very strange occurrence.

"Not strange at all," they assured me, "we have a very large population of Polish ex-POWs who never miss the wrestling.

With your vastly arrogant mannerisms, blond hair, blue eyes, and your black leather boots, trunks and jacket, all decorated with skulls and wings, they claim that you are the closest thing they have ever seen that resembles an ideal portrait of the dreaded S.S. They all call you the S.S. Man." They told me.

I had to laugh, but, only for a second or two, until the full impact of what I had just been told penetrated. I admit that I was always on the lookout for new ways to demand attention, and even shock my audience. But not like that, I would have to go back to the drawing board and find a different way to achieve my objective I determined.

EXCALIBER

Can you imagine any passenger in any country in the World, being allowed to walk onto an aircraft carrying a 4 foot long Samurai Sword – even more especially from Northern Ireland into Britain? But, this was still in the 60s. I had acquired this wonderful weapon in an old Antique shop near the Shankhill Road in Belfast. Four feet long, a blade made of the finest steel ever made, with the Hilt, Tsuba and Sheath carved from an ivory Elephant's tusk. The whole surface was deeply and beautifully carved with Medieval Japanese figures, Armored Samurai Warriors, and their Kimono clad Ladies. Every chink in the armor, every glint in their angry, ferocious eyes, every fold and design on the Ladies Kimonos were etched in the finest detail, from the embroidered flowers and writhing Dragons on their costumes to the grain and decorations in their ornate ceremonial wigs. The Antique dealer had demanded the princely sum of 30 pounds for this murderous, medieval work of art, but after 20 minutes of hot haggling I had talked him down to 20 pounds. On the plane back to England, French wrestler Robert Durant offered to buy it for 30, an American tourist who was also admiring it offered 50 and the auction was on. Durant offered 55, the American 60, Durant then bid 100 pounds and the American bid 150, but there was no way I would have parted with my newly acquired treasure. I had worked very hard as a very young kid to build up my collection of Antique weapons which I had truly loved, but this one was the very best I had every owned.

The first thing Mickey Muldoon wanted to know the first time he saw it was,

"How much do you want for it?!"

But it was very much not for sale. Mickey hated to be outdone, and could be very jealous of most things. This prompted him to search for, and purchase a pair of matching Indian Daggers which he proudly displayed by hanging them on the wall over the fireplace in his lounge. He was very disappointed that he had to draw my attention to them when next I was visiting, but quite honestly they were not worth a second glance. Every weapon I had ever owned had possessed both History and mystery, they were real, and these shoddy Indian daggers were modern, produced cheap by the thousand for the tourist trade, and were total crap. My Samurai sword was unique, possessed a pedigree, a one of a kind a weapon to be proud of. In my opinion Mickey's Indian Daggers not only lacked interest and character, but would even prove to be totally useless as weapons, that was my honest opinion – BUT, on the last count, time would prove me to be very wrong.

AMANDA LOUISE

"Here we go again!" announced Jean.

"Here we go where?!" I wanted to know, yet another Baby was on the near horizon I was told.

'I've got to get a house of our own.' I thought for the thousandth time.

"Save 1,000 pounds," my new mentor, and old enemy George Kidd advised me, "the first 1,000 is always the hardest, the second is twice as easy, and the third thousand is easier still." He assured me. I really wanted to heed his advice but it wasn't easy.

I was so full of apprehension when I remembered the life and death struggle, and the almost day and a half delivery period of our last Baby Vince, that I really wondered if I, let alone poor Jean could take a repeat episode. Plus, this time she was all set to give birth at home. I was with Jean and the Midwife in the bedroom; Adrian and Vincent were playing in the lounge when the Baby arrived. I don't know if either 4 year old Adrian, or 2 year old Vince appreciated the possible gravity of the situation. But I do remember only too well, the look of sheer panic on both their little faces as I attempted, but was prevented by the emotion and the tears that poured from my eyes all down my face. As I tried to tell them both that they now had a little Baby Sister. And I had the little Daughter, that I had not really realized that I had always craved, until she arrived that afternoon on the 11th of May 1967. We named her Amanda Louise.

****

Sandra Muldoon was persistent,

"Who were my two new male models?" she inquired – again!

"Wouldn't you like to know?!" I thought. I was introduced to Bob and Sonny by Jimmy's house guest 'AWOL' Danny, and they both proved to be as good at their job as Danny had promised they'd be.

"Where do they live – when are you going to take some more

photos – are you going to take them in that blond pouf's house?!" She quizzed me endlessly as I was once again sitting on the floor at Mickey's house, sorting through the stacks of photos I had taken the weekend before, and was popping them in sets of 5 into their cellophane envelopes. "If you tell me exactly where Eric lives," she was telling me, "I'd come around and meet them next time you're taking photos."

'YES, - RIGHT! That's just what I thought you'd do,' I thought, 'NO WAY!' Thankfully Sandra didn't know where I took most of the photos, and there was no way I wanted her to know in fact even Mickey didn't know where Eric lived.

"I don't mind posing with them." Sandra offered.

"No, I'm sure you wouldn't," I replied, "and I'm sure that Mickey would be thrilled to bits when I sold him the photos."

"I could wear a disguise," she responded, "I've got loads of different colored wigs."

"Yes," I agreed, but added, "wigs that Mickey bought you to wear when you posed for him."

"Well even if you didn't take any photos, you could watch, couldn't you?" she persisted. Unlike Mickey I had never had the slightest interest in watching,

"Mickey has really done a complete job of corrupting you – hasn't he?" I replied in a quest to divert the subject from my new Male models.

"HUH! More like the other way around!" she claimed.

"I don't believe that for one second," I told her, "you were only 16 when I first met you and you were already married to Mick." But to prove her point she went on to tell me that her Mother had left her Father taking Sandra with her, and gone to live with her Dad's own Brother when Sandra was about 10 or 11 years old.

"Every day when my Mother went to work, Uncle Sid and I would get naked." Sandra claimed.

"So you were corrupted by a dirty old Uncle?" I inquired.

"It was a six of one, half a dozen of the other arrangement." She concluded.

Mickey in the meantime was demanding more and more photos; while I as a result of my increasing status in the World of Wrestling, was finding that I had less and less time or incentive to take them. By now Mickey was running a photographic studio equipped with all the latest state of the art machines, and had gone into business with a fellow pornographer named Evan Phillips. As Mickey's interest in pornography grew, mine waned, and I promised myself once again that very, very soon, I would be taking my last photo for Mickey, just as soon as I had enough money for a deposit on my own house. The next time Mickey came around to pick up my latest negatives he was so excited I thought he must have won the pools.

"No, - better than that," he claimed, "take a look at these photos I took!"

Well I looked and looked again; Mickey's new male model was enormous.

"Are these photos real?" I inquired.

Mickey must have anticipated my response,

"Get your movie projector set up," he demanded, "and watch these movie films I took, you can see for yourself." I set up the projector and watched in disbelief at the new male movie star of Mickey Muldoon's stable – and believe me, this guy definitely belonged in a stable!

"His name is Wally," Mick told me, "he's a total idiot, thinks he's a real film star."

"I'd be inclined to agree with him." I replied.

"He brought a pair of horn-rimmed glasses with him last time I filmed him," Mickey giggled, "asked me if it made him look more sophisticated, like Cary Grant. I told him, who the fuck do you think is going to be looking at your fuckin' face, you fuckin' idiot?!" I looked through the stack of photos again, and noticed that Sandra was extremely conspicuous by her absence. I wondered if she had managed to get close and personal with Wally behind Mick's back yet, as she had with most, if not all of Mickey's other male models. If she knew about Wally and his gigantic equipment, I'm sure that she would do everything possible to track him down, as there was nothing that would make that greedy Bitch's tail wag more than a really 'Big Bone'.

The last time I remember Sandra during that period was when she was offering her opinion on my latest Female model.

"Look at the size of her fuckin' mouth," she exploded, "she looks like Mick fuckin' Jagger!" Well Jill did have very full lips, but she had a very full everything else too – especially where it counted the most. She was barely 5' tall, but had a bust that measured over 40-inches, a tiny waist, very shapely legs, and a bottom like a ripe peach. Mick was flabbergasted when I showed him the first photos I took of her, and his enthusiastic response was not lost on his very jealous Lady Wife.

"Could you imagine a film of her and Wally together?! Mickey gushed, "It would be un-fuckin' believable!!!" I did see Mickey's point, but as he stated, it would be unbelievable, as Jill would never agree to be penetrated by anyone, let alone a human battering ram like 'Whopping Wally'. I had only ever taken photos of Jill on her own, and considering what she brought to the party, that was plenty – and then some. Plus I would never ask someone to do anything they didn't want to, and penetration was definitely out of the question as far as pretty Jill was concerned.

I was well aware of Mickey's views on anyone pirating his merchandize; nevertheless, I had views of my own on that subject. I had never really believed Mickey's story concerning the rolls of blank negatives that he had produced, and used as an excuse not to pay me. Negatives that had cost me precious time and money to produce, not only in film, model's wages and traveling expenses. But also in all the photographic equipment that I found necessary to purchase in order to discover for myself if my camera was misfiring, or if Mick was pulling a fast one. After I had made the necessary investment and processed the film myself, I never had another blank negative – not one, so I am certain that you can see what conclusion I came to. So from the first time I owned my own equipment, I began printing and then photographing the very best of the photographs I took for Mick, and built up a library of my own negatives, before I sold the original negatives to Mickey. Very soon I was making more money selling photos myself than I was making from selling the negatives to Mickey, and under the circumstances felt more than justified in doing both. I never tried to sell photos to any of Mickey's customers, I didn't know, or even want to know who they were. A small percentage of my customers were amongst the wrestlers, who purchased them for resale. But that was small change compared with the sales I made when ever I wrestled at any of the many Army, or Air-force bases, which in comparison made my wages for wrestling at the same venue look like chicken-feed. As a result, at last, I had saved enough money for a deposit on my own house.

TELFORD AVENUE

107 Telford Avenue was a 9 roomed terraced house, counting kitchens and bathroom, close to the bottom of the avenue, and just across the road from the edge of Tooting Beck Common, it was just perfect for our needs. It had a small front garden domineered by a beautiful Rose bush, and a Hydrangea. There was also a fully enclosed back garden with a very large Hydrangea, and an old Apple tree. For me the closeness of the Common was as desirable as the house itself. It took less than one minute from our front door to cross the quiet, narrow road and walk along the grass, or many pathways of a very large, and very green, park like area. It was generously dotted with large trees, wild flowers, ponds, Ducks, a kids playground, with slides, swings, see-saws, and other such rides. There was an outdoor swimming pool, and further on, across another road, there was a continuation of the common that contained a one quarter of a mile running track, complete with changing rooms and showers.

We had already moved most of our belongings from Beechdale Road to Telford Avenue when I received a phone call from Jill who told me that she was in London for the day, and asked if I would like to photograph her. Although I had not yet informed Mickey of my decision that I wouldn't be taking any more photos for him, it crossed my mind that a few extra quid would definitely come handy at this time. So I told her that I would meet her at Beechdale Road. Jean and the kids had already been deposited in our new home, and all that was left in our old flat was a few bits of furniture. As the flat was now empty, I decided to take the photos in a bedroom on the top floor, rather than make the short trip to Eric's house. I had barely closed the door after Jill's arrival when someone began knocking on it; I reopened it to find a disgruntled Andy. His disgruntlement he soon revealed was caused by the fact that both he and fellow model Tony had been eclipsed and usurped by 'Whapping Willie Wally'. I invited him in, introduced him to Jill, who he had lusted after from the first time he had seen her photos, but had never, until that day met in person. Well it seemed to be a very hot combination of love and lust at first sight – and for both of them, not just Andy, especially after they had both undressed and checked each other out. I was quite amazed by Jill's enthusiasm to pose with Andy, and Andy's most outstanding quality was much more outstanding than ever before. But she was still very adamant about the 'no impalement clause'. Lack of impalement or not, in no time flat I had gone through 3 rolls of film, and I knew that I had taken the best photos that I had ever taken for Mickey Muldoon. As both Jill and Andy still only had eyes for each other, and I had other things to take care of, I told them it was time for me to leave, and suggested that they could lock the doors behind them whenever they left. So I went home to Telford Avenue and left the lovebirds to it.

It seemed as though Andy's enthusiasm was highly contagious as the very next day Mickey, accompanied by Andy came to collect the new photos.

'It was very fortunate,' I thought, 'that I had not only processed the film the day before after I had returned home, but had printed a copy of every photo that would enable me to reproduce another set of negatives for my own future use.' The extreme physiques possessed by both Jill and Andy had really made these photos special. But for me the real icing on the cake was the real genuine enjoyment that had been displayed, so much so that they had both seemed totally oblivious to the fact that I was even there with my camera. The newly effervescent Andy still gushed with post action enthusiasm when the wrong phrase he used suddenly sent Mickey off the deep-end.

"WHAT DO YOU MEAN THERE WAS NO FUCKIN'?!!!" Demanded Mick of Andy - pale complexioned Andy went whiter still, He had been in the middle of boasting,

"Adrian says they were the best photos he ever took, even though we didn't actually fuck." That was what caused Mick to explode.

"I've told you before Mick," I interceded, "Jill refuses to be penetrated, she'll do anything else, and quite charmingly I might add, but that's why she's always posed alone." Mickey glared first at Andy who blanched and recoiled as though Mickey, who obviously wanted to, had already struck him a vicious blow to the chops. Then Mick snatched the negatives off the coffee-table and looked as though he would have hurled them across the room, if he had not caught a warning shot from my eyes that arrested that action in favor of him slamming them back onto the table.

"YOU CAN KEEP THE FUCKIN' PHOTOS," Mickey yelled, "I CAN'T USE THEM IF THERE'S NO FUCKIN' FUCKIN'!!!"

"Please yourself Mick!" I began to tell Mickey, but finished telling it to the door that had slammed behind him. Poor Andy just stood there speechless and pathetic, he must have been certain that this batch of photos would have gone a long way towards helping to restore his former value and status with Mick. I was a little disappointed that I wasn't going to receive the 30 pounds I expected, but shit on it, I wasn't planning on taking any more photos for Mickey anyway. Mickey pulled up again outside my house while I was still saying goodbye to Andy on the doorstep.

"I'll give yer a tenner for the lot." He told me.

"Sorry Mick," I told him, "they are not for sale, and I'm not taking any more photos for you, ever." A couple of weeks later, Andy and Tony came to see me again,

"Mickey has been arrested," they told me.

****

Making a name for one's self in my business was not easy, nurturing and protecting that name was a never ending battle. Especially considering that every single one of my peers were franticly attempting to do the very same thing, and the very nature of my business meant that every step forward for one wrestler often meant a step back for another. My relationship with George Kidd was a little different. Just being deemed worthy enough to step into the ring and wrestle against The World's Lightweight Wrestling Champion gave his opponent a huge amount of credibility and prestige whatever the result. In my own case I was scoring almost as many victories over the World Champion as he was scoring over me. So my battles against George Kidd almost overnight elevated me from a good wrestler and performer to a virtual World beater. True Kidd's loss to me today in any given arena would give the World Champion a much greater victory down the road, especially as it would almost definitely be a successful title defense, and another arena packed to capacity.

I was making headway in the South, but at a Snail's pace compared to the North, thanks in no small part to George Kidd. Again and again I made requests to the powers that be to book me against Kidd in the South, but they just looked at me as though I was asking for the Crown Jewels to use in order to complement my latest ring robe.

Ken Joyce told me point blank that I didn't mean enough in the South to even be considered worthy of a match against the great Man. As I have already mentioned, Ken Joyce's biggest claim to fame was the fact that he had actually wrestled against George Kidd, so who was I to try to put myself on a par with him. But eventually he did concede and I was billed in a Main Event contest against George Kidd in London's Wimbledon Palais. Especially, as Wimbledon was virtually in my own back yard, George Kidd himself suggested that I should win the contest, but Ken Joyce would not hear of it. To him it was bad enough that I would be in a position to equal Joyce's career high-spot, but to surpass him by scoring the victory that he had failed to achieve – Oh no! That would be far too much for Ken Joyce's fragile ego to absorb.

Nevertheless, even a match lost against George Kidd did a lot towards causing all the Southern promoters to eye me in a new light. Particularly as George Kidd went out of his way to make certain that I got the Lion's share of the match, and came within a hair's breadth of defeating him before I was finally subdued. But, just think of the gift that George Kidd had offered Devereaux Promotions, only to have it refused by an egotistical old fart like Ken Joyce. If I had won that contest, as George had suggested, not only could that have paved the way for an arena stuffing 'Title Match', but also to a whole series of grudge and revenge matches that could have gone on for a decade or more, as our contests North of the Border were destined to do. AND – do you think that the success that that would have resulted in, would go unnoticed by all the other Southern Promoters?! It would most certainly have spelled big-BIG money for them – maybe only a little more for me, but a shit load of a big stride in my career in the South. But as I had already learned, that often in the wrestling game, ego came before financial gain. Even when they had a star in the making, someone who could consistently put arses on seats, instead of the powers that be aiding in any way they could, they simply hurled obstacle after obstacle in their path. Especially with 'Niggely' Mick at the helm, no one would ever be allowed to come close, let alone threaten his throne.

****

From the very first time that I appeared in Hove Town Hall as a rookie wrestler, the crowd had really responded to me, so much so, that in those days Hove became one of my favorite venues. To begin with I was the ultimate good guy, and the crowd would erupt at the very mention of my name. Everything I did in the ring was so well received that I felt in that particular arena I was already years ahead in my game. When my image took a turn towards the mean and nasty in most other venues, I was at first loathe to display my arrogant and sadistic side to my loyal and adoring fans of Hove - BUT, WHEN I DID – WOW! When the young clean-cut, friendly, modest, agile athlete, suddenly turned into a spiteful, cocky, selfish braggart who would cut any corner in order to gain the upper hand, their love immediately turned to hate. I had betrayed their trust and had hurled their adoration right back into their faces. Nevertheless I had suddenly become a bigger drawing card in Hove Town Hall as a Demon than I ever had as a Saint, and everyone wanted to see my big, fat swollen head brought back down to size.

I had been fortunate to have had a whole string of great opponents over a period of time that had aided me very much in adding to my ever growing status, so much so, that I would physically feel a tingle and a thrill of excitement whenever I received my monthly date-sheet and found that Hove was amongst the venues that I would soon be appearing at. On this occasion I arrived to find my opponent to be Dick Conlon, although I could manage him handily he would definitely not have been my first choice of adversary. He was flighty and clumsy and almost on every occasion we both got hurt, me due to

Dick's clumsiness, Dick due to my immediate retaliation. Outside the ring I liked Dick Conlon a lot; he was very amusing and entertaining to be around, his signature greeting to any of the many pretty Girls at the arenas,

"My name is DICK – do you like it?!" was a classic, and never failed to make us laugh, especially too from some of the Girl's responses to his question. BUT, inside the ring for me was an entirely different World. We were the last match on, that was okay, we were told to do a draw, that was not, then when referee Captain John Harris said,

"I want you to give the audience a nice little 'send them home happy match,' to simmer them down after a very controversial, rowdy, roof-raising Main Event." That was definitely not okay!

"Dick does a great little comedy type match," Captain John added, turning to me, "that will finish the night off perfectly."

"I don't do comedy," I answered sulkily; "I'm a villain."

"The Main Event was a villain match," replied Captain John, "we don't need another one, what we do need is a nice little 'send 'em home happy' comedy match and that is what we'll give them. Is that okay with you Dick?" he asked my opponent.

"Yeah – great! That's okay with me." Confirmed Conlon.

In one sense, I couldn't blame referee John Harris, for the sake of the show it would help balance the evening's entertainment, and as he said 'send the fans home happy' after a controversial villain oriented main event. But, that was not the only motive behind John Harris' request.

Schoolteacher, John Harris was the founder of the famous 'Symbic Wrestling Club' where he trained many great professional wrestlers, which included both of the Cortez Brothers, Leon Fortuna, Young Robby Baron, Dave Larsen, even my own tag-partner 'Bad-Boy' Bobby Barnes, and last but definitely least in my book was, Dick Conlon. So in another sense I couldn't blame John Harris, as he was obviously trying to look after one of his own. – BUT, NOT AT MY EXPENCE, DEAR JOHN!

"Well, it's NOT okay with me." I replied, and repeated, "I don't do comedy, I'm a villain." He tried the argument concerning team spirit, and I responded by pointing out that not only was I not a 'team-player', but I had no conception at all of what 'team-spirit' actually was. There was no more time to argue the point; it was time to go into the ring, and I was all over Clumsy Conlon before the vibration died away from the sound of the opening bell, and I stayed on him until the bell's final vibration died away to end the match. Back in the dressing room Conlon was silent and subdued, Captain John Harris on the other hand was furious and wasn't shy in expressing it. I was totally unrepentant,

"I didn't come into this business to become a comedian's stooge," I stated, "I came into this business to become a wrestler, I don't have nice little matches designed to 'send 'em home happy' and I don't pull my fucking horns in for anybody, if you book Adrian Street – you get Adrian Street!" I told him – "And there's nothing you, or anybody else can do about it!" I added for good measure.

BUT BOY! Yet again, - was I ever wrong about that one!

****

"Hi Mick, when did you get out?" I asked Mickey Muldoon in way of greeting as I opened the front door in answer to his knocking.

"This morning," Mickey replied, "I came straight here to see how you've been getting on." Mickey came in and joined us for lunch; I believe he said he had been imprisoned in Chelmsford. We must have chatted for a couple of hours when Mickey told me that he was going to visit his partner Evan Phillips, and asked me if I wanted to go with him? I can't say that I was particularly fond of Evan, but on the few occasions I had met him he had given me a large stack of photos and a few Blue movies, which I had sold for a fairly tidy sum. With that in mind, and as I wasn't wrestling that night, I decided to accompany Mickey. I had never visited Evan's home before, but I believe we ended up somewhere near Kew Gardens before Mickey parked his car outside his partner's house. Mickey was laughing at something I had been telling him as we came to a glass windowed porch and rang the bell, and a half a minute later the front door was opened by a popeyed, open mouthed Evan. He quickly ducked back behind the door, with nothing but one glittering eye staring through the very narrow gap.

"OPEN THE FUCKIN' DOOR!!!" Mickey demanded, his former jovial demeanor evaporating in a flash. Evan shook his head back and forth in way of refusal; I could still only see one of his eyes.

"OPEN THE FUCKIN' DOOR, YOU FUCKIN' ARSEHOLE!!!" Mickey roared once more. Evan shook his head more frantically in denial; - Mickey then reached into his pocket and quickly retrieved it with a revolver in his fist,

"OPEN THE FUCKIN' DOOR, YOU FUCKIN' FAT CUNT, OR I'LL SHOOT YOU RIGHT THROUGH IT!!!" Mickey snarled. Evan began to shake his head again, but then suddenly flung the door open, and with the falsest and most sheepish grimace on his greenish, white face greeted Mickey as though he was his long lost favorite Brother,

"Hey, Mickey mate, - how are you?"

'Shit! Evan's acting is great!' I thought, as Mickey and I entered his home, I didn't think he had it in him. I had often seen wrestlers put on similar charades, in an attempt to fool younger wrestlers who were new to the business, not with guns of coarse, but threatening mock violence, as though all hell was about to break loose, and then laugh hysterically at the shocked and intimidated youngster's reaction.

Then Evan still in character of a terrified victim called up his stairway,

"Stay up there Sandra darling - it's just Mickey – he won't be staying long!"

'Oh my God!' I thought, 'if Sandra has been messing with Evan while Mick has been in jail, this might not be a joke!' Then a very high pitched Women's voice called down, "Oh, Evan darling what on Earth is going on down there?!"

'Reprieve,' I thought, 'that is not the voice of the Sandra I knew!'

Correct, - it turned out that Evan's Wife was also named Sandra,

'Ha – I knew it was just a joke!' I thought again.

"GIVE ME ALL THE FUCKIN' MONEY YOU OWE ME, YOU FUCKIN' FAT BASTARD OR I'LL SHOOT YOU, AND THEN GO UPSTAIRS AND SHOOT YOUR FUCKIN' WIFE –

AFTER I'VE FUCKED HER!!!" Mickey roared.

'OOPS! Now that didn't sound like a joke!' I thought, 'even by a wrestler's outrageous standards.' Then as though to cinch my thoughts Mickey strode over to a glass drink cabinet and smashed his fist which still gripped that nasty looking gun right through the glass, before he grabbed a bottle, unscrewed the top and began guzzling,

"WANNA DRINK?! He asked me. Which was the first time he acknowledged my presence since we had entered Evan's house. I declined, this is serious I decided at last – 'duh!!!' What I eventually learned was that one of the agreements of Evan's and Mickey's partnership was, that if either one of them fell foul of the law, the other would still pay him his end of the deal for the whole duration of his incarceration. Evan had been instructed by Mickey to pay his Wife, Sandra Muldoon his cut, while Mickey was in prison. Evan had only paid her for the first week, and had then totally defunct on their agreement. Mickey demanded that Evan was to pay him 5,000 pounds immediately, but Evan claimed he didn't have that kind of money in readies to give him. Mickey then threatened Evan that he would not leave until he got it, or at least a very large down-payment. Evan then produced about 900 pounds which Mickey snatched out of Evan's trembling paw and stuffed into his pocket after counting it all out on the coffee table.

"That's not enough!" he growled at Evan, "call your partner and tell him to bring the rest right now!" It took hours for Evan to track down his original business partner and ask him to bring all the cash he could possibly lay his hands on, and deliver it to Evan's home as quickly as he could. By this time the banks were already closed so Evan's partner Bob, who seemed to believe that Evan needed the cash to close some mutual and very lucrative business venture agreed to do his best. Bob, as Evan's partner was not only aware of the deal that Evan had had with Mick, he was a part of it. So Evan was very careful not to reveal the true reason for this financial emergency as he knew for certain that Bob would not come within many miles of his house if he knew that Mickey was there. Evan didn't warn his partner of Mick's presence, even after he had opened the door to him, and had allowed him to lead the way right into Mickey Muldoon's face.

Talking about faces, Bob's face registered a look of shock and horror that suggested that someone had suddenly stuck a red-hot poker about 2 feet up his arsehole!

"Mick how are you – when did you get out?!!!!" Bob Managed to splutter at last, as his face did enough frantic aerobic exercises that it could have instantly removed 20 pounds of blubber off Evan's fat gut. At the same time he dropped the contents of a cardboard shoebox he was carrying on the floor, which resulted in a moderate sized hill of small banknotes on the carpet in front of him.

"How much have you got?!!!" Mickey demanded and after counting it Mickey discovered there was a little over 1,400 pounds.

"When am I going to get the rest?!" Mickey wanted to know, Evan promised to phone and let him know within the next couple of days, so at last we left Evan's house. Mick with his pocket full of money, me with no free photographs, or Blue-movies to show for a very disturbing evening.

True to his word – for once, the thoroughly intimidated Evan did call Mickey to make arrangements to pay him off once and for all – and a couple of days later here was Mickey banging on my door once again asking me to accompany him while he met Evan to collect his dues.

"I'm going to meet him," as Evan had insisted, "in a very crowded pub in Soho," Mickey told me, "Evan is too scared to meet me anywhere private, I told him he has to give me a total of another 3,000 for keeping me waiting." Mickey giggled gleefully.

I immediately declined Mickey's invitation, as there was no promise of reward for possibly putting myself in harms way. Plus I had the legitimate excuse that I was wrestling that night, and would soon be leaving for Dale's office to catch my ride to that nights venue,

"In fact," I told Mickey, "you can give me a lift down to Dale Martins on your way to meet Evan in Soho." Mickey agreed, but decided to pick up Andy and Tony on his way. I couldn't imagine why he felt he needed company as I am certain that Mickey was capable of totally demolishing both Evan and Bob in one minute without even breaking a sweat. Although, Mick never missed out on a chance to act tough, even more so if he had an audience.

Mickey came around again the next day to give me a blow by blow account of what had occurred the day before, just outside the Soho pub.

"Did you have to bring a couple of thugs with you?" Evan asked Mickey, no doubt a little emboldened by the immediate proximity of large crowds of potential witnesses who were crowding the streets of Soho,

"Just give me the fuckin' money, shut your fuckin' fat mouth and then fuck off!" Mickey suggested, - Evan seemed more than happy to comply. I had rarely seen Mickey in such a jubilant mood. So jubilant in fact that even taking into account that he had just recovered all the money he had owing him, to me his mood seemed disproportionately jolly. My assessment was correct,

"My mate Gerry is getting out of nick next week," Mickey told me, he's going to work for me."

"Doing What?" I inquired.

"Posing and watching my back." Mickey replied.

"I thought you had plenty of male models?" I said, "You'll never get one to replace 'Whopping Willie Wally." I laughed.

"I have!" claimed Mickey, "compared to Gerry, Wally looks like a little Boy!"

"Bollocks!!! I told him in total disbelief, as a picture of Wally in hot action past my mind's eye, "I'd have to see that to believe it." And as Mickey didn't have any movie or photographic evidence about his person, I did continue to disbelieve his claim.

BUT – once again time would prove me wrong.

****

After 3 straight weeks wrestling up North, tonight was going to be my last match before returning home to London. I had traveled to Darlington by train, and upon reaching Darlington Station I lost no time in purchasing a one way ticket, that included a sleeper-compartment. That would be a most relaxing way to complete my journey to London after the wrestling matches had concluded that night.

I was going to be wrestling in the Main-Event contest against World's Lightweight Wrestling Champion George Kidd in Darlington's Baths Hall. I was going to be wrestling against the

World's best Wrestler and refereed by Brian Crabtree the World's best referee and I thought, 'Things don't get much better than this.'

But things did, as I won the contest and challenged The Champion to defend his title on the very next show in Darlington. It had been a challenging match – pun intended. But not challenging enough to tire me as much as I wanted to be, to ensure a good night's sleep on my train ride back home to London. I was excited with my match and excited about going home to my family after 3 weeks on the road, and I needed to simmer down if I was going to get a good night's sleep on my train journey back home.

Obviously the Main Hall that contained the biggest pool was being used to stage the wrestling show, but there was also a smaller pool that we wrestlers had full access to. I knew from past experience that swimming could really tire me if I hadn't swam in a long time. I hadn't, so I really went nuts, driving myself to the very brink of exhaustion. I was just about ready to drag my bone weary carcass out of the pool when I was joined by Brian Crabtree who gave me a lesson in diving, which he excelled at, as I didn't.

Well if I'd wanted to be tired I'd achieved my goal, and then some. But I hadn't finished yet by a long shot. I'd noticed a very nice looking Italian Restaurant just across the road from the Baths Hall which I had decided would be a perfect way to end a most memorable day before making my way to the station to catch my train home. Little did I know that my day was destined to become much more memorable still.

A huge plateful of tomato, mushroom and garlic saturated pasta, and a Steak that must have been generously carved off a very large Elephant, washed down with 2 bottles of Chianti, and I was ready to hit my mobile bed and snooze away the miles to London. If I could possibly stand up and successfully navigate my way from my table to the Restaurant's exit. I walked slowly up the hill towards the station, yawning deeply as I staggered on, 'My biggest ordeal now,' I thought, 'would be trying to keep my eyes open long enough while waiting on the platform, to know when my train had actually arrived.'

When SMASH – MY FACE EXPLODED! – Just before the

back of my head bounced a foot off the hard, unyielding pavement. What the HELL just happened?! – A horde of fierce Vandals armed with a giant iron tipped battering-ram must have just mistaken my face for the main gate of the Ancient City of Rome. I tried to roll onto my hands and knees when a cannonball missed Nelson's Flagship, Victory and plowed right into my ribs helping me to achieve my goal. Now on my hands and knees, I tried to focus, and when I did I saw a large black boot which was becoming very much larger – BOOOOSH – WOW! Fireworks everywhere – it's November the 5th and the 4th of July all rolled into one. As I shook the last sparks of the firework display out of my eyes, I once again spotted that big boot getting much bigger, as it slowly began to dawn on me that I ought to try to do something. 'I don't much like this,' I thought and managed to grab onto the leg of the trousers just above the big boot that had just bounced off my face for the third or fourth time. But here comes the other boot – SPLAT!!! In spite of all the sparks, I still managed to grasp onto the other leg, and hand over hand used them to try to aid me in my very slow and very painful ascent. Slowly I dragged myself back to my feet, serenaded by an explosion of fists beating out a tempo on my face which sent my head spinning from left to right and then back again for every single inch of my slow motion ascension. When at last I found my feet I went on the attack – by pathetically trying with both hands to squeeze my aggressors throat while he just kept up the barrage of his pounding fist which continued to smash my head from left to right again.

Beginning the very next day, and lasting for many years to come, I tried in retrospect to analyze my response in that situation. For someone like myself with so much experience, and with so many lethal weapons in my arsenal, I was totally disgusted and could not imagine why my performance up to that point was so very pathetic. Was it the wine, the power behind his first punch, or both?! A final mighty punch sent me flying backwards, returning me with another violent crash back onto the pavement. Then instead of continuing his assault as I imagined he would, my attacker picked up my case containing my wrestling wear,

"I'm taking this!" he told me, speaking for the very first time.

"OINK – LIK – OINK – OINK – OINK!!! I replied viciously, or at least that's what it sounded like, - what I tried to say was, "Leave my bag, you fucking arsehole!" but there was something wrong with my nose. "OINK – LIK – OINK – OINK – OINK!!! I repeated, but instead, still in possession of my bag he walked around the corner and was gone. "OINK – LIK – OINK – OINK – OINK!!! I roared with added authority and was after him like a Bat out of Hell. To my surprise he too was running like a Bat out of Hell, down a hill which ran at right angles to the road that I had been walking up when my attacker had suddenly, and without warning, punched me in the face. The cause of my surprise was, that after what he had just done to me, why was he running away? He'd smashed me to pieces, and I'd retaliated with all the fury and effectiveness of a badly wounded Butterfly.

'What the fuck am I going to do when I catch him?' I wondered, 'he'll bloody well kill me!' As I chased him down the hill, I tried to look for some kind of weapon that would give me some kind of chance against such an opponent, a stick, a brick, a milk-bottle. But my vision was very badly impaired by what seemed like a fan-shaped fountain of blood, spraying out of my nose just below my line of vision. I could see clearly ahead, but if I tried to look down it was just like trying to see through a dense red curtain. At the bottom of the hill my quarry ran into the entrance of a wide cobble stoned Alleyway, just as a plan of action finally formed in my befuddled brain. It was a tactic that had paved the way for many a previous victory. When I faced him next, as I was determined to do, I would take a dive at his legs as though I was attempting to take him to the ground. But, it would be a purposely half-hearted attempt. This would allow my opponent to counter the move by reaching over my back and locking his arms around my body below both of my arms in order to prevent me taking him off his feet. With that accomplished, I would then lock both my arms above his elbows to prevent him retracting them. And then jerk him off his feet towards me, and as I lifted him, I would throw my feet into the air and drop backwards, breaking my own fall onto the solid cobbles with the back of my adversaries head. This maneuver in professional wrestling was called a 'double-elbows', I was very aware of its effectiveness, as I had put it to great use on many occasions after first seeing it performed in the ring by none other than Bert Assirati.

Well that's what was supposed to happen. A few more yards into the alley and the thief spun around and attempted to hit me with my case, and had inadvertently placed himself at the very angle that I would have been looking for. Unfortunately with the momentum I had achieved by tearing at full speed down the hill, prevented my clever approach, and instead the impetus of my mad charge sent me crashing right into him with so much force that we both ended up rolling over and over on the cobbles. After a brief struggle I was fortunate enough to get on top, but before I could take advantage of my position he managed to struggle out of my grasp and stood up facing me. I was dumbstruck, as when ever I managed to take someone down, it was normal for me to be the only one who could get up after I had done with them. He lashed out with one boot in an attempt to kick me between the legs, it missed and I tried to return the compliment with the same result. Missing the target as he had just done reminded me that kicking my adversary in the balls was not part of my normal repertoire. Not because I didn't want to, its just a lot more difficult to do effectively than most people imagine it to be. So when ever he aimed a kick at my crotch and missed, I retaliated by smashing my foot into his knee or shins. It proved to be effective, so effective in fact that it caused him to throw caution to the wind when he tried to grab hold of my head. Instead I used his forward impetus by grabbing his head and smashing it into the side of a brick built house behind me. I attempted to repeat it, but he placed his hands against the wall, straightened his arms which prevented me being able to do it again without a very strenuous struggle. So instead I attacked his legs again by kicking them right away from under him, he tried to roll away but I ran in and caught him with a tremendous kick right into his face.

'Wear that you fucker.' I thought. I ran at him to send another kick chops-ways, but was halted by a car that suddenly appeared around the corner and almost ran over me. The Thief took advantage by leaping up, and once more throwing a roundhouse kick at my crotch. Once more it only caught me on the thigh, while my answering kick must have almost severed his kneecap. He yelped and bit the cobbles as the car backed back around the corner and sped off. I dove in and delivered another kick with my left foot which sliced across his head, and sat him down with a bump on his arse. He attempted to rise, and I stepped forward and threw everything I had into one big fight finishing kick with my right foot, just as another car came hurtling around the corner and screeching to a halt two steps away from hitting me. My foot past harmlessly past the thief's face, and my shoe shot right off my foot and sailed off into the darkness somewhere behind the car.

Now I panicked, my most effective weapon so far in this encounter had been my right foot, now my shoe was gone, and my best offensive with it. As the second car backed out of the alley, I launched myself into the air and landed bodily on top of my adversary just a second before he managed to stand. I grabbed a huge handful of his thick black hair with my left hand, stuck my right hand down the back of his collar, and twisted the necktie he was wearing around my clenched fist with all my strength. As I held him face down on the cobbles I bit into his left ear, and gnawed on it like a hungry Hyena while I continued to choke the life out of him with his own necktie. Soon I felt his body go limp, but I still tore away at his ear that was squirting blood like a ruptured oil well. When I finally did release his torn and tattered ear, and his throat it was to roll him over and go to work on his face. Conscious or unconscious, it was now ground and pound time, but with a subtle twist. Okay it may not have been subtle, but there was definitely a twist, a twist of my thumb as I forced it into his eye socket and attempted to pull it out. Then I began punching down onto his face again, but with the same bloody thumb extended so that it repeatedly stabbed his other eye, while my fist spread his nose over his face. I have to admit he had upset me a trifle, and I was finding it very difficult to find forgiveness in my heart, or a good reason to stop punishing him. But finally I stood up parted his legs and stomped on his balls as though I was squashing a ripe Tomato, just to bid him a final fond adieu.

I had already forgotten him as I searched in the darkness for my case and my shoe. As I was slipping my shoe back onto my dainty kicking foot, I heard a noise behind me, I turned quickly To see Lazarus rise from the dead, mumble,

"You Bastard, you've done my eyes!" And then disappear around the corner.

Was the would be thief the toughest man I had ever fought, or was it down to the fact that he had almost knocked me unconscious with a punch I wasn't expecting, coming from nowhere out of the darkness after I had eaten and drank too much? – I'll gnaw on that one for the rest of my life. After hearing this tale, many have asked me why did I risk life and limb chasing after someone who had already inflicted so much damage, when all that was at stake was my case containing just one set of the many wrestling outfits I owned? Well my reply to that is, even if the case had been empty I could never allow anyone to steal it from me in such a fashion. The fact that it was not empty, but contained an expensive ring jacket and boots, would add to my determination not to lose it, but there was an even more valid reason.

Just imagine when the thief opened my case and discovered my very unique ring-wear; it would only be a matter of time before he also discovered that it had belonged to the wrestler Adrian Street. Adrian Street? Oh yes, that Adrian Street, the same wrestler who had just defeated George Kidd, the World's Lightweight Wrestling Champion, and challenged him to defend that title on the very next wrestling show in Darlington Baths Hall. The same Adrian Street who just a couple of hours after beating the best wrestler in the World, he had beaten like a Dog and walked off with his case, leaving Adrian Street laying and bleeding in the gutter. Oh no, that could never happen, I just had to have my case – AND my revenge. I was not just fighting to get my property back; I felt that even more importantly I was fighting to retain my own credibility, George Kidd's credibility, and even the credibility of professional wrestling in Darlington. No damned Thug, never mind how tough he may have been would ever enjoy the satisfaction of accomplishing that foul deed, and no one, while I still had a breath of life left in my body ever would!

"What happened to you, did you just fall off your bike? – Ha-Ha-Ha!" asked the ticket collector as I handed him my railway ticket at the station gateway.

He quickly handed it back, and even more quickly moved aside to let me pass, after seeing the expression change on what was left of my face, and me step into his, as my right hand balled into a fist. I was not in the mood for a worn out witticism.

It wasn't until after I had entered my Sleeper-compartment and closed the door securely that I felt the muscles in my clenched jaw and balled fist relax. But when I examined my reflection in the mirror over the washbasin, I really wondered what the fuck was looking back at me?! My nose was still basically in the centre of my face, in spite of the fact that everything that surrounded it was discolored, swollen, lopsided and covered with blood. My hair was spiky and stiff with dried blood, every line and crevice was etched dark red, still glistening in patches with fresh blood that continually oozed from a multitude of cuts and scratches all over my face. I filled the basin with water and began to gingerly splash its contents onto my face, and watch as the basin turned quickly from white, to pink, to bright red. Eventually most of my face seemed much cleaner, except my nose that just looked like someone had just stuck a half eaten tomato onto it. I continued to splash it with water, but the big bloody blob just wouldn't seem to dissolve never mind how much I soaked it. So I tried to get a grip on the blob and pull it off but it just kept slipping through my fingers. With a huge sigh of impatience I filled both my cupped hands with water and hurled it in my face, and was horrified to discover that the big bloody blob I had been trying so hard to pull off the middle of my nose, was the middle of my nose. I refilled the basin with clean water, submerged my face into it for a full minute, then quickly looked in the mirror, and for a quick second could actually see white bone showing through two parallel gashes running vertically down my nose before the blood once again welled up to hide it.

In courtesy to the railway, I opened my case and draped my own damp towel over my pillow before laying my painful, leaking face and head onto it. I thought about all the wounds I had just sustained, and imagined all the fantasies I could have woven around them and the lies I would have told as a child. About my death defying battle with an enemy War-party, or the giant Grizzly Bear that had caused them - to me – the one who was destined to become the most famous War-Chief in the whole World. Then I fell into a fitful sleep as the train chugged on through the night to London.

The next night I was wrestling in Bath, I had already successfully succeeded in horrifying Jean, and startling my Kids with my 'New Look'. I don't think Mandy even recognized me, but the two boys recovered quickly, as they were both big fans of the old black and white 'Horror Movies' that were often shown on TV, and thought that having their own scary Monster for a Dad was really cool.

I had arrived in Bath early, I really loved that City, and enjoyed exploring it on every opportunity I got. It was dark by the time I made my way back to the Pavilion, that's when I had become aware that someone had been following me. I increased my pace, the sound of the footsteps behind me also increased; I slowed up and so did the sound of my pursuers footsteps. I again increased my pace as I began to cross the bridge leading to the Pavilion, and began to feel my blood tingle as the footsteps behind once again mirrored my own. I was aware that I couldn't see another living person anywhere, I went faster, so did my pursuer. My heart was in my mouth when I stopped dead, and a very tall, slimly built man walked by me. He suddenly spun around to face me and I must have jumped about a foot in the air, but instead of the attack I was expecting he lisped,

"Excuth me Dear, - have you got the time?"

"TIME FOR WHAT?! FUCK OFF YOU FUCKING SCREAMING PANSY!" I screamed into his face, "OR I'LL RIP YOU IN HALF AND THROW THE PIECES OFF THIS FUCKING BRIDGE!" He fled in terror, 'but,' I thought, 'he'd have to run awfully fast if he wanted to match my heartbeat as he had my footsteps.' It was quite a while after the Darlington incident before I returned to my normal, overly confident, completely oblivious to any kind of possible danger mode – and I really hated that.

In the dressing room before the match I began to liberally apply the make-up that I had brought with me for the purpose of disguising the extensive damage to my face. I knew that the make-up would rub off, and that at least a few of the many cuts would reopen during the match. But I thought it would be much more desirable to give my opponent the credit for causing the injuries, than to appear to be so badly injured before I had even entered the ring. My ruse worked, my wounds didn't show until after I had tortured my opponent unmercifully. He had rallied and made a vigorous and valiant comeback, which caused the make-up to dissolve, the bruises to glow and the blood to flow, the audience screamed and lots of fun was had by all.

But, something had occurred that night, which caused yet another metamorphosis surge in my forward and upward character development. In spite of my very best attempts to disguise my injuries, I had also hoped that the make-up I applied for that purpose would not be too obvious either. But, on my way to the ring, I began to hear a murmur erupt amongst the audience,

"Is he wearing make-up – WHAT NEXT?!"

WOW! Now that gave me food for thought!

****

Andy and Tony had not been at all happy with their working conditions since the introduction of Whapping Willie Wally. Now since the arrival of the even more formidable competition 'posed' by 'Gigantic Gerry' they were both at their wits end. Their present role in Mickey Muldoon's ever expanding empire seemed to have dwindled from 'Super-stud-stardom' to part-time gofers. Whilst Tony suffered the added indignity of his Wife Pauline working overtime posing with the company's two new juggernauts while he just twiddled his thumbs on his own at home, or carried out menial chores around the studio when Mick took photos. I was quite certain that as Pauline was libido wise, of a very similar ilk to Sandra that she would not be in the least bit unhappy with the new arrangements. But that would obviously add a heap more insult to injury as far as the poor dejected Tony was concerned. Tony's distress was not lost on Sandra who had long coveted Pauline's role, and she began to taunt poor Tony unmercifully, very soon both Mickey and Gerry got in on the act. Whenever Tony was present, Sandra and Mickey would enjoy observing Tony's mounting discomfort. They encouraged the Stallion like Gerry to pullout all the stops and to batter the living daylights out of pretty Pauline until her squeals of shear delight could have been heard on the Moon.

"I'll bet you can't follow that Tony!" Sandra would snicker maliciously.

"What can I do for you?" I asked Andy and Tony after admitting them to my home.

"We want to offer you a deal." They answered in unison.

"What kind of deal?" I inquired.

"A partnership," Andy replied.

"We want to leave Mickey and start our own business," Tony added, "All you have to do is take the photos and keep Mickey off our backs, and we'll split the profits three ways, between you, Andy and me, wadda ya say?"

"I say the same as I told Mickey," I told them, "I've finished taking photos."

"We'll make a fuckin' fortune." Tony coaxed.

"None of Mickey's customers like him," Andy chimed in, "I know they'd rather buy from us."

"We've already straightened out the law," Tony added, "they'll give me 'n' Andy a license no problem."

He went on to tell me that in order to do business with the Soho bookshops without being nicked or molested, one had to buy protection from the Police or the Krays.

"Better to pay 'Old Bill,'" Andy advised, "The Krays are never satisfied."

"If you are already going to pay for protection, why do you need me?" I wanted to know.

"'Old Bill' can't protect us from Mickey and Gerry." Tony claimed.

"Why not?" I wanted to know, "if they can protect you against the Krays, Mickey and Jerry shouldn't be a problem."

"That Black Bastard, Gerry used to work for the Krays," Tony told me, "but they let him go 'cos he was even too much of a loose cannon for their firm!"

"I'll be honest with you Adrian," Andy pleaded, "we are shit scared of Mickey and Gerry, but if you're with us, I know they'll leave us alone."

"I'm sorry, but I'm not interested." I told them.

"We'll give you 50-percent and me 'n' Andy will split the rest." Tony offered.

"I'm not interested," I repeated, and then added in an effort to divert the subject, "is Gerry the Monster Mickey's made him out to be?"

"Hung like a fuckin' Horse!" replied Tony in utter disgust.
"Bigger than 'Whopping Willie Wally'?" I asked.
"A fuckin' lot bigger!" Tony claimed morosely.
"Has Sandra got to either of them yet?" I inquired.
"What do you think!?" Tony replied.

In truth I had intended to stop taking photos, but Kalman had introduced me to a photographer named Kenneth, who at first had seemed very interested in purchasing my negative library. After seeing the quality, he had instead invited me to join him and a group of photographers who practiced their art every weekend in a house in Belgravia. Most of their models were Strippers, and were recruited by Kenneth's Girlfriend, Tooee, who was also a Stripper. There was usually anything up to a dozen Strippers posing every Sunday, and almost as many photographers all snapping away at the same time. My involvement with the Belgravia Brigade only lasted a few weeks, owing to the fact that I discovered that all kinds of illegal drugs were being used there. I knew nothing at all about any kind of drugs, in fact I still don't, and don't want to. I've always claimed to be a natural dope, and have no need whatsoever of any unnatural stimulant to be every bit as silly as I want to be. I had become discontent and disillusioned with the group from the time of the very first session, owing to the fact that I could smell food cooking which made me so hungry that I could have eaten my camera. And yet after taking photos for hours no one ever offered me a bite to eat. From time to time little groups of both Male and Females would disappear into other parts of the house, the tantalizing aromas would become almost unbearable, and no one gave me a crumb. I was convinced that just about everyone was taking time out to eat, and for some reason I was the only one not invited to join them. When I eventually did complain, it was explained to me that what I could smell was not food, but some kind of 'wacky-backy' and I was suffering from the second hand effects that was making me so ravenously hungry. I was totally paranoid concerning drugs, and that would have been enough to make me quit the club. But when Kenneth became deathly ill after accidentally taking some kind of aphrodisiac that he had meant to feed to one of the Strippers that he fancied, I was certain that it was time to say 'Adios Amigos' – so that was what I said. The whole Belgravia affair would have been a complete waste of time, but for meeting Big Abe there. Abe was a huge overweight Jewish Porn-peddler, whose 'Blue-movie' wholesale prices left plenty of room for making some excellent profits. But, as far as Mickey Muldoon's unhappy models were concerned I was finished with the business. I did like Andy and Tony a lot, and was sad to see them so distressed as they were normally a lot of fun, and very comfortable to be around, but I had made my mind up and that was definitely the end of that. BUT, once again I was 'dead' wrong – or at least, could have easily been made that way.

CAPTAIN'S REVENGE

I was certain that my last performance in Hove when I had wrestled against Dick Conlon had done very little to enhance my image there. But, thanks to my total lack of cooperation in that match I felt that it had not been damaged too badly either, and tonight I planned to really make up for it, and make the fans forget all about my last appearance in Hove Town Hall. I had not crossed paths with Captain John Harris since the night in question, but nevertheless, I smiled disarmingly at him in way of greeting as I entered the dressing room. I got a very strange look in return, one that at first I couldn't really decipher, until I had fully scanned the room and my eyes locked with those of Wigan's own 'Stiff-Cliff' Beaumont. What was the last thing that I had said to Captain John? - Oh yes,

"I came into this business to become a wrestler, not a comedian's stooge, I don't pull my horns in for anyone, if you book Adrian Street, you get Adrian Street and there's nothing you, or anybody else can do about it!" Yeah right - obviously I couldn't have been considering 'Stiff-Cliff' when I made that statement – OOOPS!

I glanced back at Captain John, and hated the smug look of triumph decorating his leering chops as he observed me digesting the situation. So I took myself into the furthest corner of the room, sat down in disgust, and prepared myself for my match like a prisoner on Death-Row prepares himself for his own big event. I thought I may have got somewhat of a reprieve when the gaunt, grey haired, raw boned Wigoner strode over to me, and after puffing a few times on his foul-smelling, ever present Woodbine, he said,

"I've heard you only wrestle as a villain now?"

"Yes, that is correct." I replied.

"Good, wrestle villain tonight - we'll have a great match." He told me.

I felt so relieved that I forgot to wonder who had told him that 'I only wrestle villain now.' Okay, well this gets very, very painful, so let's make it as short as possible.

I marched to the ring serenaded by the same hostile chorus from my Hove Town Hall admirers as I had grown to expect, so far so good. I entered the ring and received even more verbal abuse during and after my introduction. All's good so far – then something happened that spoiled everything, and from then on it went downhill very fast.

Did I hear you ask what happened? – Oh yes, sorry about that – Right, I'll tell you what happened – the fucking bell rang that's what happened. Out of his corner bounded 'Stiff-Cliff' we briefly touched, but that was enough to send me hurtling skyward with enough velocity for the bottom of my feet to smash into one corner of the ring-lights and send a shower of ancient dust cascading down all over my ever-loving fans. At first screamed, and then violently coughed their abuse. From then on I rode the 'Stiff-Cliff' special, which is the fastest, most hectic and violent Roller-coaster rides in the World – and all for free – WOWEEEE!!! After what seemed like about 25 years, Cliff grabs me and whispers,

"Okay now go villain." And before I had chance to flutter an eyelash, he grabbed hold of me, pulled me towards him and draped himself back over the ropes.

"BREAK THAT HOLD!" The referee ordered. But I couldn't as 'Stiff-Cliff' hung onto me like a limpet, he was so damned greedy he was even doing my villainy to himself for me, and merely using me as a prop. "BREAK THAT HOLD!" The ref repeated, as he forced his way in between us prizing us apart.

Then WHOOOOSH! Off we go again, spinning, crashing, bouncing, getting swooped up, flying, somersaulting – WOW! This would be great if some TWAT named Isaac Newton hadn't invented gravity – CRASH!-CRUNCH! That's the bit I hated most.

Then I get scooped off the canvas, dragged back across the ring where I'm once again playing villain draped all over Cliff while he's holding himself back over the ropes.

"BREAK THAT HOLD!" The ref screams into my cauliflower ear, but this time 'Stiffy' doesn't wait for a repeat order, or for the ref to push in. He places his hand between my legs and attempts to hurl me right over him and the ropes out into the raging fans. 'YEAH, RIGHT - NO FUCKING WAY!!!' 'Stiff-bloody-Clifford' would have had to have cut all my fingers off to loosen my grip on those ropes! – AND that was that – I still got aimed from arsehole to breakfast time that I couldn't prevent, but try as he may he couldn't throw me over the top rope, and I found that as I had now completely lost interest in the procedure, and refused to engage him, 'Stiff-Cliff' was having a more and more of a difficult time trying to manhandle me. 'Stiff-Cliff' won the contest by two falls to none, but even after such a devastating loss I still managed to piss-off all the fans, and Captain John by completely ignoring the fact that I had lost so thoroughly and decisively. I strutted around the ring with arms raised as though in victory, and marched back to the dressing room like a conquering hero with huge smiles of triumph for all and sundry.

Fuck the lot of you I thought, especially you Captain John – and of course you too 'Stiff-Cliff' I'm going to remember this – and this time I was dead right!

****

I had found my first afternoon riding Horses so exhilarating that the Stables Joe Quesek had introduced me to had become one of my favorite haunts. Soon after I had interested Bobby Barnes in joining our little equestrian group, and we began riding at every opportunity we got. We decided that as we were so enthused, it would make sense to learn everything we could at a proper Riding School, so that we could learn to be as courteous and mindful of our mounts as we should, as well as becoming very proficient Riders. Iggy Borg told us that his Father-in-law owned a Riding School in Brixton, so we all went along with the idea of learning everything there was to learn. Unfortunately after all the helter-skelter galloping through the woods and meadows we'd grown used to, had completely spoiled us for the mundane, mindless boredom we experienced at the riding school. We all agreed that after just one boring lesson, that ignorance was indeed pure bliss, and we went right back to what we called riding. We began leaving early for wrestling shows if there was a good stable in the same area, and if we were in places like The New Forest for a number of consecutive days, every fine morning and afternoon would be spent in the saddle. It was at our favorite New Forest Stables where I met my favorite mount 'Brigadier', a giant Chestnut Charger that would have done credit to a Military Hero like the Duke of Wellington.

****

I had mentioned before the statement made by Ronnie Kray in reference to Peter Rachman's enforcers and rent collectors, many of which had been wrestlers. Wrestling's sudden increase in popularity had robbed the Demon Landlord of their services and had left him vulnerable to people like the Krays,

"Rachman's Boy's were big - my Boys were bigger!" – He had claimed, But his Boys had only got bigger AFTER Peter Rachman's wrestlers had left him to wrestle full time. I had seen both the Kray Twins many times in 'The Cromwellian Club' and had wondered if they had ever attempted to put the screws on the Club's owners. I very much doubted it, as the owners were none other than the ex-owners of 'The 2Is' coffee bar, wrestlers Paul Lincoln and Big Ray Hunter. Plus the 'Cromwellian' was always teeming with wrestlers – and many of them were VERY BIG BOYS.

It was about that time when Ron and Reg may have thought that if they couldn't beat the wrestlers, why not join them, and they decided it might be a good idea to get into the wrestling business as promoters.

Tony Scarlo told me that the Krays paid him 25 pounds to wrestle and act as match-maker for the wrestling shows they ran in York Hall in Bethnal Green, Canning Town Hall, and Hackney Town Hall. Another wrestler on their card was one of their own enforcers 'Chopper' Levac, who used to referee for Dale Martins as Stan Howlett. Tony had been introduced to the Krays by another of their enforcers, Roy Smith who also wrestled as the Midget 'Fuzzy-Ball' Kay. Fuzzy-Ball was a vicious little Demon, but was punished very viciously himself when he did something to upset his bosses. They ordered him to break into a house where Jack 'The Hat' was being held, he was half way through a ground floor window, when they pulled the window down trapping him. Then they pulled his trousers down and slashed his arse 50 times with a razor. Well I guess that proved they could handle little wrestlers.

There had been an attempt by another Gang to extort protection money from The Cromwellian Club, when Raymond Nash sent some of his heavies around there to give them 'an offer they couldn't refuse'. But refuse they did, so they pushed past the Club's Doorman with the idea of performing a little demolition in order to promote a little more incentive. One Thug got as far as ripping a phone out of the wall when the Doorman punched him so hard that he acquired an instantaneous Cauliflower-ear, and was still walking around in La-La-Land for many eons after regaining consciousness. The Doorman was none other than the huge and ferocious Russian, Heavyweight Wrestling Ogre. Yuri Borienko.

After a very brief inquiry, Raymond Nash discovered that not only was Yuri Borienko a force that it was better not to reckon with, but that he was a very good friend of Peter Rann and 'Mad Fred' Rondell, which definitely put The Cromwellian Club off limits to extortionists. Amongst the other Clubs that all London Gangsters learned to leave alone was, 'The Churchill Club' in Bond Street, because Peter Rann's Wife Gina worked there. 'The Eve Club' in Regent Street, because wrestler Tony Cassio's Wife Frankie worked there. 'The Topaz Club' in Mill Street because Wrestler Spencer Churchill's Wife Jean worked there, and they were all friends of Peter Rann and 'Mad Fred' who no one wanted to upset. Raymond Nash decided it would be a very good idea to try to cultivate Peter Rann as a friend. He even moved into a Basement Flat directly below the Flat where Peter and his Wife lived - that proved to be a very bad mistake.

Peter didn't like Raymond Nash, but pretended that he did, he even invited him to parties that he often threw at his home. That was the only times I ever remember meeting Raymond Nash myself, while he entertained Peter's party guests by playing all night on the Bongo-Drums. I would often pose his efforts some very serious competition by taking along an 8 mm film projector and a small case full of 'Blue-movies'.

In spite of the very close proximity of his new found friend, Nash was soon running scared, as Peter convinced him that some vicious gang was out to get him. No such gang even existed, but all kinds of destructive and annoying things kept happening to Nash's property. Valuables went missing; his car was continually vandalized and sabotaged. Al Miquet and his Dad, 'Gorilla' Don Mendoza was kept very busy indeed repairing Nash's car on Peter Rann's recommendation. The penny finally dropped for Raymond Nash, one night when upon returning home found that after unlocking his front door, it simply refused to open. The reason he was to discover was that 'someone' had nailed it shut with six-inch nails, in losing his temper, and attempting to kick the door open Nash cut his leg very badly on one of the nails. He then discovered that one of his windows had been left open, he entered his Flat through the window, and walked to the light switch to turn on the lights. They wouldn't come on, as 'someone' had removed the light-bulbs. Although Nash didn't realize that at the time, and thought instead that the electric meter needed some money put into it. On his journey across the room in his quest to feed the meter, and then again on his way back to flip on the lights he became aware of a crunching and cracking sound with every step he took. He discovered what the crunching and cracking was after turning on the lights, and learned that 'someone' had laid out his entire collection of very valuable records all over the floor. That was when the penny dropped, and furious, he ran back to the still open window, leaned through it as far as he could and screamed his protest up to Peter Rann's flat,

"I KNOW IT WAS YOU RANN!!!" Peter had been leaning through his own window waiting for just this moment, and emptied a big bucketful of piss that he had been collecting and saving for this very occasion all over Raymond Nash.

Not only had the penny finally dropped, but Raymond Nash had finally got the message – PISS-OFF! – Or was that Pissed-on?!

The Cromwellian Club was in Cromwell Road right opposite one of my favorite haunts, 'The Natural Science Museum'. Upon entering The Cromwellian Club for the first time, I was very impressed by the décor. Especially an excellent reproduction Medieval Suit of Armor, although its style would have dated it a few centuries earlier than Oliver Cromwell and his 'Ironsides' I still thought that it added a nice touch to the overall atmosphere.

There were very many 'Showbiz celebrities' amongst the

regular clientele, Peter Wyngarde, Lionel Blair, then Jonathan King, Long-John Baldry, Rod Stewart, and Elton John had their own little corner table and amused themselves by addressing each other with Girl's names. Harry, better known as 'Harriet' who used to serve behind the bar in the Gay-Club 'The Golden Guitar' later renamed 'The Masquerade' was the number one 'Barmaid' in the main barroom.

I was traveling to Rochester with Peter Rann and Mad Fred one Friday night, completely oblivious of the startling events that would unfold just moments after we arrived at the arena. Upon entering the dressing room, Mad Fred pushed past me walked up to Uri Borienko who was sitting on a bench against the wall, and slapped his face so hard it almost shook the building.

"STAND UP!" Fred ordered. If he had stood up Uri would have towered a half a foot taller than Fred, but Uri wouldn't budge.

SMACK! Mad Fred's huge paw exploded once more into Uri's face.

"STAND UP!" Fred ordered once more, but Uri only leaned forward and stared at the floor leaving his face completely unprotected as yet another blow struck the giant Russian resounding like a clap of thunder. Frustrated at Uri's lack of response Mad Fred grabbed the Russian's big leather bag containing all his wrestling ring wear, which included his trunks, boots, his long red Cossack jacket and his black Cossack hat.

"I'm keeping these," Fred announced, "If you want them back you can fight me for them." Big Uri had to borrow boots and trunks from another wrestler that night to wrestle in, while Fred tried to sell all Uri's equipment to Ivan Penzekoff, a bogus Russian from Bolton in Lancashire. Ivan politely and carefully refused the offer as he didn't want to offend either Uri or Mad Fred for personal health reasons. Talking of reasons – I couldn't imagine for the life of me why Fred, who I thought was a great friend of Uri Borienko would abuse and belittle him that way? A few days later when I was traveling back from a match with Peter Rann, Peter enlightened me.

Mad Fred had began frequenting The Cromwellian Club, but as Fred was known to suffer from chronic Homophobia, and the Club was a popular haunt of so many 'flamboyant' show-biz characters, it was figured only a matter of time before there could be an embarrassing, violent or even a deadly confrontation. In order to prevent such an occurrence, the Doorman – namely Big Uri Borienko had been given the unenviable task of barring Mad Fred Rondell from the Cromwellian Club for life.

Whilst on that subject I quizzed Peter on the fact that so many tough guy characters, himself included were known to carry knives, guns and own vicious dogs for protection if they were indeed supposed to be so tough. In Peter's case he owned a very large and savage Doberman. Peter replied that in his time employed by Polish Peter Rachman as enforcer and rent-collector, he would often find himself in very rough areas, dealing with very rough characters, whilst carrying large amounts of cash. Plus as a well known associate of Rachman, and many other dubious characters he could well be under threat even while sleeping peacefully in his own bed.

CLICK–BANG!

After stepping out of Dale's dreaded Van and attempting to stretch a little life back into my limbs, I made my way down the hill and around the corner to the entrance of 'The White Rock Theatre' in Hastings. The moment I rounded the corner I spotted Mickey Muldoon standing outside the Theatre flanked by Tony and Andy.

'Great', I thought, 'at least I won't be traveling back home in that bloody awful van.' It wasn't unusual for Mickey to drive to some of the matches I was appearing at, watch the show and then give me a lift back home when my contest was over. Although I hadn't seen him since the time I had told him I was finished taking photos for him. Mickey's smile of welcome was huge, and my own must have mirrored his, as relief swept over me at the very thought of not having to return to London in Dale Martin's mobile Navy-blue box of pain. My return journey would also prove to be a great ego-booster, as Mickey would always chuckle all the way as he gave me a blow-by-blow account of everything I did in the ring that amused or impressed him. I noticed in contrast that both Tony and Andy seemed to be very quiet and subdued, and I wondered briefly if they might still be upset with me for turning down their offer of a partnership on the last occasion I had seen them. My whole mood had improved immensely, but that would prove to be very short lived indeed. In fact it only lasted until I entered the dressing room, picked up a program containing that evenings line up, and learned who my opponent was to be. 'SHIT!' I thought, 'Another unmistakable message from Mick McManus – 'don't try to fly too high little Boy – 'cos I can ground you with just one stroke of my pen.' – I was royally Pissed-off!

There would be no showing off to impress Mickey, Andy and Tony tonight, or any one else in the packed Theatre, and if there was any chuckling it would be at me, not with me. I changed reluctantly into my ring wear without one single smidgen of enthusiasm whatsoever. Under normal conditions I couldn't wait to get into the ring and begin my performance, especially when I had friends to show out to, 'but not tonight Josephine, - definitely not tonight!'

As I made my way to the ring, the crowd erupted as was normal at the very sight of me, this was good, but unfortunately this was about as good as it was going to get. My opponent was already in the ring waiting for me, I looked at him in disgust and thought,

'This is the only time anyone can see him when he isn't sucking on one of those vile, stinking Woodbines.' The match was to be the best out of three falls, or one knockout in a 4 x10 minute round contest. The result I was told would be a knockout finish for my opponent in the third round, with no falls for either of us before hand. My opponent chose to knock me out with a dropkick, which was about as decisive as it gets. Unless of course your opponent happened to be 'Stiff' Cliff Beaumont, when it gets considerably more decisive still. The bell sounded to begin a contest that I had already lost interest in, as my opponent advanced towards me I compared his appearance to my own. I looked Young, Blond, muscular and well tanned, and he looked old, grey, gaunt, and very much to me as though he had taken on the appearance of one of his own clientele. One who he and his Brothers made the wooden overcoats for. Nevertheless, I knew only too well what that walking, talking, chain-smoking cadaver was capable of, and I didn't want any of it. Which was just as well as the greedy bastard always demanded the Lion's share of the match – and then some. So I thought,

'Fuck him! I'll make sure he gets the Lion's share of the match – AND THEN SOME!' When ever I heard other wrestlers discussing the phenomenal skills of 'Stiff' Cliff Beaumont, one thing they all seemed to agree on was, 'don't ever attempt to block one of his throws, unless you're tough enough to suffer the consequences'. Cliff without a doubt was the most skillful, trip - hip-toss - cross-buttock, monkey-flip artist I ever, or would ever see. As any wrestler who had ever shared the ring with him very soon discovered the hard way was, if you succeeded in blocking just one forward trip, he instinctively tripped you backwards in almost a reflex movement. One thing was certain when 'Stiff' Cliff Beaumont even touched you, you were airborne, no ands, ifs, or buts.

Cliff did touch me, and I was airborne, but I knew that I would be so I fought against any instinctive resistance on my own part. Instead threw myself into the flow that Cliff had created with all the velocity I could muster. I don't know who was the most shocked, the audience, Cliff, or me, when instead of smashing into the mat with all the bone-jarring force that we had all expected, I was propelled into a graceful dive which brought me right back onto my feet on the opposite side of the ring.

Even though I was normally despised by the Hastings fans, many applauded me vigorously - Cliff was in my face in a flash,

"OOOOOPS – HERE WE GO AGAIN!" And once again I didn't only go with the flow, I embraced it. I dove into his throw with all my might, and there I was once again landing on my feet right across the ring. Cliff then began demonstrating what must have been his entire repertoire, but I was putty in his hands, no resistance from me whatsoever. The more he threw me, the more right it felt to me, I turned to water and flowed easily in any direction Cliff directed me. And it was easy, by now, I or most other of Cliff's opponents would really be beginning to feel the stress, soon they would become exhausted, but I felt as though I could go on all night.

"Grab a hold!" Cliff ordered at last.

"No thanks Mate," I replied, "you're doing fine." Cliff grabbed my arm and wrapped it around his own head – can you imagine? He used my arm to put a headlock on himself. I just stood there as nonchalantly, and as expressionless as I would have been if I had been waiting for a bus, I even used my left hand to stifle a yawn with my right arm just loosely draped across my opponents head. He suddenly exploded like a steel spring, and once more I was flying, but flying strictly under my own terms, easily finding my feet once again on the other side of the ring.

"Wrestle!" demanded Cliff as he dove at me.

"Nah, I don't think so," I told him, "I know you like it all, so you can have it all with my blessing." I knew that 'Stiff' Cliff was capable of taking it all, with or without my blessing, but I had definitely succeeded in presenting him with a problem tonight. Cliff got mad, I didn't care, I was pissed-off too, so why not share it? Dale Martin's had given me an insurmountable obstacle to scale so I wasn't even going to try, I was disgusted, and my performance was disgusting. That was the way the match continued, when the third round came, and it was time to end the match, I turned my performance down a notch – no, make that two notches. 'Stiff' Cliff grabbed my arm, propelled me into the ropes and caught me with a beautifully delivered drop-kick which should have lifted me right off my feet and out of the ring. Instead I tottered around drunkenly, sunk down in slow motion to the mat, rolled underneath the ropes onto the ring apron, and then made a big deal out of making myself comfortable by placing both my hands behind the back of my neck and then putting one foot up onto the bottom rope and crossing my other foot over it. I just lay there until the referee finished the ten count, and then immediately threw my feet off the ropes landing me beside the ring where I raised both arms, as though in victory and sauntered back to the dressing room.

Cliff was in another dressing room on the opposite side of the building, so there was no ensuing confrontation with him, but the referee wasted no time in bursting first into the dressing room and then my face and demanding to know,

"WHAT THE FUCK WAS THAT?!"

"My brand new patented 'Stiff' Cliff format." I informed him.

'Take that back to Mick McManus!' I thought. Well that was definitely the easiest match that I ever had against 'Stiff' Cliff Beaumont, but also most definitely the worst match I had ever had so far for Joint Promotions and I was not happy about it at all. I washed, dressed and left the building, collecting Mickey, Tony and Andy on my way.

Mickey started up a conversation as we rounded the corner, and we made our way up the hill towards where Mick had parked his car, but I was hardly aware of what he was saying as I was still fairly deep into my own dark thoughts. Suddenly Mickey pulled his revolver out of his pocket and shot me point blank in the face, my head instinctively shot back as Mickey turned and fired another shot up the hill, and I heard the bullet ricochet into the distance. Luckily for me, the first bullet was a blank, but the second one wasn't.

Mickey began to laugh, but not for long – if that was supposed to be a joke he could not have chosen a worse time to pull it. I grabbed hold of him, spun him around, snatched hold of the back of his collar with my left hand, and with my right I reached up between his legs and grabbed a handful of his balls, which I used to upend him face first into the pavement. I then wrapped my right leg over Mickey's left leg, and twisted it so viciously that he almost lost his own shoe up his arsehole. He screamed out loud as I snatched the revolver out of his hand and threw it as hard as I could over the back of the houses that lined the right side below the road.

"You ever do anything like that again you prick, and I'll stick your fucking gun so far up your arse it'll knock your fucking front teeth out!" I told him.

"OH, YOU NEARLY BROKE MY FUCKIN' ANKLE, - YOU KNOW I'VE GOT WEAK ANKLES!" he complained as he staggered back to his feet, and began hopping and limping around in a circle.

I wondered briefly what the conservation would have been like concerning the unusual match I'd had with Cliff Beaumont that night, but all the way back to London Mick never stopped moaning about his weak ankles. I barely answered him as I tried to analyze events. I came to the conclusion that somehow Mickey had learned about Tony's and Andy's proposition to begin a partnership in opposition to him, and this was his way of demonstrating to them and to me how easy it would be for him to nullify any protection I might afford them. At the same time, for my benefit he tried to make the incident appear to be no more than a joke – an ill timed joke as it happened. In the mood I was in after my match in Hastings he could not have chosen a worse time to make a pathetic power play. Nevertheless I had received two warnings from two Micks in one night – one from McManus, and the other from Muldoon, but in my own way I had sent two messages back.

I got my MUCH anticipated phone call from the office; Jack Dale wanted to see me – NOW! I hoped that Mick McManus would be present in Jack's office when I received the Bollicking I was expecting, as it would not only give me a chance to clear the air between Mick and myself, it would also make Jack Dale aware of McManus's dubious methodology. Mick was in the office he shared with Jack Dale but the Bollocking had nothing to do with my atrocious behavior in Hastings, but instead with my atrocious behavior in a new Club where Dale Martin's had just began promoting.

My match had been the fourth and last match of the evening, and I was wrestling against Al Miquet, who was a contrast in every way to 'Stiff' Cliff' Beaumont, and had everything in aces that the Wigoner lacked. He was young, dark handsome, a very skillful and entertaining wrestler who possessed an almost indecent helping of charisma. Also in contrast, whereas a match against 'Stiff Cliff', for his opponent was an impossibly difficult and unpleasant experience. Sharing the ring with Miquet was a sheer pleasure with the guarantee that you were going to be one half of the best match of the night.

The ring was set up in the centre of the Club, the room was very large and was packed Sardine tight with an extremely enthusiastic audience. But – the Club's ceiling was so low that both of the very tall heavyweights who had wrestled in the contest before ours had to be careful not to jump too high during their match in fear of bumping their heads on it. Al Miquet and I did not allow the very low ceiling to hamper our performance; on the contrary, we made it the main feature in our match. By the time I had disrobed, posed, skipped gracefully around the ring the fans were already incensed enough to scream their abuse at full volume. After punishing my opponent with a barrage of powerful forearm smashes, spiteful, sniping kicks to his thigh, followed by a submission with a one legged Boston-crab, the fans were really yelling for my blood.

Miquet looked as though he was already through, as his second struggled to assist him back to his corner. I was staining like a mad Dog on a leash ready to burst out of my corner at the sound of the bell and continue the mayhem. The bell rang, I charged, but was caught by my opponent as he stabbed me under the ribcage with an upward thrust of both hands which lifted me high above the ring and my head crashing right through the hard tiled ceiling. I landed flat on my back in the middle of the ring as the remnants of the shattered tile landed on top of me, the crowd went insane. I no sooner found my feet and shook the cobwebs out of my head, when Miquet stepped in smartly and repeated the maneuver. Lifting me high and crashing my skull through the ceiling, smashing another hard tile in the process, down I went again showered with shattered tile. The audience went mad with delight, as they began to scream at my opponent whilst pointing to their own personal tile of choice that they wanted him to smash with a little help from my head. Up I'd fly, SMASH went my head though the ceiling, and one after another the hard brittle tiles would explode all over the ring. Eventually as I began to struggle off the canvas after my latest collision, Miquet took advantage of my dazed condition by leaping over me, grabbing me on his way and equalizing the score with a neatly performed double-leg-nelson. The crowd went Ape-shit!

I was so far out of it I could hardly make it out of my corner as the bell sounded to herald the next round, as the fans yelled their choice out of the 3 or 4 tiles that still remained in what used to be a ceiling.

"Which one do you want next?!" Miquet called to the crowd as he pointed to the ceiling. The fans made their choice, and yet again I was propelled skyward with the force of a rocket-engine, exploded into the ceiling and crashed once more into the mat.

"Now which one do you want," Miquet demanded of the blood crazed mob, "this one or this one?!"

"THIS ONE – NO – THAT ONE!!!" They screamed back. Their choice would prove to be superfluous, as while both my opponent's and the referee's attention was on the fans, I picked up the largest piece of tile I could find and smashed it into the back of Miquet's head. Everyone except my opponent and the ref witnessed the dastardly deed, and screamed their outrage at double full volume. I pounced onto their fallen Idol to score the third and winning fall.

I strutted back to the dressing room with both arms held high in triumph, leaving my opponent to be swept up with all the rest of the debris that was heaped up all over the ring. And talking of ring – the Club's manager was on the phone to the office the very next day demanding immediate restitution if Dale Martins wanted to continue promoting wrestling at what was left of his club. Jack Dale was not happy with me at all, but I thought I may have justified my action when I claimed,

"I don't know why the manager was upset Jack - not only was that the best match on the card, it will probably be the best match he ever sees in his life. - We got so much reaction from the fans it literally raised the roof – BY ABOUT THREE FEET!

YOU MAKE ME SICK

Well I guess that wasn't terrible, nevertheless I was happy to take refuge up North for a few weeks. I was wrestling the first week for Relwyskow, and on the Monday, Bob and I were main event in Leeds Town Hall, the next night we were main event in Aberdeen, Scotland. Normally when we traveled from Leeds to Aberdeen we would leave early on the morning of the show. But owing to the fact that promoter George Relwyskow had a new Lady friend who lived in Aberdeen, he wanted to leave on the night before, right after the Leeds show had ended so that he could spend more time with his latest interest. Many of the wrestlers were not too enthusiastic about those arrangements. After traveling all day to get to Leeds and then wrestling, all the wrestlers wanted to do was eat, drink and then sleep – not travel all night to another town hundreds of miles away. But Relwyskow knew exactly how to bribe us and make everyone happy – including himself – or at least he thought he did.

Beaming all over his chops, Relwyskow announced to the dressing room that when the Leeds show had concluded, all the wrestlers that were due to travel up to Aberdeen that night were invited to eat at a very nice Greek Restaurant. And, that the entire bill would be picked up by George himself. Now wouldn't you think that a promoter with George Relwyskow's experience of professional wrestlers, would have had more sense than that? Especially as he went home to prepare himself for the trip rather than join us in the restaurant and keep his eye on the wrestlers. Unsupervised wrestlers are ten times worse than unsupervised children – even more so when there is abundant alcohol to be had – make that FREE abundant alcohol to be had, and you'll get the picture.

Very many bottles of Retsina and Demestica were ordered and greedily consumed. It had been announced in Leeds Town Hall that night that the wrestlers were going to eat at that particular Restaurant, with the result that the eatery was jam-packed with wrestling fans who wanted to get a closer look at their heroes. A bottle of wine was delivered to our table with the compliments of a table full of fans; we all stood and drank their health. That started a virtual avalanche of booze in quantities sufficient to have drowned both Amphictyonis and Dionysus in their favorite juice, and it flowed freely from table after table, from every corner of the restaurant. – CHEERS-HIC!

We had been told by Relwyskow that he wanted as all to meet at the Leeds office no later than 11.30pm, where a bus would be waiting for our transportation. It was now almost midnight, the restaurant phone rang – Relwyskow wanted to know where his wrestlers were. Jon Cortez answered the phone,

Relwyskow – "Why are you still at the restaurant? You were supposed to be at the office half an hour ago."

Jon – "Well it's like this George – there's been a Police raid – they've arrested everyone."

Relwyskow – "OH NO – WHAT AM I GOING TO DO?!"

Jon – "Don't worry George – just leave it to me, I'm sure I can sort it all out – we'll get to the office as soon as we can." Jon puts down the phone and shouts out,

"That's it – no more wine for anyone!"

"BOOOO!!!" All we wrestlers shouted back.

"No more wine for anyone Jon insists – waiter Ouzo all round – and George Relwyskow is paying for it!"

Strangely enough when Bobby Barnes and I did eventually leave the restaurant both clinging to each other for dear life in a monumental effort to remain on our feet, the Police were sitting in a car right outside the entrance. Considering the state we were in I'm amazed that they allowed us to enter Bob's car and drive away. But they followed us all the way to the office, as Bob drove as slowly and carefully as he possibly could. At least their presence must have added a little credence to Jon Cortez's story.

Nevertheless George Relwyskow was beside himself, he had wanted to leave for Aberdeen by 11.30pm and now it was almost 3.30am. There were also a number of other wrestlers who would be traveling up to Aberdeen who hadn't been wrestling at Leeds, and they too were furious that they had been kept waiting for hours by the group of noisy drunks that at last arrived shouting, singing and dancing. Amongst the revelers was George Relwyskow's nephew Douglas Relwyskow, sarcastically christened by fellow wrestlers as 'The Aggressor', due to his incredibly mild and timid persona both inside and outside the ring. The bus that was to transport us all to Scotland was now parked right outside his home, and he amused and amazed all of us when both his wife and Mother came out of his house and demanded an explanation concerning his present condition,

"BOLLOCKS – FUCK OFF!!!" He told them.

"You just wait until you get back from Scotland they both threatened.

"BOLLOCKS!" He repeated. At last we were on our way, and Relwyskow was well prepared. He had laid out a comfortable sleeping bag between the driver of the bus and the front side passenger seat, with his feet facing in the direction we were traveling. He had taken a very strong sleeping pill, so that he would be well rested for his romantic rendezvous at our destination's end. It was just as well that George was well drugged up as the noise made by all his dinner guests was quite colossal. Especially by me, I sang and danced like a Dervish. Bob told me the next day that he had watched me performing, and wondered how long it was going to take for my head to fly off my shoulders. Eventually everyone was snoring soundly, and as I now had no one at all to perform for, I sat down next to Bob and joined the crowd. Some time later I awoke bursting, I called to the driver, "Piss-stop!"

"You'll have to open the door and piss as we are moving," the driver replied, "the boss's orders is we don't stop for anything!" I stood and staggered to the door, there was a step down, I opened the door, unbuttoned. I was just beginning to enjoy the relief when the Aggressor, who was sitting in the seat next to, and facing the door, leaned over the chrome rail in front of him and threw up all over me. I placed my left hand on his face, and pushed him back into his seat as streams of red hot vomit squirted between my fingers, up my sleeve and all over my chest and shoulder. I was stuck temporarily where I was, as my right hand was still occupied. I called the Aggressor everything for what good that did, he was completely out of it. So I slammed the door shut, staggered back to my seat, composed myself, and tried to go back to sleep. I got as far as beginning to doze when the sickly smell of the Aggressors vomit overcame me, and I shot out of my seat, and made for the door again as quickly as I could. But not fast enough unfortunately, for me, and even more unfortunately for George Relwyskow, as I emptied all the food, wine and ouzo he had bought for me all over his head. Fortunately for me – unfortunately for George, thanks to the sleeping pills he had taken, he slept blissfully right through the deluge. I was able to creep quietly back to my seat, and hope that the Aggressor would get the blame as he justly deserved to.

I didn't come out of that episode Scot-free, as I swear I must have been drunk for about 4 days, and I also swore that I would never, ever drink ouzo again as long as I live.

Well I seemed to be blotting my copybook in both the North and South, so we decided to flee the country for a while, give Britain a break and hope that absence did indeed make the heart grow fonder

SPANISH-FLY

Spanish-flee may have been more accurate, as we didn't actually fly to Spain, we traveled by car. We had called the wrestling promoters in Barcelona and Valencia, and were invited to wrestle for them both. We decided to combine business with pleasure and have a working holiday. Bob would take his brand new Wife Jan with him, and I would take Jean. Mam and Dad agreed to house-sit our Streatham home, and look after Adrian Jr. – Vince and Mandy for the few weeks we would be in Spain.

We took a ferry over to France and drove almost to the Spanish border in one go. We slept for a couple of hours in the car, crossed the border next morning, and arrived in Barcelona the next afternoon. It took us hours to find the promoters office, and after we did we were told that we were wrestling for Gil Espaza, the Valencia promoter for the first couple of weeks. Then coming back to Barcelona for a short tour, before returning to the Valencia territory where we would wrestle till the end of our Spanish trip. So off we sped again. After arriving in Valencia, we met up with Gil who directed us to a hotel where his foreign wrestlers usually stayed. He told us to return to his office the next morning so that he could direct us to the offices where we could obtain our Spanish Wrestling Licenses. After we had received our licenses, Gil told us to get ourselves a meal, and then we were to drive South once more to Alicante. We would be wrestling that night in the local Bullring after the Bullfighting had finished. Three of Spain's premier Matadors would be fighting that evening. Manuel Benitez, better known as 'El Cordobes', Angel Teruel and another master Matador who's name now escapes me. Gil advised us that it was a must see event. The Bullfights always began at 6pm and you could set your watch by their punctuality, we were quite amazed that the Wrestling matches in Spain didn't begin until 11pm, and if you were the last match on the card – as Bob and I usually were, it was not unusual to enter the ring in the very early hours of the next morning.

I found the spectacle of Bullfighting both exciting and

sickening, Bob didn't like it – full stop, and I could understand his view very well. As exciting as it was, plus the colorful, sparkling costumes, it still couldn't really justify the slow and cruel slaughter of such beautiful and powerful creatures. Gil defended his country's favorite spectacle by countering that the people of Spain viewed the British 'Grand National', as equally or even more barbaric, I wouldn't argue with that viewpoint either, but to each his own.

The Hell's Angels or 'Los Angeles del Infierno' as we were billed as in Spain was to be pitted against Spain's own, Nino Pizarro and Braulio Veliz in the Main-Event.

At first I thought the Spanish fans must have watched British TV wrestling tapes, as they erupted like a volcano on steroids the second we appeared, and made our way to the wrestling ring. The ring was set up in the very centre of the Bullring where we had watched the Bullfighting just a few hours earlier. The hostility was immense, and as villains it was just the way we liked it. It meant that we were already recognized as 'the bad-guys' which would make it unnecessary to use foul tactics in order to establish the fact. When the Spanish team made their appearance the cheers shook the foundations of the Bullring. Then it dawned on me, that just like a non Scot wrestling against a Scottish wrestler in Scotland, in Spain as a foreigner you were automatically cast as a villain if you were pitted against a Spaniard. Good – that would make life much easier.

Just as I always did in Britain, I scoured the faces of the audience closest to the ring in order to see who demonstrated the most response to our actions against their heroes. There were many, but my favorite of all was a large jet-black haired man, who reminded me very much of the Giant villainous actor Eric Campbell who appeared as Charlie Chaplin's nemesis in many of his old silent movies. He sported a matching set of jet-black moustache and eyebrows. His dark eyes smoldered with hatred as he snarled something intelligible at me. I responded by pouting as seductively as I knew how, and his smoldering eyes burst into flame. His response to everything I did was so huge that I must have concentrated most of my outrageous theatrical gestures in his direction. I blew him kisses to punctuate each kick I delivered to my floundering Spanish opponents, and licked my lips, and fluttered my eyelashes at him as I twisted Spanish heads and limbs. He reacted by clawing at the air around him, as smoke seemed to billow out of his ear holes. I occasionally alternated my attention on some of the more vocal fans, but Mr. Moustache was my undisputed favorite. I returned my attention back towards him again and again – a kick or slam for my opponent, a blown kiss or a sultry pose directed at Mr. Moustache. I thought that he was going to have a fit!

Bob and I won the match as savagely as we were able. To add as much insult to the very excessive injury, The Los Angeles del Infierno, raised their arms in victory, and strutted arrogantly all around the ring, before leaping out of the ring directly in front of Mr. Moustache. Upon leaving the ring we had no sooner lowered our arms than they shot back up again – the reason being that we were at once surrounded by a swarm of uniformed and heavily armed Police, with all their rifles pointing right at us at a range of no more than a few inches – OOOOPS?!

Mr. Moustache turned out to be Alicante's Chief of Police, and we were about to be arrested. Too late I remembered a story that Abe Ginsberg had told me, when a few years earlier he had toured Spain. In response to the Spanish fans continued jeering, Abe had put both hands against the sides of his head and stuck his forefingers up in order to mimic a Bull's horns. He began scraping one foot on the canvas before bellowing and charging at his opponent with his head lowered, ignorant of the fact that in Spain those actions were interpreted as the most vile and obscene insult. On that occasion the law didn't even wait for the conclusion of his contest, but stopped it instead, arrested Abe and took him straight to Prison where he spent most of the rest of his Spanish tour.

"What's up Mate?!" I asked Mr. Moustache. Not being fluent in the Spanish language, his verbal response went right over my head, but his facial expression left me in no doubt that we were in deep shit! We learned later that the promoter Gil Espaza had been watching our match, but as soon as he witnessed our apparent arrest, had for some reason completely disappeared. Just when it looked as though all was lost, the Cavalry arrived from a very unexpected direction. The Spanish wrestler, Vincente Castella, who had been my first opponent ever, for Relwyskow Promotions in Leeds almost 4 years earlier pushed his way between the Police rifles and myself. I didn't understand what he said to Mr. Moustache, but I imagine that he asked what the problem was. During their conversation I became aware of a word used most frequently by Vincente that sounded like 'Plastique'. After an argument, that probably seemed much longer than it actually was, we were allowed to return to the dressing rooms with Vincente, who told us that he had vouched for us, and had promised to keep us out of further trouble. I asked him what he had meant by 'Plastique' and Vincente said that he had explained to 'Hairy-lip' that in Britain I was a very famous Male-model. All my strange, sexy and sensuous poses and gestures, was just part of my image while exhibiting some designers new line, as I strutted my stuff up and down the runway, and I was absolutely not, under any circumstances after Mr. Moustache's fat arse.

In the shower room, I was somewhat taken aback by the fact that I found that every one of the carcasses of the 6 Bulls that had been killed in the Bullring earlier, were hanging up where they stretched from ceiling to the floor, and I almost had to squeeze between them to take my shower.

It was so late by the time we got back to the hotel in Valencia, that I decided to forgo going to bed and decided instead to go and lay on the Hotel's flat roof and wait for the Sun to come up. That turned out to be a scenario that I repeated more often than not.

Our Spanish working holiday didn't turn out to be much of a holiday, as we found that we were wrestling every night, or should I say very early every morning. Most of the trips were no longer than the ones we were used to in Britain, but believe it or not most of the roads were even worse. To be fair it became very tiring for everyone, but more especially for Bob, who never stopped complaining that he was the only one driving every day. The reason for that was, that at that time, Bob was the only one of us who knew how to drive. The furthest south we wrestled was Cartagena, where I was thrilled to see Palm Trees growing wild for the first time in my life.

The most memorable matches we had was against Nino Pizarro and his Brother Gomez. Both Pizarro Brothers were huge idols in their hometown of Valencia. Their savage defeat at the hands, knees and feet of the hated 'Los Angeles del Infierno' guaranteed a packed arena in Valencia's 'Plaza de Toros' when they challenged us to a return contest which would take place after we returned from our tour of the Barcelona territory.

I very much liked the City of Barcelona, especially the area known as 'The Ramblas', there were very many interesting shops and excellent restaurants. My own favorite eatery was 'Carracoldes' meaning 'Snails', which was one of their specialties. The first time Jean and I ate there I was surprised to find they knew exactly who I was, with the result, when I asked for a big Steak, I received a BIG Steak. It was served on a huge rectangular wooden platter, and I swear the only thing missing was the hide, horns and hooves. I washed it all down with a large pitcher of Sangria – that was the first time I had tasted Sangria, but it most certainly would not be the last. In spite of the fact that I had been pre-warned that Spanish cuisine could have a very unsettling effect on a stomach unused to it, especially if you were going to be wrestling later the same night, I became amazingly adventurous. Fish of all kinds, including huge Shrimp, Squid, Octopus and even Carracoldes smothered in Garlic all became part of my favorite diet.

Amongst the venues promoted regularly in the Barcelona territory, was Palma which is on the Mediterranean Island of Majorca, which meant all four of us flying out from Barcelona Airport on the smallest Airplane that I had ever traveled in up to that time. Parts of Majorca were very mountainous which contributed to so much turbulence as we approached, and then began to fly over the island, it felt more as though we were aboard a giant yo-yo. We would shake shudder and tremble, then drop like a stone, serenaded by the terrified shrieks of many of the passengers. I had never ever suffered with airsickness, but I'm certain that I would have, if I had remained on board for any more than another 15 minutes. Fellow passengers began vomiting all around us in such small and stuffy confines. When we at last landed Jean, and I couldn't wait to get off the plane and into the fresh air. I was surprised that both Bob and Jan didn't seem as eager to evacuate and instead told us that he would meet us shortly in the airport building. The mystery was cleared up later when Bob explained that as the turbulence had been so very severe, the deeply plummeting plane had caused the elastic to snap in Jan's knickers, and as they expected fell down as soon as she stood up. As she was wearing a very short skirt both Jan and Bob thought it might be more prudent to wait until everyone else had not only left the plane, but also the area near the bottom of the stairs that descended from the plane to the runway.

At first I was both shocked and dismayed to discover that the City of Palma seemed to cater so strongly towards foreign tourists. Everywhere you looked there were pubs and restaurants with very British titles, like 'Freddie's Fish and Chips' and British Beer sold here. But thank goodness after a bit of searching we found some very good local Spanish eating places, which were fortunately well out of smelling range of all the greasy and unimaginative English fare.

That night upon entering the dressing room I spied amongst its occupants Yorkshire's Steve Beresford, son of Promoter Ted Beresford. He wrestled professionally as Steve Clements, in order to disguise the fact from the Yorkshire wrestling fans that his Dad was the promoter. It was good to see a face we recognized, especially from Britain, but no sooner had we dispensed with the greetings than Clements who spoke Spanish fluently began making fun for the benefit of the Spanish wrestlers. Although I was far from fluent, and was unable to put any more than a few words together, I understood enough to appreciate that Clements was going too strong with the piss-taking. A few of the Spanish wrestlers seemed to laugh obligingly, others looked a little embarrassed. I smiled at the Spaniards, walked over to where Clements was standing, and slapped him so hard across his face that he fell onto his seat which toppled over and emptied him onto the concrete floor. I hoped that Ted Beresford's stupid son might be one of our opponents, but fortunately for Clements we were once again wrestling against an all Spanish tag-team.

The thought crossed my mind that even though we were now in Spain that I was still risking blotting my copybook back in Britain with Beresford promotions, but thankfully the incident generated no repercussions whatsoever.

After returning to Gil Espaza's territory we made our main headquarters in Benidorm for most of the remainder of our tour. Although it was our return match against Valencia's Pizarro

Brothers that was to be the highlight of our tour. The Giant Bullring was packed to capacity, and bearing in mind that the actual Bullring itself was also packed with seats, as well as all the stands we actually outdrew 'El Cordobes' himself.

Our success also drew the promoter from Madrid who asked us to come and wrestle in his territory. Although he offered us much better wages than we had so far enjoyed, I turned him down flat, we had come to Spain for a working holiday, and so far it had been nothing but work, and not one single day off, I'd had enough. A few more days in the Sun and then back home. Then Bob had another plan, his old school teacher and wrestling instructor – wrestling M.C. and referee, Captain John Harris was holidaying in a town near San Sebastian, on Spain's North Atlantic Coast. Bob asked me if I was willing to travel a wide detour in order to visit him on our return journey. In spite of the Dick Conlon and 'Stiff' Cliff incidents John Harris and I had both buried the hatchet, but more to see a different part of Spain than a chance to visit John Harris I agreed to go the long way around. John Harris used to rent the same apartment in Spain every year; I was surprised to find that he always took a number of his schoolboys there to holiday with him. Jean and I had enjoyed our Spanish tour in spite of the fact that it had been mostly work, but what we both missed most of all were the Kids, and now we just couldn't wait to get back and see them again. Being as impatient as we were you can imagine how we both felt when just a few miles up the road after we had driven off the ferry on the British side of the channel, that Bob's car broke down. We called a taxi which took us the last 30 or 40 miles, and I thought once again that it might be time to learn to drive and get a car of my own.

VIOLENCE

On the whole our Spanish tour had been somewhat therapeutic, but it was great to get back to familiar territory where our absence had been noticed, and our return to British rings seemed to generate more reaction and controversy than ever. But as my notoriety increased so did the fan's violence by leaps and bounds, often and especially after a controversial win a villain would have to brave a virtual gauntlet of hostile fans in order to make the journey from the ring back to the safety of the dressing-room. Fans who would attempt to punch, kick, pinch, grab hair, stub out lighted cigarettes on bare flesh were now becoming the norm. I have even been stabbed in the back of my shoulder with a nail-file. I simply refused to tone down the persona that was designed to entertain the majority of the fans just because a number of idiots amongst them wanted to get overly violent – I would not be controlled by a bunch of hooligans. We had been warned by many of the promoters not to retaliate, but thankfully not all. I remember one night Jack Dale punching with one fist, and using the leather bag that contained that night's takings, as a weapon in the other, while he stood shoulder to shoulder with Bobby Barnes and myself as we attempted to batter a pathway through a lynch-mob of angry fans. Another night Jack Atherton leapt out of the crowd that I was trying to beat a pathway through, and hyped a hooligan about 6 feet in the air a split second before he was about to smash a heavy wooden chair down on the back of my head.

Even away from the arenas we were not always safe. We were wrestling one freezing winter's night for Jack Atherton in Dumfries in Scotland, and before the matches began Bob and I decided to take a walk to a nearby café for a cup of coffee. We sat down on a very low and soft bench with its back to the window; the table was quite high and was fixed firmly to the floor. No sooner had we been served our coffee when two men walked up to our table, one leaned into my face and assaulted me with a loud but undecipherable verbal barrage. Although his accent was so strong, and I could not understand what he actually said, I could tell by its tone that its owner bore me no good will. I responded by informing him that I found the smell of his breath extremely hostile and strongly suggested that he should "Fuck off!" He responded by smashing a bottle of coca-cola over my head. I was in a very disadvantageous position, trapped down low on a soft seat with a high immovable table in front of me, so I responded by grabbing a fistful of his shirtfront before hurling my scalding hot coffee right into his face. He screamed and leapt back from the table dragging me out of my seat and across the table as I clung onto him. Now unconfined I punched and kicked the living shit out of him, punctuating my assault by picking him up and slamming him down onto the hard café floor. I dove down onto him, now it was ground and pound time, and I took no time at all getting busy. The next thing was, what I thought to be my victim's friend dive down heavily onto my back, and I wondered why Bob had allowed him to do that. No more time for wondering, I threw myself backwards with all the force I could muster, and smashed my attacker into a shelf like table that ran along the wall on that whole side of the café behind me. As I began to drive my elbow repeatedly into the guts of my attacker, I looked across the café at Bob in an effort to decipher why he had not prevented this second attack by my first assailant's friend. To my surprise I was confronted with a sight of both Bob, AND my assailant's friend, both wearing a look of distinct shock. Only then did I notice on the floor in front of me a checkered Police Officer's hat. I turned around and attempted to pull the bruised, battered and disheveled policeman to his feet, but before he was even upright he was screaming excitably into his walkie-talkie for immediate backup. I could never have imagined that immediate backup could be so immediate; it seemed that within seconds the café was filling up with large blue uniforms, in a scene reminiscent of the Keystone-cops, only on this occasion I wasn't laughing. I was grabbed and manhandled out of the café and towards a police car that stood parked against the curb right outside the café, Shit these guys were on the ball. The Police Officer who had come so sadly unstuck was still in a very highly agitated state, and was pushing and pulling at me with all his might. The café was situated on a steep slope, and the pavement was covered in very slippery ice. I was certain that I was in great danger of falling if this very excitable policeman didn't ease up. I told him a number of times to stop pushing and pulling or I would fall down, then I grabbed him, and added that if he caused me to fall on that icy sidewalk I would make sure that he would be underneath me when I landed. It was only then that I was allowed to enter their car under my own steam, from where I was transported to the Police station. The Desk-sergeant seemed very somber, and I was left in a large room with him as my sole companion. He suggested that I might like to use the adjoining washroom to clean myself up, as my head and face was covered with blood from a large gash on the top of my head made by the coke bottle smashing to smithereens on impact with it. After I returned he left the room for well over an hour leaving me alone. When he finally returned he told me that Jack Atherton had turned up, and asked if it was at all possible for him to 'borrow' his Main-event wrestler for a couple of hours, and that he promised to bring me back as soon as the wrestling show was over. He was also much less somber – even friendly, and upon receiving statements from the café owner, and a number of customers who witnessed the fracas learned that I had been defending myself after an unprovoked attack. On further investigation they learned that my assailant was a local thug very well known to the police for his frequent violent behavior.

"That'll teach the little Bastard a good lesson!" The desk sergeant beamed, who then gave me one of the two apples he had on his desk and told me I was free to leave.

That night Bob and I wrestled against Bert Royal and his Brother Vic Faulkner – a team we were guaranteed to generate huge reaction with. But tonight the crowd got an extra bonus that no one except I expected. Five minutes into the match the gash on my head that had remained well hidden by my hair, reopened and poured blood all over the ring, and over everyone in it. The fans imagining that the bloody wound had been inflicted by one of their heroes screamed their approval until they were hoarse.

The following Tuesday we wrestled against Bert and Vic again, this time in Lime Grove Baths in London's Shepards Bush. Action had been hot and heavy since the opening bell, we had young Vic trapped in our corner, and we were swapping tags fast and furiously. I was tagged in, and was in the process of gently tearing Vic's face off his skull, when my own skull suddenly exploded. Blood shot into the air and poured back down over me like a rainstorm. I really didn't know what had happened to me, I just stood reeling for a second, when I suddenly felt a pain in my right ear. I reached up to touch it with my fingers only to find that my right ear was missing. I turned just in time to duck away from another vicious blow that whizzed past my face with just a fraction of an inch to spare. It was only then that I spotted a large Black man wielding an umbrella, which he was holding by the metal tip while he slashed at me with a very heavy curved wooden handle. I was well aware that the first blow I received could have killed me, and this Bastard was determined to get another one in. I went after him like an enraged Rhino, but was prevented from grabbing him by referee Don Branch, who dived between us and threw his arms around me locking both my arms to my sides. The umbrella-man jumped off the ring apron into the safety of the screaming fans, who by now were crowded all around the ring. I struggled to get free of the referee intent on going after the umbrella man, even if I had to dive on top of him from the ring. But then Vic, Bert and even Bob enveloped me as my assailant melted further back into the cheering crowd. I looked and then looked again at Don Branch, when he had grabbed hold of me just seconds earlier, he had been wearing a whiter than white shirt – now it was the reddest red I had ever seen. There was also the most blood I had ever seen, and it was still pumping out of where I used to have an ear. I decided to look for it and soon found it sliced into three jagged pieces and stuck to the side of my face. Bob drove me to a Hospital in Balham that was only a couple of miles from my home in Streatham. It took a couple of dozen stitches to put my ear back together, the surgeon did a great job, but it still bled every night for weeks as I refused to take any time away from wrestling never mind how badly I was injured – no wrestling – no money – pain I could bear – loss of wages I couldn't.

SEX & VIOLENCE

In March 1969 The Kray Twins, Ron and Reg were convicted of the murders of fellow Gangsters, George Cornell and Jack 'The Hat' McVitie, and received a sentence of 30 years to life for their trouble. Well that was 2 down, but as we all know things often happen in threes. It was a pretty spring day in May 1969 when I answered the door to a face I hadn't seen for many months, but one that had seemed to have aged a decade during that period. Tony's hand was trembling as he placed a newly lit cigarette in his trap. He was well aware of my views on people smoking around me, so he took it from between his lips, threw it down on my doorstep and ground it out with one twist of his shoe. I continued to give him that look, which prompted him to gather up the squashed cigarette and stuff into his trousers pocket. Only then did I step back and invited him inside,

"I hope you put that out properly, you don't want to jeopardize your livelihood do you?" I inquired. My attempted flippancy went right over Tony's head.

"Mick killed Gerry!" he blurted.

"WHAT?!" I replied. I had heard what he said, but obviously thought that I must have misunderstood him. He shook open a newspaper and showed me a story dominated by a large photo of Mickey Muldoon, and a smaller photo of the tattooed half-caste, Gerald John Hawley. Strangely enough the first and last photo I ever saw of Mick's latest and greatest Male-Model. In spite of reading the newspaper's version, and Tony supplying many more details, it wasn't until a couple of years later that I got a more complete picture of what really occurred from Sandra Muldoon herself.

In order to relate this story as concisely as I can, I think it would be best to combine all three sources now as I understand them, and add any other details at the future dates when and where they actually occur.

Surprise – surprise! Just as I had suspected, Sandra had got to Gigantic-Gerry right after their first photo shoot together, and he'd been banging her like a big base drum ever since. Obviously Mickey hadn't suspected a thing, and he may have remained ignorant of the fact indefinitely. But for one evening when Gerry was at Mickey's home, and they were both chatting when Sandra walked into the room wearing nothing but a very short, and very transparent negligee. Mickey looked at her in surprise; it wasn't that Gerry hadn't seen Sandra showing a lot more than that, when ever they posed for photographs. But there was no camera handy, or any other female models who would have taken centre stage to Sandra's background. Sandra cleared up the mystery when she took Gerry's hand and began to lead him upstairs,

"Me'n Gerry's going upstairs for a fuck, Mick," she announced, "You can come up and watch if you want to." Mickey wasn't happy, but at first thinking they were joking with him he began to laugh, the laugh died in his throat and was replaced by a roar of fury when Sandra added,

"Gerry's been fucking me for ages – haven't you Gerry?" Gerry's response was to grin at Mick in the same lecherous fashion that Mickey had seen him employ towards Tony, when he was deeply engaged with Tony's Wife Pauline. Poor Tony just had to grin and bear it, but Mickey wouldn't. Mickey snatched the two Indian Daggers from above the mantelpiece, and attacked Gerry like a starving Saber-toothed Tiger attacks its next meal. After stabbing him 89 times he stood over his lifeless form with blood pouring from the steel fangs he clutched in each fist.

"There was blood everywhere!" Sandra told me, "We rolled Gerry's body up in a carpet, took him out to Epping Forest, and dumped him in a ditch, then we came back home and cleaned up – there was even blood on the ceiling." She claimed.

As it was common knowledge to the Police that Gerry was Mickey Muldoon's number one model, it took them very little time to come knocking on Mickey's front door. Mickey was arrested, tried, convicted and sentenced to life in Prison. Sandra was charged as being an accomplice and got 6 months.

The cheaply made daggers that I had proclaimed to be both useless as weapons, and lacked history, now proved me wrong on both counts. So I made another prediction – that Mickey was finally out of the Pornography business for good, once again time would prove me wrong, but more of that later in my story.

GETTING INTO THE SPIRIT OF THINGS

Jack Robinson had just brought me the most exotic ring jacket to date, it had taken almost a year to complete. It was made from a rich flame colored velvet, and was so heavily encrusted with Rhinestones that it probably weighed more than 3 of my other jackets combined. The jacket was a great success, and as was usual generated almost as much attention in the dressing-room as it did in the ring.

"Oh – and what did you have to do to get that?!" the wrestlers inquired suggestively pouting their lips a flopping their hands about with limp wrists.

"Nothing at all," I told them, "although he did ask me to go to church."

"Whatcha gonna do marry 'im?!" asked Steve Logan as he took another drag of his cigarette. I explained that Jack Robinson was a Spiritualist; he lived in a very large house on the outskirts of Ipswich that belonged to a Lady who also had a Spiritualist Church in the grounds of her 4 acre estate.

Whenever Jack thought I might have been in a good mood, the kind of mood that a new jacket was guaranteed to generate, he would invite me to attend his church. Haunted and daunted by memories of Dad's dreaded Tabernacle, I always declined his invitation. I thought it better not to attend in the first place, rather than to have to make excuses later for not wanting to continue attending. But much to my amazement my declaration of Jack Robinson's religion generated more interest amongst many of my piers than my new jacket had.

The bogus Russian Ivan Penzekoff told me that he was practicing becoming more proficient at Astral-flight and did Jack Robinson have any tips on the subject?

Joe D'Orazio claimed to be so proficient at Astral-flight that he was able to choose a destination and visit wherever he fancied.

Bernard Murray told me of a house in North London that he had visited that was haunted.

He said that a gang of decorators who had been contracted to renovate had been terrorized to such an extent that at first wouldn't enter the premises alone, and eventually wouldn't work there at all, after cans of paint were seen flying across the room. Newly hung wallpaper would be torn off the walls, and handprints from invisible hands would appear then smudge and smear even as the painters were applying it to the walls.

Bernard claimed that when he visited the house he was alone, and after entering, the door slammed behind him of its own accord, and something knocked his hat off. Startled, he picked up his hat, replaced it on his head, cleared his throat, and in a loud voice said,

"Who ever is there I am not frightened of you – apprehensive – yes, but I'm not frightened!" With that, he said that every door in the house began to open and slam. Then the front door opened behind him, and he was flung bodily out of the house dropping his hat in the process. He said that he picked up his hat once more, replaced it on his head once more, then turned on his heel and marched away.

Julian Morice said that he and his young Daughter were able to read each others thoughts, so much so, that either one of them could hide any object in any room, without the other knowing which room, or even what the object was, and the other could just walk straight to where the object was and retrieve it as though they had hidden it there themselves.

Les Kellett told me that he was a practitioner of the occult, and a collector of the bizarre, including Taro-cards and such. He claimed that the star item of his collection was a set of Taro-cards designed by the self proclaimed Great-Beast himself, Alistair Crowley.

TALKING OF LES KELLETT

Les Kellett basked in a reputation of being the hardest man in Professional wrestling, and maybe he was, he most certainly possessed a tolerance to pain that was legendary. Although he assumed an air of modest indifference to his almost superhuman toughness, in reality he never missed an opportunity to demonstrate it to the full, as he strived to nurture an image that would equal if not surpass that of Bert Assirati.

Tales of Kellett's extraordinary pain threshold were ten a penny. Like the time when he, and a number of other wrestlers were engaged in some repair and maintenance work in Norman Morrell's gym. A heavy steel girder fell onto Les's foot, and squashed it like a pancake, it took a few wrestlers just to lift it off in order to free him, and Blood was oozing right through his boot.

"Are you alright Les," the other wrestlers asked, "let's take your boot off and have a look at it!" - "Best take him straight to Hospital!" another wrestler advised.

"No, no," Kellett replies, as calmly as though nothing had occurred, "we told Mr. Morrell we'd get this work done, so we'll do the work first, and take a look at my foot later."

Hours later, the only way they could remove Kellett's boot was to cut it off his foot, as it had swollen to twice its normal size, and was glued to his boot with congealed blood. Obviously everyone was mightily impressed. Another story that took place in Norman Morrell's Gym was when Les was in the ring wrestling against Norman Morrell himself.

Kellett found himself outclassed and tied up by his smaller adversary, who in an attempt to gain a win grabbed one of Les' Banana sized fingers and threatened to break it if Kellett didn't submit,

"BREAK IT!" Kellett invited, - he didn't believe in submitting.

Les lived on a Smallholding on the Yorkshire Moors where he raised various farm animals including pigs. One morning whilst feeding them, a huge tusked Boar bit him savagely on his hand. Apparently, all Kellett did was to wrap it up to stem the bleeding, and then go about his chores as usual. By the time he arrived at the venue where he was wrestling that night his hand looked more like a boxing glove, and after relating the story to a dressing room full of wrestlers, he presented his swollen paw for their inspection. The wrestlers were horrified by the sight of his mangled hand, so much so that his opponent that night told him,

"Nay Les, you can't wrestle with your hand in that condition!"

"Yes –yes," Les agrees, "I think you're right – so what I'll do is to put my hand down on the floor, and you stomp on it to get rid of all that swelling."

"Nay Les," his opponent replied, turning green at the prospect, "I can't do that!"

"I don't understand!" queried Kellett, "you just told me that I can't go in the ring and wrestle with my hand like this, and I agreed with you. So I'd like you to stomp on it to get the poison out, then I can go in the ring and wrestle can't I?"

"Nay Les," his opponent repeated, "I just couldn't do it!"

By now Kellett had the full and undivided attention of everyone in the dressing room so he replied,

"Well if you won't help me out so that I can wrestle tonight, I'm going to stamp on you, and then you won't be able to wrestle tonight either."

Les placed his hand on the floor and his opponent stomped on it.

"Harder!" Les ordered.

STOMP! – There was blood and pus all over the floor around his mangled hand.

"HARDER!" Les ordered, "You have to make sure you get all that poison out."

Then there was the time when we were wrestling for Wryton Promotions in the middle of winter, in a big corrugated tin shack in the middle of nowhere. Outside was freezing, while the wrestlers in the dressing room were huddled around a hot smoky cast iron stove trying to keep warm. When all at once our misery was rudely interrupted by 'Jumping' Jim Hussey, who burst into the dressing room. He was closely pursued by a large, and very hostile member of the audience, who had become so incensed at

Jumping Jim's treatment of one of the fan's favorites that he was totally intent on meting out revenge on the perpetrator himself. As Jim scuttled into a corner the avenger's path towards him was suddenly blocked by Kellett, who suggested that the trespasser would be wise to vacate the wrestler's sanctuary. Not only did the avenger reject Kellett's sincere advice, but made the monumental mistake of taking a swing at him. Kellett grabbed the avenger in a skull crushing headlock and placed the unfortunate heroes head over the red hot stove. Immediately the room was inundated by the unpleasant aroma of burning hair and flesh, but even as Kellett roasted the avenger's head like a marshmallow, big blisters began to appear all over his own arm and shoulder without appearing to cause Kellett the slightest sign of distress. Some then thought that Les must have had a sudden attack of compassion when he picked the avenger up and threw him through the only window, outside into a snowdrift to cool off. Having made his point – not just to the avenger but to all wrestlers present, Kellett sat back down and continued to warm his hands by the stove. The wrestlers recovered their composure quite quickly,

"Thanks a lot Les" they moaned sarcastically, as they too huddled closer to the stove in response to the icy wind that now howled through the broken window.

This kind of behavior was designed to intimidate his peers, and succeeded to such a degree that I have actually heard other wrestlers speculating who would come out on top if Kellett and powerhouse George Gordienko got into a serious fight. When asked for my opinion on the outcome I truthfully replied,

"Are you fucking nuts, how could Kellett possibly last half a minute with George Gordienko, he couldn't even beat Norman Morrell who was only a Lightweight."

By the very next day Les had been told of what I had said,

"So you don't think I could last half a minute against Gordienko?!" he accused me.

"No I don't - do you?" I replied.

I thought that I had received rough treatment when Jack Dale had put me in the ring with an Olympic wrestler who had outweighed me by about 30 pounds to determine how well I could handle myself in a shoot match. But that episode paled into insignificance when compared to the tryout of another young hopeful.

The young wrestler, like myself before him, had been wrestling for independent promoters, and now wanted to move up to the big time. Jack Dale invited him to come and tryout at their gym. Unfortunately for the newcomer, the only wrestler available for him to tryout with when he arrived that day was Les Kellett. Well to cut a short story even shorter, Kellett stepped into the ring with the youngster and almost murdered him, within seconds the kid was screaming for mercy. Jack Dale called a halt to the massacre, but Kellett's blood lust had been aroused and he intended crippling his victim. Jack and others had to jump into the ring and pries him off his pray. An ambulance had to be called to take the ex-hopeful to Kings-Cross Hospital with a dislocated shoulder – plus a shattered body and shattered dreams.

There was a period when Les was wrestling in the South, when we found that there was only the two of us traveling in one of Dale Martin's vans to each night's venue.

When wrestlers were asked to drive Dale's vans, even though they were only paid a couple of pounds extra for that service, there was never a shortage of volunteers as we were all believers in earning as much as we could by whatever means possible. It was during this period that I learned a lot about Kellett's early history right from the tough man himself. I would sit in the passenger seat and listen for hours as Les talked and talked about his favorite subject.

He claimed he had been brought up in the wilds of Yorkshire by his Grandparents, where they had no electricity, no running water, and lived only on what they could grow, and by what edible plants and herbs they would gather in the woods.

"I was brought up hard," he claimed, "if there was a hard way to do a job, or an easy way, I would always choose the hard way."

"Why would you do that?" I asked, "Surely if you found an easier way to do a job, you could finish it faster, and then have more time and energy to do something else.

I was missing the point – being hard and doing everything the hardest way possible was much more compatible with the 'Super Human' myth he was attempting to weave around himself.

He told me he bred Rabbits for their fur and meat, and also Dogs for Ratting and they, just like the young hopeful who met his Waterloo at his huge rough paws, had to pass a test if they wanted to move on. He had a small barrel full of water and a big barrel that would contain live Rats. When the young Pups reached a certain age he would drop one into the barrel of Rats, if it killed Rats it was worth keeping, if it didn't he would use the smaller barrel containing water to drown the Pup.

"Why would you do that?" I wanted to know – surely you could find someone who wasn't plagued by Rats who would be happy to give it a good home." But no, that would scar Kellett's unyielding, uncompromising image,

"It does the job, or its no use." He growled.

I asked him why he had treated the young would-be wrestler so harshly in Dale's gym,

"You've got to hurt them for them to know they've been beaten." He replied.

'He had demonstrated that quite adequately when he roasted the fans head, and launched him through the window.' I thought. But in order to make his point, he continued by telling me a story that happened to him during the period he had been employed as a Merchant Seaman, when he was wandering around some dockland area late one night. He was attacked by some huge thug who got the surprise of his life to find himself flat on his back with Les on top of him, completely constraining his slightest movement with comparative ease.

"I explained to him," Les explained to me, "that as he was now pinned to the cobbles and was unable to move a limb, and that he was now beaten by someone who could very easily do him a serious mischief if that someone chose to do so. I then asked him if he agreed, and that he would behave himself in future if I let him up and allowed him to go about his business. He agreed, so I helped him up – and up he came – foot first right into my balls. I woke up early next morning covered in blood and bruises, and made my mind up there and then, that from that time on – YOU'VE GOT TO HURT THEM, FOR THEM TO KNOW THEY'VE BEEN BEATEN" Although I thought that was a lesson worth remembering – I still wondered what that had to do with a young wrestler trying to advance his career.

Another aspect that had me puzzled was the fact that after being called up by the army during World-War II, this violent brute claimed to be a conscientious objector and flatly refused to fight.

"I had it very hard in the army," he told me, "I was put into a Military Prison, and was beaten up regularly at first in an attempt to make me retaliate, which would have cast doubt on my claim that I was a pacifist. Then I was placed in solitary confinement and fed slops which I refused to eat. I told them I was a vegetarian, and would only eat fresh, raw vegetables. At first they told me I could starve, but after days of refusing any other kind of nourishment, a guard came and opened my cell door and threw a cabbage at me,"

"Hey Rabbit," he called me, "here's your dinner!"

"Then every day for the rest of the war they would come and throw a cabbage or a lettuce at me and shout – Here's your dinner Rabbit!"

"Yes," Les claimed, "I had it very hard during the War."

Maybe I was still smarting over the horror I felt when he told me of his treatment of Puppies who lacked a sufficient measure of the killer instinct to be deemed worthy of remaining alive. Maybe it was the thought of Soldiers like my own Father, and many other Fathers, Sons and Brothers, who had the guts to fight when I replied,

"Personally Les, I think it was much harder for those in the trenches trying to dodge bombs, bullets and bayonets than sitting in a dry safe cell dodging an odd lettuce or a cabbage."

Not only was that the end of our conversation for that day, but the next day as I sat in the passenger seat next to 'The Hardest Man in Wrestling', he said,

"Some of the Boys like talking and telling jokes to pass the time when they're traveling to the shows - I'm not like that – and I prefer to keep my own counsel. So, I'd appreciate it if you don't talk to me, and I won't talk to you!"

"That's fine with me Les," I told him, "in fact I'd prefer to sleep." Having said that I vacated the passenger seat beside Kellett and walked right to the rear of the van where there was a seat long enough to stretch right out on.

Les spent the whole journey swerving and slamming on the

brakes, which suggested to my satisfaction that my remarks the day before had succeeded in hurting the unhurt-able. I didn't give a damn about my lack of diplomacy dealing with such a savage ogre, as he weighed well over 200 pounds while my own bodyweight hovered between 150 to 165, so I knew I was in no danger of ever having to share the ring with him – or so I thought!!!

****

Although the life of a professional wrestler could be very hard, and I could have found much to complain about, such as, the endless long trips, often weeks away from home, violent fans, and constant exposure to second-hand tobacco-smoke, I was living the life I had always wanted since I was just a young kid. But the fact that as a result of my profession I saw so little of my own Kids was most probably the hardest part of all. When I did get home as often as not instead of being met with a welcoming smile by Jean, I got a grumpy scowl. She seemed to imagine that my life as a wrestler was just one eternal holiday, while she just sat at home and lived a life of continual boredom. The moment I walked in through the door she'd start, and yes 'other girls' was still a main feature in her repertoire. But now the undisputed new kid on the block when it came to disagreements were the Kids.

"That bleed'n Adrian and Vince have been playin' me up rotten," She'd complain, "you want to have a go at them tomorrow – I told them you'd give them both a bleed'n good hidin' when you came home!"

"Why did you tell them that?!" I wanted to know.

"Well they won't listen to me, so you need to have a go at them!" she insisted.

"Don't you dare make me into a Bogeyman to my own Kids," I'd warn her, "I want them to look forward to seeing me when I get home, not be frightened!"

To be honest my Kids spoiled me, from the time each of them had been born. I can never remember having one single sleepless night, and even at the time Jean wanted me to discipline them, all I'd have to do if they were getting a bit rowdy or misbehaving is to tell them,

"That's enough," or, "tone it down a bit." And that was that.

"Yes, that's ok for you, they listen to you, but they won't take any notice of me when your not here!" Jean would complain. So I would call Adrian and Vince and tell them,

"Listen you two – don't play your Mother up ever – especially when I'm away wrestling."

"Ok Dad." They'd reply.

"You need to belt them!" Jean would shriek, "I told them they would cop it when you got home!"

"Well don't ever tell them that again." I'd warn her, "I'm their Father not a fucking Bogeyman, I only see them once in a blue moon, I look forward to seeing them, and I want them to look forward to seeing me – so that's that! – Then to Adrian and Vince,

"Let's go for a run over the running track Boys – bet you can't catch me!"

Jean would be furious with me for not disciplining them, and I would be furious with Jean for using me as a threat. I still don't know if I was right or wrong, but I knew how much I disliked my own Father's company, and did not under any circumstances want my own Children to ever feel that way about me.

DRIVING FORCE

"Ok, start it up." The driving teacher instructed.

"Ok, how do I do that?" I asked. I had been traveling in various vehicles back and forth, to and from wrestling venues for a dozen years, very often sitting right next to the driver. I was now 28 years old, and I didn't even have the slightest idea of what to do to turn a vehicle on in the first place. I had never had the tiniest interest in motor vehicles of any kind, and anything to do with them went completely over my head.

The Instructor showed me where the ignition key went, and how to turn it on. Then explained how to put the thing in gear, how to use the mirrors, and where to look, then finally how to put the contraption into motion. I was instructed to drive out of the Side Street and right onto Streatham High Road, and into bumper to bumper traffic; my heart was in my mouth. The traffic picked up speed – so did my heart rate,

"Go a bit faster." I was instructed. I complied.

I began to sweat, my knuckles were white.

"Speed up a bit." I was told. We seemed to be flying, there was traffic all around me doing the same thing. I remembered that I would probably feel a lot better if I actually began to breathe again, then another thought crossed my mind and I asked,

What do I do if I need to stop this thing?"

Just a couple of weeks later my instructor asked me if I would like to take my test,

"You won't pass," he explained, "but the experience will be beneficial."

He was quite correct, I didn't pass, but I did come close.

"You did great!" he told me after he had received my results.

His praise prompted me to go shopping for my first vehicle. I was shocked and horrified, I could not believe how expensive cars were, even a new Mini cost over 1,000 pounds.

"I'll never, ever pay as much as 1,000 pounds for a bloody car!" I stated with conviction. As you can see I still didn't appreciate inflation. The vehicle that caught my eye was a red and white Triumph Herald Convertible, but even a second-hand, or even third-hand model was so far out of my price range, I decided to forget flashy, and settle for a set of cheap wheels that would hopefully get me to and from where ever I wanted to go. I finally decided on a little Dark-Bronze Hillman Husky, which I chose mainly because it was cheap, and also with the back seats down there was room back there for a blow-up mattress which I thought might come handy. I continued taking lessons in my own car and passed my next driving test with comparative ease.

EXOTIC FISH

Although I very rarely, if ever got a day off from wrestling, I wanted to visit The Ideal Home Exhibition that was held once a year in Earls Court. The reason being, I had began redecorating our new home and was looking for new ideas. I didn't have the day off, but the fact that on that night in question I would be wrestling in London, gave me all the rest of the day to take Jean and the Kids with me to check out the exhibition, and then take them all to the local venue to watch me wrestle afterwards.

The exhibition was very impressive indeed, and a dozen new ideas flooded my mind, but they all evaporated the second I saw 'The Marine-Tropical Fish exhibit'. I had seen, and admired tropical Fish before, but I had never ever seen Marine Tropical Fish outside special aquariums in the Zoo. I was awestruck by the blinding colors and bizarre shapes of these fantastic fish, and determined to make my own Tropical-Marine aquarium a major feature in our main room. The vendor gave me his card, and I was delighted to find that his shop 'Seaquariums' was in Croydon, and only a few miles away from my home in Streatham. For months to come Seaquariums almost became my second home. I received most of my advice, and was usually served by a pretty girl with long dark hair named Linda, who I naturally took an instant fancy to. So much so, that I would have continued to frequent Seaquariums with or without the fabulous fish.

I built a 60 gallon tank into a recess, and clad it with York stone which I continued on across that side of the room to form a new stone fireplace. Then above its marble mantelpiece was the very large plate-glass mirror that I had bought from Mike Dimitri, the rest of the walls on that side of the room I clad with Cedar.

I wasn't blessed with beginner's luck, and my first attempt at keeping Salt-Water Fish was marred by many casualties. Which prompted me to suggest to Linda that she only sold me sick fish, so that I would have to come back and see her in order to replace the ones I continually lost. Although I probably startled her at first with my bizarre sense of humor, we soon became very good friends, and I felt that she enjoyed my company almost as much as I enjoyed hers. It was not unusual to find the shop void of customers, and in order to pass the time Linda would make small models, or base-reliefs of her favorite fish, out of some kind of modeling clay. She was an excellent sculptress, but complained that she was unable to obtain as much detail as she would have preferred with the clay she had been using. I began bringing her various modeling agents in the form of clays, wax and so on. Including a variety that she became particularly fond of, which didn't only give her models the fine detail that she had desired, but could be baked in a regular oven in order to make it permanently firm. which she then painted to match the living fish. I found the little sculptures she produced almost as delightful as I found the Sculptress. I invited her to come and watch me wrestle, especially when I was appearing at The Fairfield Hall, which was only a short walk away from 'Seaquariums',

"Yes, I'd like to see you wrestle, but is it alright if I bring my husband too?" She asked,

"No! Its not alright," I told her firmly, "I like you very much, but I don't like husbands at all." I would have been horrified to meet her husband just in case I did like him, as that would have put a giant dent in my aspirations concerning beautiful Linda. Linda lived in West Norwood, just 2 or 3 miles from Streatham, and I would often give her a lift home when she finished work. But, she would never accept a ride unless I had my kids with me. Although I left her in no doubt concerning the nature of my interest in her, I also explained that she would be as safe with me alone in the centre of the darkest forest as she would be in Seaquariums with a shop full of customers.

"I can be persuasive," I told her one day as I tried to coax her into the car beside me, "but I would never do anything that was not welcomed with open arms – or any other limbs that might be available."

She laughed, stooped down and kissed my hand, then ran to the bus stop to catch an approaching bus to take her home.

CARNABY CAVERN

I was introduced to Colin Wilde by Joe Quesek, Colin owned Carnaby Cavern, a Boutique that specialized in creating costumes that were Wilde, even by my own exotic standards. Colin was an ex-Male dancer, and dressed as though he was his own best customer. His jacket would taper dramatically from shoulders down to a waistline that he boasted measured a dainty 26 inches, and his skin-tight pants flared out enough to almost entirely obscure his fancy high heeled boots. His shoulder length hair and beard were bright red, he loved Horses, and bragged that he had just bought his latest mount for no other reason that its beautiful chestnut coat matched his hair and beard exactly.

"When people see me riding by, they are amazed!" he'd shriek.

Glam-Rock was in its infancy, but maturing at the speed of light. I was asked during an interview many years later, if I had invented Glam-Rock. I modestly denied the charge, but added, that although I didn't invent Glam-Rock we 'borrowed' very heavily from each other. For instance, I immediately began designing my own clothes that I had made by Carnaby Cavern, and later by 'Granny Takes a Trip' in Kings Road, Chelsea.

Many of my designs were copied for Adam Ant, David Bowie and Gary Glitter. I designed a black velvet suit decorated with Birds of Paradise made entirely from Rhinestones down the outsides of the jacket sleeves and trouser legs. While it was being made I was touring up North, and by the time I got back to London and went to collect my suit, I was told by the owner of the Boutique, an American named Lee, that Elton John had seen my suit and had wanted to buy it. After it had been explained to him, who the suit had been made for, Elton very wisely had a similar suit made for himself instead of buying mine. His suit differed only in the basic color and the in the Birds of Paradise that were replaced by Music-Notes. When asked during an interview where he had got his ideas for make-up and stage costumes, T-Rex's Marc Bolan replied,

"By watching Adrian Street wrestling on TV."

As the Glam-Rockers began wearing more and more make-up, my own use of cosmetics increased dramatically, I was determined to stay ahead of the pack whether they were wrestlers or Rock Stars. The mere hint that suggested that I may or may not have been wearing make-up, gave way to the most colorful, garish, and exotic designs I could devise, I added glitter, and even began gluing sequins and rhinestones around my eyes. Once again many referees and even opponents were very reluctant to go into the ring with me, but the fact that my constant evolution had propelled me into one of Britain's biggest box office draws gave me a much bigger voice. I was also proud of the fact that the other of Britain's biggest Stars, like Pallo and McManus were well into their forties, Les Kellett must have already been in his fifties while I was still in my twenties.

My ever expanding wardrobe gained so much notoriety that I was contacted by a shoe company who asked me to model their new line of shoes and boots. I did and the stores began to fill up with platforms that were risky to walk in, but could add as much as 4 to 5 extra inches to the height of its wearer. This was the style I had been waiting my whole adult life for; all of a sudden I was eye to eye with many big wrestlers instead of looking up their nose. The shoe company offered me the pick of the shoes I had modeled for them and I chose a pair of Black and Blood-Red shoes that elevated me to a height of over 6 feet – WOW! Talk about being lightheaded! Very soon my collection of platform boots made from multi-colored Snakeskin began to match my collection of exotic suits, themselves all made from exotic fabrics, velvets, metallics and multi-color brocades.

Since the death of my great friend Charles Mascall, Master of Ceremonies Mike Judd had taken over his role as well as continuing in his own role as Ring Announcer. As I continued adding to my sartorial splendor, he thought it would be a great idea to drop the title 'Nature-Boy' Adrian Street awarded me by Charles Mascall, in favor of 'Adrian Street Esq.' I wasn't over the moon concerning his idea, I had been thrilled to bare the title of one of my old-time favorites, Nature-Boy' Buddy Rogers, and Esquire meant nothing to me whatsoever. I knew that Esquire was a title held by young Noblemen going way back in history, but nowadays I wasn't sure what it was supposed to mean. Nevertheless, I did remember Les Martin's reaction to my rejection of his idea of naming me Stuart instead of Street, so I decided to humor Mike Judd and allow him to have his way. I had lost a great champion in Charles Mascall, but I knew that as one of Dale-Martin's under-bosses Mike Judd would want his own ideas to bear fruit, which could only work in my favor. It was only for that reason that I agreed to become Adrian Street Esq. Another idea attributed to Mike Judd was, in order to emphasize the new Monika, the Master of Ceremonies to initially introduce me as 'Nature-Boy' Adrian Street, and I would arrogantly correct them, and even refuse to continue until I was introduced as Adrian Street Esq. What I found amazing was the way I was now perceived by many wrestlers who had known me from the time I had began wrestling for Joint-Promotions. I was traveling in Dale's van to a venue with a number of wrestlers from Wigan, who were in the midst of grizzling about the shoddy treatment and poor wages they were receiving from Joint-Promotions. I agreed with them wholeheartedly, but reminded them how much better off they were now than when they were all coal-miners.

"What the fuck do you know about coalmining?!" they all wanted to know.

"Quite a lot," I told them, "I worked down the pit for a couple of years after starting work in the colliery at the tender age of 15."

"BOLLOCKS!!!" They all responded, "You've never even been down the pit in your life!" - "You'd shit yourself if you did!" another added for good measure.

They were beginning to sound just like the miners I had worked with who all had predicted that I would never become a professional wrestler. After explaining so many details concerning the art of obtaining coal, details that no one but a miner, or ex-miner would know, I almost had them believing me, until I spoke about the underground stables and the Pit-Ponies.

"Now we know you're full of shit!" They told me, "They haven't had ponies down the pit for decades!"

"Maybe not in Lancashire or Yorkshire," I agreed, "but in Wales they still use pit-ponies to this very day."

"What a load of crap!" they told me, "you've never been down the pit!"

It wasn't just the ex-miners, but all at once even the other wrestlers seemed to imagine I had been brought up with a Silver-Spoon in my mouth. –

"More like a rusty shovel." I assured them.

"Well yer fuckin' mouth is big enough!" agreed Iron-man Steve Logan as he drew another drag of his fag.

****

I imagine the road from London to Salisbury must have been built over the original road built by the Ancient Romans, as in the old Roman style it was as straight as a billiard cue. Although the road lacked bends it did not lack hills, and I was driving up a very steep one of these one Saturday afternoon on my way to Salisbury. As I drove over the crest I almost collided with a car that had stalled just beyond the crest, and had been out of sight until the very last second. I swerved to the right and slammed on the brakes and missed the stalled vehicle by inches. I began to breathe a huge sigh of relief, but didn't get the chance to complete it, as another car shot over the blindside behind me and crashed at full speed right into the back of my car. The impact was so huge that my seat broke, it completely collapsed and I found myself laying almost upside-down and struggling like an upturned Tortoise as my car hurtled down the hill in front of me. I righted myself just in time to see that I was heading straight towards a stampede of oncoming traffic. At first there was nothing I could do about it, as I was almost sitting in the back seat and unable to reach the steering wheel or the brakes. I dove forward swung the steering wheel hard left, shot right off the road, and straight into a grassy bank. Again the impact was so great, that my body hit the door so hard that it shot open, and I was thrown right out of the car and onto the side of the road.

'Well that was exciting!' I thought as I picked myself up and walked back up the hill to check on the other vehicles. The driver of the car who had back-sided mine, had his door open and was sitting sideways with his feet outside on the road. Booth his shins were bleeding, but were in much better condition than the front of his car which was completely caved in. The driver of the stalled vehicle that had caused the crash had got his car going again, and drove off down the road as though nothing unusual had occurred.

After returning to my own car and attempting to force the seat back into a position where I could actually reach the steering wheel, I started it up, but it fizzled out again. I started it up once more and managed to get it going, but it limped, popped and farted all the way to Salisbury, where I eventually arrived with barely enough time to wrestle in the last match. It must have taken 3 times longer than normal to drive back home from Salisbury, and the next day I was already out shopping for a replacement. My next vehicle was a white Singer-Vogue.

The first venue I drove my new car to was Bedford, and I parked it in the car-park which was on the opposite side of the road from the Town Hall where the wrestling matches were held. I was in the Main Event, and my contest was the third match. After it concluded I showered and dressed as quickly as I could so that I could get out of the hall before the last match ended, and beat the crowd of fans that would soon come streaming out of the Hall. As I entered the car-park I noticed a man taking a piss, and remembered that I should have had one myself before I left the Hall, but had forgotten due to my haste. I walked up next to the man, unzipped and began to piss all over his trousers. He leapt about three feet in the air and screamed,

"HEY – FUCK – LOOK WHERE YOU'RE AIMING – YOU'RE PISSING ALL OVER MY PANTS!!!"

"Yes, I know," I replied, "and you were pissing all over my car."

LINDA

Soon after Linda had begun working at Lester's Riding-School, Peter and Marion Larrigan, an ex-Circus family took over the management. A couple of decades later their Daughter Tanya represented Britain in dressage at the 1984 Olympic Games held in Mexico.

There were a number of famous actors that frequented the school who Linda would take out for rides including James Villiers and Terence Stamp, who was perfecting his equestrian prowess, which greatly enhanced his performance as Dragoon Sergeant Francis Troy in the 1967 movie 'Far from the Madding Crowd.' Linda also taught Michael Caine how to ride for his part as British Officer, Gonville Bromhead in the 1964 movie 'Zulu' that elevated him to superstardom.

Next she applied for a job in Battersea Park, working in the Zoo from spring till the end of summer, and then in the gardens until the beginning of the following spring. After the first year Linda would work in Crystal Palace Zoo during the Winter, and then return to Battersea Park each Spring. It was during a summer period in 1965 that Linda met and eventually became engaged to a security Guard at Battersea Funfair. Then when their affair ended, on the rebound she married a welder whose Father had been contracted to work on the Park's fences. She and her husband lived in West Norwood and she continued to alternate working between Battersea and Crystal Palace until in 1968. Then she saw an advert in 'The Horse and Hounds' for a job in 'Seaquariums' which she applied for and secured.

As well as various modeling materials that I introduced Linda to, I also brought her many modeling tools that I myself used to achieve the greatest detail on my ever expanding historical military miniatures. I was a little taken aback by Linda's slightly brutal criticism of my cavalry's Horses when I first showed them to her. But then Linda was a perfectionist, and nothing less than perfection would suffice when it came to her all time favorite Beast. I took her criticism to heart, and my Cavalry thanks her for it very much for their improved and smarter mounts.

On September 9th 1969 I was wrestling against the West-Indian Middleweight Star, Linde Caulder in Croydon. As always when ever I wrestled in that venue I would invite Linda to the show, and as always she would decline the invite. But on this night as I raised my arms in acknowledgment of my introduction, I also raised my eyes which focused on a lovely looking Girl sitting in the balcony. I refocused my eyes and realized that the lovely Girl was Linda, and that night I wrestled for her.

In spite of being one of the nicest guys in the business, my opponent was also one of the greediest for glory. He was highly competitive, and any adversary had to work his arse off in order to gain even the slightest advantage. With Linda in the balcony watching our every move, even the powerful fast moving Linde had his work cut out to keep up with me on this night, and after 7 hard fought rounds I emerged the winner.

During the match I had scrutinized all the fans sitting near Linda for anyone who may have turned out to be her husband, but was optimistic when I saw no likely candidate. After I showered and dressed I went to join her, and she introduced me to a friend named Carol who had agreed to accompany her, and had brought Linda to the matches in her car. I thanked Carol, and invited them both to join me for a drink in the Greenroom Bar. Linda was wearing a dress under a light jacket, and I realized that this was the first time I had seen her when she was not wearing jeans. Her legs were beautiful, long and shapely with calves like a dancer.

I naturally imagined that it would be me who would be taking Linda home from Croydon, and was thrilled to think that at last she trusted me. I wasn't given the opportunity to prove my trustworthiness however, as only when it was time to leave, I was informed that Linda would be going home the same way she came – with her chaperone Carol. Disappointed, would have hardly described my feelings – I was royally pissed off!

****

Although I no longer took pornographic photos, I was not completely out of the business, if there was money to be made, I still had an interest. I would pay Big Abe 2 to 3 pounds each for movies, which I would resell for 10. I also had customers who would exchange the movies I had previously sold them for new ones every week, and pay half price for each exchanged movie. I carried out that business on a very small scale, as I realized that the bigger you got in that profession the more undesirable attention you potentially attracted from both sides of the law.

OCTOBER 14th 1969

I hadn't visited Seaquariums to see Linda since before she came to Croydon with her chaperone Carol, partly because I was still mad at her, but mostly because I had been spending so much time wrestling up North. I was tempted to pop in and tell her that I was once again appearing on another TV show in Croydon on the 14th of October, but with the memory of the last episode still fresh in my mind I decided there wasn't really much point. When I arrived at the Fairfield Hall on the night in question I suffered disappointment number 2 when I found that I would be wrestling against the spoiler himself, Peter Szakacs. Definitely not my first choice of opponents, especially on TV. We had an all action match, but as it was being viewed by a huge television audience we were both determined to domineer our contest, which resulted in a lot of extremely hard work. Nevertheless, I emerged as the victor, and I lost no time strutting my stuff around the ring with raised arms, serenaded by my favorite tune, namely the booing of the crowd, while I braved the scowling countenance of my badly beaten opponent. It was only then that I glanced up into the balcony and caught sight of Linda sitting quietly amongst the screaming fans.

Speculation was running high after showering, dressing, collecting Linda, and escorting her to the Greenroom for refreshments when I discovered that this time there was no chaperone in tow. Would she risk my offer of a ride home alone with me in the car, or would she announce that she would use the bus, taxi, or that someone else would come and pick her up? After coming straight to the point and inquiring how she intended getting home, and fully expecting another last minute double-cross, I was happy to learn that she hoped that I would take her.

Speculation was speeding up and gaining altitude!

I turned on the ignition, very much aware that this was the very first time that Linda and I were alone together in my car.

"Do you want me to take you straight home, or would you like to go for a ride somewhere?" I inquired.

"We'll go for a ride somewhere." She replied.

Now speculation was really flying!!! So much so, that I didn't really know where I was driving to, and still in a dream state eventually found myself driving past Purley Orchid Ballroom. I decided to get off the main road, and after a few twists and turns I finally pulled to a halt in the centre of a football field. I thought I'd test the water when I asked,

"Shall we stay in the front, or make ourselves more comfortable on the back seat?" She removed her panties and replied,

"The back seat." - Speculation exploded!

****

For the next few days, as I was wrestling each night close to London, I would pick Linda up from Seaquariums and take her to the venues with me. Everything went great until one night after wrestling 8 rounds at the arena, Linda and I decided to see how many rounds we could do in the car. After finally calling our contest a draw we were both shocked to find it was gone 3am, and Linda should have been home hours ago – doesn't time fly when you're having fun?! I sped towards London as fast as I could, and Linda instructed that I should drop her off a few blocks away from where she lived. We had hardly kissed and wished each other a good night when another car hurtled around the corner and Linda hit the deck. The other vehicle slowed and I saw the face of a bearded man glaring at me through the window.

"Quick move!!!!" Linda demanded, "That's my husband!!!" I did, like a shot from a cannon, and didn't stop until we were in the middle of Crystal Palace.

"What now?" I asked her.

"I can't go home now." She told me.

"That sounds reasonable enough," I agreed, "but where do you want to go instead?" She decided to call her Mother who lived in Fulham, and stay with her until she was able to sort everything out, so that is where we made for. What Linda's Mother thought when Linda arrived at her home about 5am, in the company of a strange looking guy with long platinum blond hair is anyone's guess, but we had hardly stepped through the front door when the phone rang!

"What are you doing around your Mother's house, why aren't you here!" her husband wanted to know – and then before Linda could reply he added, "And what was Adrian Street the wrestler doing in a car parked around the corner from the apartment?!"

"How would I know?!" Linda lied.

"When are you coming home?!" he inquired.

"I'm not." Linda replied – and she never did.

****

Rather than risk her husband suddenly appearing at Seaquariums and causing a scene, Linda quit her job there. So from then on, in order to meet her I would have to pick her up from her Mother's home.

In a few more days it would be Linda's Birthday, and I would be going back up north for a week. So I decided to take Linda to one of my favorite restaurants, and then a hotel the night before I left, as I wouldn't be seeing her again until my northern trip had been completed.

It was a Spanish restaurant near the corner of Earls Court and Kings Road, all the waiters were incredibly gay, and the food was incredibly good, so it promised to be a fun evening. I wondered if Linda would be too shy to eat, so I ordered a huge jug of ice cold Sangria to help relax her. I had nothing to worry about, first she ordered Mussels simmering in Garlic sauce, I had a main course Paella as an appetizer. I swallowed my first mouthful and passed judgment,

"MMMM! This is really tasty." I told Linda.

"So WAS mine." She replied.

'What do you mean WAS?!' I wondered.

I looked to where seconds earlier, Linda had a big dish of hot steaming Mussels, now she was mopping up the last drop of Garlic sauce with a large chunk of crusty bread, which I swear she must have swallowed whole without even chewing it. Talk about fast! I was amazed that she didn't begin crunching up the Mussel shells, which was all that remained. Instead she observed,

"That looks nice!" and speared a large juicy Prawn right out of the centre of my Paella. I knew I should have whacked her hand with my fork immediately, but was too shocked to act before she had devoured more than half of my appetizer. Her hand and mouth coordination was amazing to behold. Then she scanned the restaurant, caught the waiter's eye and gave him that, 'Come on – what's next?!' look.

A large Steak each with all the trimmings later, and Linda was eating the first of a multitude of deserts, which she got through washed down with Coffee, Spanish Brandy, and another glass or maybe 6 glasses of Sangria, and all before I finished eating my Steak! There had been none of that romantic small talk that I had expected over our meal. Linda's chops had been otherwise occupied non stop from the time we sat down in the restaurant until it was time to leave. And, even then, as we were leaving the restaurant I caught her looking longingly at the desert trolley!

'Goodness gracious!' I thought, 'this Girl can surpass all my appetites!'

"Okay," I told her now's the time to find a hotel and work off some of those calories."

"Could you stop the car first!" she replied. She rushed out of the car and lost the last of her many deserts.

"Are you ok?" I inquired, "are you up to this, or should I take you home?"

"I'll be fine," she assured me – and then, "COULD YOU STOP THE CAR AGAIN?!!!!!!!!"

That was the name of the game for the next couple of hours, but by the time she lost the Mussels in Garlic sauce, she had the bloody cheek to ask me,

"Do you know of any restaurants that might be open this time of night?" and added, "I'm hungry again."

I sighed and replied, "The only thing open for business tonight my dear, is going to be you." Next morning we showered together and then breakfasted. I would be driving up to Leominster, the first venue of my northern tour, and Linda would begin looking for a new job while I was away. But, the sight of my bathing partner that morning inspired a much better idea, "Why don't you come with me?" I suggested.

We really lucked out with our choice of hotel in Leominster. Not only could we get up for breakfast as late as we wanted, but breakfast included a mixed grill, which consisted of steak, pork-chops, lamb-chops, liver, kidney, bacon, eggs, mushrooms, tomatoes, beans, toast, muffins and hot, strong coffee. Even though my next venue Malvern, was a little out of the way we returned to the same hotel the next night. After Malvern came Bolton, and the rest of the tour was in the Manchester area, where we stayed in the same hotel each night. My last venue was Altrincham, where we also lucked out as I met a fan named Dan Murray, who owned rental property all over Manchester, and offered to rent us a flat for what ever duration we wanted it. If I was wrestling down south for an extended period we would give up the flat, and then rent a different one from him next time I was in that area, we both loved the idea. In fact Linda loved it so much that she filed for divorce, and changed her name by deed pole from her married name of Linda Barbara Lever to Linda Barbara Street.

BOSTON BLOODBATH

Linda and I had arrived at Boston early, and had a few hours to kill before the matches began in Boston's Regal Cinema. We had just had a bite to eat, and were now window shopping as we slowly made our way back to that night's venue when we were both suddenly accosted by an extremely Butch Policewoman.

"I believe your name is Susan Jenkins, you are 14 years of age, and have run away from home?!" she accused Linda, as she glared at me, and flashed me her finest Medusa impersonation. Her inquiry was directed to Linda, but as she was glaring at me, I replied,

"Sorry Cunt-stable, but I believe you believe wrong, this is Linda Street, she's 24 years of age and she is with me." She didn't believe me, and we were both escorted to a nearby Police Station. After sharing her beliefs with other Police-people at the Station, they began to question us both, so I suggested that it might be a good idea to phone the parents of the runaway girl and let them talk to Linda. Eventually they took my advice but couldn't get a reply, again I got glared at as though it was my fault the runaways parents weren't at home. So I suggested them calling Linda's Mother, and allow her to confirm Linda's identity. Eventually they did, but wouldn't you know it? – Linda's Mother wasn't at home either!

Although we had wanted to kill a few hours, this was not the way we had in mind. Linda was 5' 6" tall, sporting a 39 inch bust and 10 years older than the runaway and these fools were going to make me late for the matches that night if they didn't hurry up and get their shit together. EVENTUALLY – after many attempts, they managed to get through to Linda's Mother who after talking to Linda, EVENTUALLY convinced most of the Police-people that she was not the runaway, and we were allowed to leave.

"I'm still not convinced!" The Police-woman stubbornly stated as her parting shot. - "What a pity." I replied.

That night I was in the Main-Event match against 'Cry-Baby' Jimmy Breaks. He was a great wrestler, and was I very happy to have him as an opponent. I was very happy, but Jimmy wasn't, and I can't say that I blamed him at all. From the first time I had wrestled against Jimmy, or even watched him perform, I had regarded him as a first class wrestler. Up until recently he had been one of the good guys, but now he had changed his image from fan favorite to a skillful but spiteful villain. The change had been an excellent career move, as he was really beginning to register with the fans. But – there was very little that was capable of derailing a villain's momentum more efficiently than to wrestle against another villain and lose, and that was what was going to happen tonight. I did sympathize with him, I had often found myself in the same dilemma, but a result that was bad for Jimmy's career was good for mine, so I didn't sympathize with him too much. Jimmy was so distraught that he asked me to do him a very special favor, which after a little consideration, and out of the goodness of my heart, I agreed to do for him.

As the bell sounded to begin our contest Jimmy went on the attack, he dived in grabbed me in a vicious headlock then spun around me in a flash and secured a bone-bending hammerlock. I retaliated by hurling a back-elbow which smashed right into Jimmy's nose which burst, and filled the air above us in a scarlet haze. As my opponent landed flat on his back, I threw myself backwards and dropped like a bomb, elbow first straight into Jimmy's newly shattered trumpet. WOW! I thought I'd struck oil as the blood shot right up into the air. Again Jimmy fought back, he even seemed to be out-wrestling me, but every time he trapped me in a painful hold, I would hurl a forearm, a head-butt, a knee, boot, or on the blindside of the ref, a fist right into Jimmy's bloody, flattened nose. There was blood everywhere, Jimmy was covered, I was covered, the ring was covered, and even some of the ringsiders were getting splashed. When Jimmy attempted a comeback I stopped him in his tracks with yet another vicious blow to his nose. When I went on the attack I zeroed a relentless blitz directly into the scarlet facial fountain that continued to squirt out of the middle of my opponent's face. There was so much blood that the referee had to stop the contest in my favor.

It doesn't sound as though I did him much of a favor does it?

But that was what he asked me to do, if he had to lose to another villain he figured that being stopped in that way would do less damage to his reputation than being pinned or forced to submit. In the same manner, a Boxer like Henry Cooper, on the rare occasions that he lost a match, it was usually due to cuts around his eyes that cost him the verdict. That way his biggest fans could still boast on his behalf – 'IF' he hadn't been cut the verdict could have well gone the other way. Even before this match I was well aware of Jimmy Breaks' skill and toughness, but to purposely suffer a badly broken nose just to preserve, if not enhance his image in one average sized arena elevated him to a whole new level in my books. He really was one tough little bastard.

A MARS A DAY

Linde Caulder had been contacted by Mars Incorporated, and invited to feature with his Tag-partner Leon Fortuna in a Mars-Bar television commercial. Linde's and Leon's team were known as The Sepia-Set, and they were to be the latest add in the 'A Mars a day helps you work, rest and play' series. In the Sepia-Set's commercial the 'work' would consist of Linde and Leon engaged in a wrestling contest, the 'rest' would be relaxing in the dressing-room, while gnawing on a Mars-Bar, and 'play' would be what ever each of them did for fun in their own time. The Sepia-Set needed a pair of good opponents, and Mars had left the choice to Linde who asked me if Bob and I would be interested.

"Bloody right we would!" I assured him. He arranged a meeting for us to ascertain that Mars Incorporated would approve of his choice of adversaries. Not only did they approve of his choice, but decided to give Bob and I the Star-role that had been originally offered to Linde and Leon, and give them the lesser role of opponents instead. For 'work' we would be wrestling 'The Sepia-Set', for 'rest' we would be gnawing on Mars-Bars in the dressing-room, and they asked if we had any suggestions for play? I suggested Horse riding and they loved the idea.

Mars decided that it would be good if we had female companions for our horse-riding scenes, and left the choice of companions to us. Bob had already taught his Wife Jan to ride, but as I knew that it would be next to impossible to get Jean interested, and Linda was not only a horse lover, but also in need of the fee, I put her in as my companion. We were all very pleased and excited by the prospect of appearing in the commercial, not only for the initial fee, but we would get paid a fee every time the commercial was played on TV. And, even better the publicity could only do wonders for our careers. For the dressing-room scene I had already acquired a few huge wrestling posters to adorn the walls in the background with 'The Hell's Angels' name and our photographs plastered all over them. In preparation for the Horse-riding scene Linda, Jan, Bob and I rode when ever we could spare any time at all in order to make sure that our equestrian skills were fully honed, we could hardly wait.

Then just a few days before we began filming I received a call from Mars to tell me that the whole deal was off, and would I please inform all the others who were to be involved. When I called Bob and gave him the news, he responded by pleading,

"Please tell me you're joking – Please tell me you're joking!"

"Unfortunately I'm not." I replied. I had asked Mars for the reason of the cancellation, as they had told us previously that they were more excited at the prospect of filming our commercial than any of the others that they had ever been involved with. The reason I was informed was, that one of the top guy's wife had objected. She didn't think that anything involving violence would be good to advertise their product. I knew that 'Mars' had got its name from the founder Forrest Mars, but couldn't resist pointing out that 'Mars' was also the God of War.

"You can't get much more violent than that can you?" I remarked.

STRIKE!

In spite of the fact that Dale Martins seemed to be running more and more venues, there were many very good, seasoned wrestlers getting less and less work from them. Their numbers were not only being made up, but increasingly surpassed by much cheaper raw recruits whose performances often left a lot to be desired. It also appeared that the more established wrestlers were expected to both train and carry the newcomers on the job whenever we were matched against them. We began to think that we might be coaching our own cheaper replacements as we were all well aware of Dale Martin's insatiable greed.

After considerable discussion, Clayton Thomson, Wayne Bridges and I started recruiting like minded wrestlers, and began arranging meetings where possible solutions to this problem could be ironed out. At first new members were invited to join us, but as the would-be rebel's numbers grew, the attitudes of many began to become much more aggressive, and attendance by absent wrestlers was demanded. The sad thing was, that all of a sudden there were dozens of wrestlers who had long ago been fired by Dale Martins for various reasons. Then scores of independent wrestlers who had never been deemed good enough to wrestle for Dale Martins in the first place. In fact wrestlers whose performances would not have been any better than the cheap raw recruits who had promoted our outrage to begin with. Even worse, these infiltrators who had nothing whatsoever to lose by their insubordination, were usually the ones with the most to say. And the ones who demanded the more outrageous forms of retaliation against Dale Martins, and against any wrestlers who had so far not joined us in what was fast becoming a full blown mutiny.

Amongst the most militant, was part time wrestler, and full time school teacher, Irish Sean Regan who attempted to instigate a reenactment of the 'Night of the long Knives' when he drew a big axe on a blackboard and began listing the names of Wrestlers who had not joined our cause, and deserved violent retribution.

He even demanded that we should invade their homes with a hostile ultimatum. A picture formed in my brain that reminded me of the final scene in the old black and white Frankenstein movie, where the 'Monster' was being hunted down by a hoard of murderous villagers armed with flaming torches and pitchforks.

At first we thought that media interest could only aid our cause, but soon even they too were blowing everything out of proportion in pursuit of that almighty scoop. It was the newspapers who claimed that professional wrestlers were demanding better wages, and stating that professional wrestlers from coast to coast would go on strike if they didn't get more money for their matches. In reality it was only Southern wrestlers who were going on strike against Dale Martins, and not against the rest of Joint Promotions. Well we went on strike and picketed the Fairfield Hall, but thanks to the spies and double agents amongst our ranks, Dale Martins were forewarned and took their own steps to confound our move. When we arrived at the venue we did so in time to watch more than a dozen Northern scabs, who had traveled south by train to wrestle in our place. They were being escorted into the arena by scores of Police Officers who had met them at the station, and driven them to Fairfield. There were police everywhere many accompanied by trained German-Shepard attack Dogs. Of course the media was also there in droves, and as a result of we wrestlers divulging to them the exact amount of miserly monetary rewards we received, Jack Dale himself came out of the building in the centre of a police escort and attempted to break us up before we said too much. Wrestlers were not allowed to discuss the amount of wages they got – even amongst themselves. To admit publicly that although they appeared as famous household celebrities, many were living on pauper's paychecks, and that knowledge would prove to be the ultimate embarrassment to Dale Martin's Wrestling Promotions. The moment that Jack was face to face with us he spotted 'Mad Fred the ear-biter' who had come with Peter Rann and Jack Dale went berserk,

"WHY DID YOU BRING HIM HERE?!" He screamed at Peter Rann, indicating the Ear-biter – and before Peter had chance to reply he threw off his overcoat and roared at 'Mad

Fred', "I'M NOT AFRAID OF YOU!" and shocked us all by diving after him.

If I hadn't been standing there myself I would never have believed what was happening. It took a number of police officers and wrestlers to either dive in-between, or drag Jack away from actually attacking Fred. To add to our bewilderment – it was 'Mad Fred' who really looked to be quite startled by the event. But in his defense, that was probably more to do with the proximity of so many Coppers, rather than the fear of violence from our irate promoter. How much more money do you want to make all this nonsense go away Dale Martins wanted to know? 5 pounds a match for everyone the wrestlers demanded, but settled for a counter offer of 2 pounds a match! Our original concern regarding new cheap recruits just got swept under the carpet, and life just went on as before – but not quite for me! Almost every photograph that had appeared in every newspaper that glorified the wrestler's strike pictured me centre stage – and if you think for one second that Dale Martins was going to let me get away with that, then you haven't been paying attention.

Personally, even before the strike, thanks to my ever increasing drawing power, I had less to complain about money wise than most. As a result of the success of my exotic persona my own wages had gone from 10 pounds to 12, to 15, and most recently to 20, when most other wrestlers in the lighter weight divisions were only receiving in the region of 5 to 8 pounds a match. For them a 2 pound wage hike was fairly substantial. But for me increasing my wages from 20 pounds to 22 was negligible. I immediately demanded that the northern promoters round out that amount to 25 and got it, and eventually got Dale Martins to match that figure too. But on the negative side – I had been averaging at least a couple of TV matches a month from Dale Martins, and won 99 percent of all my matches. After the strike was over I didn't get one single TV show for a year and a half, and my winning ways was also placed in jeopardy. I began looking for my own methods of retaliation.

OH – LA-LA AND ALL THAT MERDE!

Julien Morice had been one of Dale Martin's seasoned wrestlers who had been getting less matches that had been lost to cheap newcomers, and as a result had began wrestling once more in his native France. As Bobby Barnes and myself seemed to have placed ourselves in Dale Martin's bad books, thanks to our prominence during the 'bogus strike', I thought it might be a good idea to take a French tour ourselves in the hope that once again a temporary absence might make the heart grow fonder. We contacted the French Promoter and were immediately invited over the channel. A few days before Bob and I were due to leave Britain, I received a phone call from Julien who was still wrestling in France, and he asked me to bring 3 blue-movies over with me as he had a customer who wanted to buy them. As I thought that we may be making regular trips over to France, I decided to take a couple of extra movies, and a few dildos just in case there was a market for such items. Although, I would have thought that with the sexy image Paris possessed, taking Blue Movies and dildos to France would be like taking snow to Antarctica.

After arriving in Paris, we were met and escorted to our hotel by Michele Saulnier, a wrestler I had wrestled when he toured Britain, but who now worked in the French promoter's office. We were received in the hotel in style, and felt like film stars, or Royalty as the hotel manager and staff were all lined up, and bowed or curtsied as we walked along their line nodding and smiling as introductions were made. We had the rest of the first day off, but would be traveling south to Toulouse early next morning for our first match in France.

I couldn't wait to explore Paris, but went out alone as Bob wanted to send postcards to his friends and family. My first priority was to attempt to find out the going rate for the merchandize I had brought over with me, so that I would have a better idea what to charge Julien Morice. I immediately made a b-line for Paris's famous Red-Light district. I had imagined that the Pigalle would be like Soho on steroids – I'll be polite and just say I was disappointed. But, I had made a very educated guess as far as gaining the information I was looking for, as I was accosted by a young scar-faced Algerian Boy who attempted to sell me a packet of 'dirty French postcards' the minute I arrived there. Although I spoke very little French and the Algerian spoke very little English, I managed to explain to him that I didn't want postcards but I was interested in buying Blue Movies. He bid me follow him, and we eventually ended up entering a seedy little bar that along with all of its inhabitants could have been the film set for a tenth-rate comic James Bond type farce. Every one of its denizens was a sleazy, villainous looking character. The Rat-faced Algerian barman had eyes as black as coal, jet black hair slicked straight back and a large Hawk's beak shaped nose. As bizarre as this Motley crew appeared to me, I still must have stood out like a sore thumb, as I had shoulder length platinum blond hair, wore a black fur coat over a bright red velvet suit, a shiny black silk shirt complete with my black and red platform boots.

After attempting to explain to him what I was looking to buy, the Barman told me that they were unobtainable in Paris; - I lied when I told him that they were attainable as I had already purchased some, and was interested in purchasing more. It was very difficult to understand each other, but it seemed that he wanted to see the movies. Whether it was to make me an offer, or just because he didn't believe I had already bought some I don't know. He led me behind the bar and through a beaded curtain into a backroom and showed me an ancient looking projector.

"Okay," I told him, "I'll be back in an hour."

When I got back to the hotel I told Bob about my adventure, and after slipping a couple of movies into my pocket I asked Bob if he wanted to accompany me. He did, and as we were about to leave Bob slipped a dildo into the inside pocket of his overcoat.

"You might as well try to find out how much these sell for at the same time." He suggested. Upon our arrival at the bar we were immediately ushered into the backroom. I placed both the movies onto the table where the projector was set up, and both Bob and I sat down while Rat-face threaded one of the movies into the projector, switched it on and let it roll. We couldn't have been two minutes into the movie when all hell broke loose, as about a dozen armed men suddenly burst into the room with handguns aimed point blank into our faces. Bob threw his hands up as he slid up the wall behind him,

"P-P-P-P-Police?!" He inquired hopefully. I grabbed both the remaining movie and the empty box that had contained the movie in the projector and thrust them into one of my fur coat's pockets, but one of the invaders tore them back out and slammed them onto the table. With guns still pointed at our heads, I was pulled out of my chair and searched. Bob was also searched and relieved of a 9-inch rubber dildo which was also slammed onto the table where it stood bravely, proudly and defiantly. Bob and I were then handcuffed together and hustled out of the backroom through the bar into the street, and into the back of one of the few parked Police cars. I did notice that so far none of the Frenchmen and Algerians who had also been present in the backroom had been apprehended. As the car sped away I leaned as close as I could towards Bob, I told him that all he knew about the day's happenings before we had gone to the bar, was that I had gone out alone. I had left him alone in the hotel, and I had returned later with the movies and rubber-ware, which I had told him I had just bought. What had happened I considered had been all my fault, and I wanted to keep Bob out of it as much as possible. Also if Bob had no other details to add, I figured it would be more difficult for the police to find any discrepancies in our stories that they could use to trip us up. I also knew that buying pornography was not a big deal in Britain, whereas selling it in those days was. I hoped that the law was the same in France.

They took us straight back to our hotel, - although we hadn't told them which hotel we were staying at, and we made an even more spectacular entrance than we had earlier. But what a contrast, earlier we had been treated like famous celebrities, now we were dragged into the foyer handcuffed together, where the cop in charge demanded the keys to our room. They found the other 3 movies and 4 dildos almost immediately, but still tore open more draws, turned the mattresses upside-down and left the room looking as though a tornado had ripped through it. By the time we were bundled back into the car I noticed it was quite dark, we were then transported to a Jail that was close to Notre Dame Cathedral on an island in the Seine. As Bob and I entered what looked like a medieval fortress I remarked,

"Shit, I thought they'd demolished the Bastille' over a century and a half ago!"

At first we were put into a narrow rectangular cell with about 30 or 40 other new inmates, most of them looked like the scum and dregs of the Parisian sewers. The cell was so crowded that we were packed together like an army of Sardines. After a couple of hours, as names were called, one by one we were taken out of the rectangular cell and then herded onto a larger U-shaped cell lined with benches. It must have been late that night when Bob and I were called out of the u-shape and marched into a small cell for the rest of the night. We were given water and a small French loaf each with a small triangular piece of processed cheese in metal foil, the bread was so hard that I told Bob that we could use it to prize the bars on the small window apart. The cell had no beds or movable furniture, only one very narrow bench that comprised of a few slats of wood bolted to a metal frame that was embedded into the wall. There was not room on the bench for both of us, so I told Bob that it was his, while I lay on the tiled cell floor and used my rolled up fur coat as a pillow.

Early next morning we were taken out of the cell, into another part of the building and were made to sit in a corridor opposite a row of offices where we would be interviewed. To make certain that we wouldn't try to escape we were handcuffed to a metal radiator. We had been given nothing to eat or drink, and complained to a guard that we were both very hungry; he brought us a ham sandwich and coffee which we were made to pay for. Eventually Bob was released from the radiator and taken into an office to make a statement, I called after him,

"Tell them to hurry up – we've got to be back at the hotel in time for them to pick us up for our trip to Toulouse!" – Talk about being optimistic! I also wondered if the promoter was aware of our predicament, and if he would be able to do anything about it? That too turned out to be no more than wishful thinking. About an hour later Bob was brought out of the office and refastened to the radiator, I was released from the radiator and taken in. I was made to sit in a chair facing a desk behind which sat my interrogator, a dark haired, stern faced Detective. I can't remember his name, so for reasons that will become painfully evident I shall refer to him as Inspector Le Douche'.

The interview began, slowly and very painfully, I think he accused me of attempting to sell the Algerians obscene items which I had imported into the country for that purpose. I told him that wasn't true and that I had bought the items earlier that day and was looking to buy more when I was taken to the bar by young scar face. Where did I buy them? He wanted to know. From a red haired Canadian man named Don, I told him. The interrogation went on and on, I understood very little of what he asked me, and I doubt that he understood my response any better, but he continued to write everything down regardless. Finally he put my statement in front of me, handed me a pen and told me,

"Sign it!"

I replied, "NO!"

"Why not?!" he demanded.

"I don't speak or read French." I replied.

"I just translate!" he told me.

"How do I know you translated it correctly?!" I wanted to know. I had fallen for this shit once before, and for complying got a few weeks behind bars and a fine for doing nothing wrong. 'Not again I thought.'

"I will not sign something I don't understand." I told him adamantly.

This went on for a couple of days, and then finally they brought in a translator in order to explain everything we said to each other. The translator was an attractive Lady who I estimated was probably in her late twenties to mid thirties. I don't remember her name either so I shall call her Fifi. Le Douche' explained the situation, and before Fifi had a chance to translate I said, "Ask him if the movies were good?"

She did as I bid, and after he finished jabbering she translated,

"He said they were terrible."

"Did I pay too much for them?" I inquired innocently. I had decided to act as flippantly as possible, in the hope that eventually they would decide that I was not a porn-peddler, and no more than a naughty boy.

"Why won't you sign your statement?" was her first question.

"Because I don't speak or read French." I replied.

"He says that your partner has signed his statement." She told me.

"My partner didn't buy the movies, I did, my partner did nothing wrong, he signed his statement, so why is he still in jail?" I wanted to know.

"If you don't sign you stay in jail!" she translated.

"If I sign right now, will I be allowed to leave?" I inquired.

"NO, YOU GO TO JAIL!" Le Douche' barked without Fifi's aid.

"Not much incentive to sign it then, is there?" I observed as I stifled a yawn.

"The Algerians said you were trying to sell them the movies". Fifi translated.

"That isn't true", I told her, "We don't speak the same language, if they thought they were for sale they obviously misunderstood."

"Why did you take the movies to the bar in the first place?" was the next question she translated.

"When I went to the bar the first time, the barman showed me a projector and seemed to want to see the movies. I was anxious to see them myself, as I had only just bought them from a man in the street, and I wanted to see the quality of the films. Or even if they were true to the photographs on the package. They may have been Mickey Mouse, or The Three Stooges for all I knew." I explained.

"Why did you want 5 godemiche'?" she translated. [She pronounced it 'gomejay'.]

"I wanted what?!" I asked.

"The 5 godemiche'" she repeated, I was completely bewildered and she began to stammer, 'That's great', I thought; 'now I don't understand my translator either.

With a huge office vibrating sigh, Le Douche' opened a draw in his desk, snatched out one of the dildos and slammed it upright on the desk in front of him.

"Looks just like him, doesn't it?!" I asked Fifi, she immediately screamed with hysterical laughter and was never right again. Le Douche' didn't even crack a smile,

"Why did he want 5 of these?!" He repeated.

"They were presents for my friends in Britain," I told her after she had translated between fits of giggling. "I was going to wrap a red, white and blue ribbon around each one to represent the tri-colors of the Republic, and pretend that I had mistaken them for scaled down models of The Eiffel-Tower." Again Fifi went into fits.

"Even he," I explained to Fifi indicating Le Douche', "must be aware of the sexy reputation that Paris has possessed for about a century or more – OOOH LA-LA and all that merde. I was just trying to bring presents from Paris that I thought would be appropriate." Fifi was still giggling, which only tends to goad me on,

"When he lets me out will he give my movies back?" I asked Fifi.

"NO!" Replied Le Douche'

"Will he return the 5 godemiche'?" I inquired.

"NO!" Bellowed Le Douche'.

"What is he going to do with them," I asked Fifi, "train them to be French Policemen?" Well Fifi must have pissed her draws laughing. Le Douche' screamed loud enough to bring a Guard bursting into the room, and after Le Douche' had jabbered a mouthful of instructions, I was hustled out of the office into the corridor where I was handcuffed to the pipe that lead to the radiator that I had been fastened to previously. But, as the pipe was only inches from the floor I was bent over sideways in a most uncomfortable position. Just then Fifi came out of the office to leave,

"Are you alright?" she asked me, obviously concerned by the awkward way I had been secured.

"Not too bad," I assured her, "but if they leave me like this for long I'll be able to get a job next door ringing fucking bells!" Fifi laughed loud enough to be heard in Le Douche's office, 'That'll go down well!' I thought.

The next day they let us out – minus the merchandize.

On our return to the hotel we found the reception very much cooler, everyone even avoided looking at us directly. We phoned the promoter's office where we found the reception better – but not much! We had missed 3 or 4 matches, each of which was main-event, they were not happy with us.

Before we had left Britain I had been looking forward to French wine and cuisine, so far all we had eaten was rock hard bread, processed cheese and stale sandwiches. Unfortunately we were picked up from the hotel and whisked off to Le Mans where we were wrestling that night before we had the chance to eat anything.

That night we wrestled against, and beat the European Champions, Guy Mercier and Gil Cesca in a non-title contest. They were both excellent wrestlers, especially by French standards, and we thought that the match may have at least helped redeem us somewhat. But we found that we were going to be made to pay the substitutes that had taken our places on the shows that we had missed. And even pay the cost of train-fare for the two substitutes that had taken our places in Toulouse, which would have been our first match. Now we obviously didn't expect to receive payment for matches that we had missed, instead, naturally our substitutes should have received those wages. But we were told that the wages they had already received would be garnished from our future wages, even though we hadn't received any wages at all so far. I was not happy and didn't mind showing it. To add injury to insult the first meal we had that day was after the wrestling was over, and was a very mediocre meal in a very mediocre restaurant. I was only slightly consoled when told that the next night we would be wrestling in Rennes, a town they claimed that sported one of the premier Fish Restaurants in France.

Well the restaurant didn't disappoint, in fact I had never experienced a better Fish restaurant before or since. We traveled from Paris by train arriving in the town late afternoon, and after depositing our wrestling gear in the arena's dressing-room we made our way straight to the restaurant. Normally I would eat very little, if anything at all before wrestling, and wine would most definitely be out of the question. But I wasn't feeling normal, and didn't give a fuck for the promoter or his promotion. I ate far too much, and although it was absolutely delicious, I can't remember what I ate as I washed the lot down with two whole liters of ice cold white wine.

We wrestled, I was very rough and dangerous to be around. I

didn't only abuse my opponents physically in the ring, but back in the dressing-room I also verbally abused the promoter, and with the same vehemence. I showered, dressed, and went straight back to the restaurant for more food, and especially wine. A liter or so of wine later, I made yet another series of poor choices. As much as I loved Seafood, I had never – ever come to terms with Crab. I found out what they were called in French and ordered the biggest Crab they had in the restaurant – and another liter or so of wine. I ate and drank like a whole squad of Sumo-Wrestlers, and must have made myself a thorough nuisance. After I had finished eating I marched behind the bar, opened my mouth and turned a beer tap on full, just as The Giant German Wrestler Kurt Kaiser opened a door and stepped into the room. The beer hit me in the mouth with such force that it shot back out in a huge jet, and smashed straight into Kaiser's rugged chops. As dazed as I was, I quickly turned off the tap, shook the beer off my face, and made ready to defend myself from a Blitzkrieg that I was sure would be forthcoming. But instead, I began to think that The Bouncing Berlin Behemoth was performing some ancient religious rite, while praying loudly to some Teutonic-Pagan God named 'Alles Schizer'.

We had a long wait at Rennes Railway Station for the train that would take us back to Paris. We were amongst a whole gang of rowdy wrestlers as we staggered onto the platform, and the first person that I spied was our promoter. He was talking to a tall elegant looking Lady who was holding a Dachshund on a leash. The promoter was very much in my bad-books, so as we drew level with him and the Lady, I pointed to the Dachshund and exclaimed in my loudest voice,

"Ha Mademoiselle, I see you have taught your godemiche' to walk – what a novel idea, I've never seen one with legs before, but I trust you find it very satisfactory!"

Bob and I were the only ones who blatantly laughed out loud, but I did detect a few of the other wrestler's hands covering their mouths as they hurried away out of my range. At first there had been very few passengers waiting for the train to Paris, but by the time the train arrived at Rennes Station there was quite a crowd. I was very disappointed to discover that there was not a bar open on the train, even though I needed more Fire-water like Custer had needed more Indians. My second choice would be a compartment to myself, or one I could share with Bob, but the train was packed. By the time the train stopped and I had opened a door all the other wrestlers, including Bob had disappeared. But in fairness to them all, after drinking as much as I had, there was very little restraint left in my good behavior department.

I must have wandered up and down the corridor for 20 minutes or more looking for somewhere to sit. Finally I came across a compartment that only had two occupants, but they were both laying full length on each of the row of seats, leaving no room for anyone else. I opened the compartment door, placed my wrestling bag in the overhead luggage rack, and hurled one of the occupant's feet off the seat, and sat myself down. The startled man said something undecipherable, but sat in the corner by the window. This gave me more room, so I lay down, and pushed my big Red and black boots towards him. He grunted, said something to the other man who was stretched out on the other seat, and moved over to his side. They both lay down with their heads and feet facing in opposite directions.

"Good', I thought, 'just what I wanted, a whole seat to stretch out on as I sleep my way back to Paris'. The carriage seemed to sway quite vigorously, but I didn't mind, 'it will rock me to sleep in no time.' But, I had eaten more than a pregnant Wolverine, and drank wine like a Camel drinks water, and with the constantly jerky motion of the carriage something had to give!

I leapt up, but too late, WWWOOOOOOOSH!!!! All over the two sleeping beauties! It seemed that I had still not come to terms with Crab. After a few more whooshing heaves, the horrified screams of the newly drenched Frenchmen woke me out of my reverie, and I shot out of the compartment and staggered down the corridor to the toilet. How long I kneeled there with my head down the toilet bowl I don't know, but when I finally opened the toilet door, both the half drowned Frenchmen were waiting for me,

"YABBER-DABBER-DABBEROOOO!!!!! They both screamed at me – or something like that, but as you can well imagine I wasn't really in the mood. "Go away you smell repugnant to me." I told them reasonably.

"YABBER-DABBER-DOOOOO!!!!!!!" They screamed and

made the mistake of stepping closer to my face. I grabbed a fistful each of their shirt collars, and began smashing them together like a set of cymbals,

"Fuck off you French cunts!" I politely suggested – and with that I threw them both away from me, and made my way back to the empty compartment.

Well, when I say empty, that wasn't quite true. The constant lapping as the Technicolor tide that was all over the compartment floor ebbed and flowed with the train's rocking motion, and kept me company all the way back to Paris.

When I alighted in Paris I saw Bob waiting for me further down the platform,

"Are you alright Ade?" He asked me, "You look awful."

In lieu of a reply I threw up on the platform, sending other alighting passengers leaping out of range. During the taxi ride to our hotel I barely managed to keep the little I had left down. I just managed to dive out of the vehicle as the taxi driver put on the brakes in time to prevent me messing up the back of his cab. Instead I threw up in the hotel entrance; - they really must have loved me!

In spite of being incredibly dehydrated I was only able to sip a very small amount of water for fear of throwing it back up. And all too soon, here comes the transport to take us to the town that we would be wrestling at that night. On the way to the town we stopped for lunch at a small restaurant where the food was reputed to be really delicious. While all the other wrestlers ate and drank, I found a vacant corner opened a small leaded widow, and gazed into a garden that was so beautiful that it belonged in the pages of a child's Fairy Story Book. I couldn't eat; I could barely stand the aroma of their delicious feast. A few matches later it was time to return to Britain, I had lost money, weight, movies, 5 Godemiche' and a future refuge, as I felt fairly certain that we would not be asked back to France any time soon.

CRYSTAL GLASS SLIPPERS

While I had been busy in France, Dale Martins had been busy too, they had a new
'Adrian Street' – at least that was how most of my peers gleefully described him. Newly arrived from Australia with Long blond hair, wearing fancy multi-colored tights, boots, and a metallic multi-colored cape. He carried a large hand mirror into the ring with him into which he would gaze admiringly, and fuss with his hair in a very-very Adrian Street like manner. In Australia he had been known as 'Murf the Surf' or 'Magnificent Maurice' but for British rings Dale Martins had renamed him 'Maurice La Rue'.

Now you couldn't get much more blatant than that, at that time there was a famous Female impersonator named Danny La Rue, NOT only that, but La Rue is French for Street, and France was where we had been taking temporary refuge. I never learned who thought of that one – which to my mind was uncharacteristically clever by Dale Martin's usual standards. Nevertheless, thankfully for me Maurice La Rue never really paned out for them. He was a good wrestler and performer, and if I had never been, I do think that he would have made a great impression. But whenever he appeared the fans were not only reminded of me, but would goad him unmercifully with shouts and jeers like,

"Who do you think you are – Adrian Street?!!!"

The fans still hated me, but they certainly hadn't abandoned me, and if I was putting arses on seats, even vindictive Dale Martins had to put the past behind them – eventually. Eventually, but not without a fight.

The West Indian Ezzard Hart was obviously attempting to emulate the extremely flamboyant Black Canadian wrestler 'Sweet-Daddy Siki when he bleached his hair blond, but failed miserably. 'Sweet-Daddy' left nothing to chance, he would swagger and strut his way to the ring waving a fancy walking stick, while clad in a glittering stars and stripes outfit and golden sunglasses. In contrast, Ezzard would slink out to the ring, almost apologetically, and then stand in the corner with his face downcast whilst the introductions were made. The only thing he achieved was remaining virtually invisible in spite of his so called metamorphosis. If that wasn't bad enough, yet another Black wrestler jumped on the blond bandwagon, and thought that the transformation may help in elevating him out of the preliminary ranks. His initial attempt at becoming Blond was such a dismal failure, turning his naturally black hair to a dirty orange, that I invited him to my home and got Jean to bleach his hair properly with the same bleach that I used myself. I don't know if he achieved what he was looking for, but it did succeed in catching the attention of the other wrestlers, who began referring to him as Guinness-Head. I had also noticed that many of my peers, especially many of the former piss-takers, after witnessing my steadily rising status had began brightening up their own act. Although nothing spectacular, a string of sequins added to the same old battered ring-jacket that they had been wearing for years, and would be destined to wear for the remainder of their wrestling career. Or maybe a new brighter pair of trunks. BUT – it was too little too late, there was only one Cinderella, one pair of Crystal Glass Slippers and they only came in my size.

QUEENSTON ROAD

The Northern Promoters were unperturbed by the events that had occurred in the South regarding the wrestler's strike, the only thing that interested them was the fact that I was consistently putting arses on seats. Nevertheless, I was determined to send a signal to Dale Martins, and in the process I hit upon a plan that killed a whole flock of birds with one stone. Although initially I had made an excellent choice by renting apartments in Manchester when ever I wrestled in the North instead of staying in hotels, I was still taking money out of my own pocket and putting it in someone else's. I realized that the rent I paid was buying the houses for my landlord, so why not do away with hotels and rents by purchasing property of my own?!

First and foremost it would be a good investment; it would be a more permanent place for Linda and I to live while in the North. If I bought a house that was big enough, I could rent part of it which would pay for the house and even add to my income. It would give Dale Martins something to think about – especially after I spread the rumor that I was considering moving North permanently. Whether Dale Martins were still mad at me or not, I knew they still regarded me as one of their major drawing cards, and would still want to use me as much as they could. But, if I moved north it would cost Dale Martins a lot more money to pay for my transport from the North to the South, plus other expenses that would be incurred.

I bought 27 Queenston Road, in West Didsbury, it had three floors and a basement, Linda and I lived in the basement and ground floor, in which I turned one large room into a weight-lifting gym. The two floors upstairs we rented out which paid the mortgage and made a profit which would also suggest a small degree of independence. But best of all, the house was directly across the road from Wryton Wrestling Promotions which was guaranteed to send Dale Martins a very concise message indeed.

For obvious reasons I vastly exaggerated the degree of independence afforded me by my property purchase, but began to wonder if the purchase of yet more property might turn my exaggeration in to a reality? Within a few months I bought 2 houses in Withington Road, 2 houses in Clarendon Road, and another in Mayfield Road. They were all large properties, in fact one of the houses in Withington Road was nicknamed 'The Beast' by the wrestlers, as it was really huge and contained 49 rooms on 4 floors.

As well as redecorating, all the properties needed appliances and furniture before they could be let. Abe Ginsburg lived at the end of Queenston Road, and was also in the rental property game. I thought he had really come to our rescue in our search for reasonably priced appliances and furniture when he claimed he could get us anything we required. Eventually we accidentally discovered his source, and also discovered that he had been reselling us the items we had purchased from him for 5 to 6 times the price they had cost him. - Wrestlers – you've got to love them ay?!

THE BIG BUILD UP

Eventually, as I thought they would Dale Martins came around, and I was told that not only Dale Martins, but all of Joint Promotions had called a meeting and had decided to give a number of wrestlers who had shown promise a Big Build up. This build up consisted of little else than a lot more television exposure for just a short period, after which if the wrestler had failed to show Superstar potential, he would be dropped from the build-up program and someone else may be given the opportunity instead. Amongst the wrestlers they chose was masked mystery man Kendo Nagasaki, hard-man Les Kellett, Black Diamond Abe Ginsburg and I. Initially I was the only wrestler in their program who was not a heavyweight, but after dropping Abe Ginsburg for not coming up to scratch, he was replaced by Brian Maxine, who they also put the British Middleweight Championship title on in their quest to make him into a star.

Needless to say, Mick McManus ruthlessly jealous and protective of his own exalted position booked me with one of my last choices of opponent – the spoiler Peter Szakacs. As if that in it self would not have been bad enough, but I had already beaten him twice on television, and out of the two new TV shots I had for Dale Martins, McManus billed me against Szakacs both times. Now if you wanted to find a more accomplished spoiler than Szakacs you wouldn't have to look much further than Yorkshire's Ted Heath, and for Relwyskow promotions I got not one but two TV matches against him also.

'Well I couldn't do much worse for Norman Morrell's promotions.' I thought, again I underestimated Joint Promotions. I was one of Britain's most hated lightweight wrestlers, so in Bradford Morrell had me wrestling against the full blown villainous heavyweight 'Honey-Boy' Zimba. If that wasn't bad enough unlike the straightforward wins I had scored over Szakacs and Heath, I would only be victorious in this contest because Zimba would be disqualified! Now how much sense does that make, how much prestige can result in winning against and opponent who outweighs me by more than 60 pounds of muscle and who has to cheat enough to get himself disqualified, Not exactly a blinding victory, aye?! Joint promotions was sometimes very hard to figure out, on one hand they tell you that you are about to be given a chance to become a headliner, and then they make it as difficult as possible to accomplish. In spite of the obstacles placed in my path posed by Joint promotion's atrocious choice of opponents, I began receiving outside help that was propelling me up the ladder of success faster than any of them could have possibly anticipated. The outside help included regular television appearances that Mick McManus or any of the other Joint Promotion bigwigs had any control over whatsoever.

The comedian Freddie Star was famous for his impersonations which included Elvis Presley, Norman Wisdom and me. I appeared on 'The Freddie Star Show' twice. On the first occasion he was in the middle of performing his Adrian Street act when I walked on stage behind him, much to the surprise and delight of the live audience and viewers watching from home. On the 'Rolf Harris Show' I was posing for one of Rolf's famous portraits, and pretended to take exception to the muscular physique he endowed my likeness with. That prompted me to grab Rolf up onto my shoulders, whirl him around, dump him onto a higher level on the stage, and render him helpless by tying his arms up with his legs. I then proceeded in taking his brush and paint, and covering up all the offending muscles on my portrait by designing a long sequin encrusted, white laced, lilac and purple gown. I liked the look of the gown so much that the next day I went out shopping, and using the money I received for my appearance on the show, I bought the fabric I needed to make the gown a reality. I cut out the fabric myself and got Jean to put it together for me, which resulted in the most gorgeous ring costume I had yet possessed.

I had proved to be such a success during my first appearance on 'Pebblemill at one' that I was invited to appear on the show any and every time I found myself in the Birmingham area around one o-clock. Believe me, I really made use of their invitation, especially as there was a decent fee attached.

HERE'S TO YOU MR. ROBINSON

Due to my trip to France and my extremely busy schedule after my return to Britain, I hadn't seen Jack Robinson for months. On the next occasion that I would be wrestling in Ipswich would also coincide with the first time that Linda would be accompanying me there. For obvious reasons I would have preferred them not to meet each other, but unless I chose to leave Linda at her Mother's home where she would have to live while we were in the South, their meeting would be unavoidable. I couldn't guess what Jack Robinson's reaction would be when they did meet, but the event did give me cause for some speculation.

I was standing at the bottom of the stairs that led up to the dressing rooms talking to Linda when I spied Jack walking towards us,

"Hello Jack," I said to him, then to Linda, "this is my friend Jack Robinson." Then again to Jack, "And this is my Girlfriend Linda." Jack just glared at Linda for one long minute then turned on his heel, walked away and I never ever saw or heard from him again. Well that was the end of my personal tailor, but I had already discovered that I was very good at designing clothes myself, much better in fact than Jack Robinson. Even before I had designed the ultimate gown on The Rolf Harris Show, I had designed a full length cape made in metallic fabric in the form of a Union-Jack flag on the outside and lined in metallic red, white and blue stripes on the inside. That particular cape came into being in an effort to bury my SS-Man image in Edinburgh without compromising my villainous persona there.

Nevertheless, Jack Robinson had played a vital part in my overall success and I do owe him a dept of gratitude,

So here's to you Mr. Robinson, Heaven holds a place for those who pray,

Hey, hey, hey – methinks you're gay?!

MY PURPLE VELVET GOWN

My 'Rolf Harris Show' designed Purple Gown proved to be a sensation. The audience reaction was incredible, and every time I strode from the dressing room to the ring just the very sight of me wearing it would set the scene perfectly for the battle that was about to commence.

More often than not I was wrestling in the main event, but I also noticed, that all at once many of my opponents seemed to be selected from the heavier weight divisions. The fact that George Kidd was one of my more regular opponents I liked to keep my weight between 150 to 165 pounds. But the very next night after wrestling against Kidd in a World-Lightweight Title Match, I might be wrestling against a Heavyweight like the 6' 3" African Witch-Doctor Masambula, or the Bell-ringer Quasimodo, or Mustapha Shikane 'The Terrible Turk'. Also, someone I had never expected to share the ring with – The Hardman Les Kellett.

On the first occasion that I wrestled against Kellett after I began wearing my Purple-velvet Gown was in Oxford Town Hall, and Kellett was already in the ring when I made my entrance. The seemingly endless applause for the popular Good-guy ended so abruptly the second I was spotted, that it sounded as though a switch had been flipped off. I was certain that my opponent would be furious, but as the sight of me in the gown began to be digested by the audience a racket arose that must have threatened to cause the building to explode. As I stepped through the ropes and into the ring all eyes were on me, Les Kellett had been totally eclipsed, thoroughly upstaged. I seized the moment and paraded around the ring in a way that would have made a fashion model look to their laurels. I looked at Kellett who had never set eyes on my new gown until that moment and I have to say that he was completely gob-smacked. I looked across the ring at him triumphantly, and he seemed to shrink and shrivel before my eyes. He approached me feebly with slouched shoulders and hanging head and inquired meekly,

"Can I try on your gown?"

What the Hell possessed me I don't know, but I shrugged off my fabulous gown and handed it to him, and realized too late that I had made a terrible mistake. He attempted to put the gown on but he had fingers as big as bananas on hands that looked like a Baseball player's catcher's mitt, so that they got stuck part way down the sleeves. He took off around the ring performing a comical mimic of my own entrance as the audience erupted with glee. Finally in an effort to extract his huge paws out of the sleeves he tore the lace trim on both sides, and once free he rolled my gown into a ball and threw it out of the ring. It was only the quick thinking and fast movement of my second who barely managed to grab the gown before my hated fans did. As I breathed an enormous sigh of relief at the split second salvation of my precious gown, Kellett slowly approached me again. I thought that he must have realized that he had gone too far, and I imagined an apology was about to be offered, instead he drew back his hand and slapped me in the face so hard it almost knocked my head off. Now I was gob-smacked – literally!

Just as he wanted the ball was back in Kellett's court, I had stupidly allowed myself to be conned and outmaneuvered, the audience was delighted, I was totally disgusted.

The very next night I was wrestling in the other famous University City, at Cambridge Corn-Exchange, and once again it would be a Main-Event contest against The Yorkshire Hardman, Les Kellett, - I was anything but ecstatic!

The beginning of the match could have been an action replay of the night before, huge reception for Kellett until I appeared, then a bigger reception as I strode into sight. I stepped into the ring, the crowd got louder, I strutted my stuff around the ring – the crowd got louder still, I sneered down my nose at my diminished opponent who once again stumbled across the ring and humbly asked,

"Can I try on your gown?"

And I replied, "No you can't – FUCK OFF!"

His meek countenance evaporated in a flash,

"Can I try on your gown?!" he repeated rearranging his features somewhat.

No you can't – FUCK OFF!" I repeated.

He glared at me murderously – "CAN I TRY ON YOUR

GOWN!!!!" He shouted.

"What part of – NO, YOU CAN'T, DON'T YOU UNDERSTAND YOU OLD TWAT?!" I replied loud enough to be heard in Oxford. I turned away from him, disrobed, handed my gown carefully to my second, and he, as I had previously instructed, took it back to the safety of the dressing room. As I had expected my opponent was not well pleased, and as I also expected his first move was that huge smack in the chops with his gigantic club of a paw - but this time there was no chops to smack. I did the unthinkable and moved. He dove in grabbed me in the referee hold to keep me grounded while he drew back his hand and threw another slap from the backyard. I stuck my elbow up and blocked it; he roared with fury and attempted to throw me onto the mat. That was not an easy task as I was blessed with abundant balance and strength. My resistance must have presented a challenge, and with renewed effort he pushed and pulled in an effort to drag me off my feet, he couldn't do it. I suddenly disengaged so suddenly that it was Kellett who lost his balance and almost fell flat on his face. He leapt up growled like a Bear and charged like a Bull, but I moved and he missed.

"COME ON LES!!!!" Shouted his fans, as they were used to seeing much more from their hero. Come on he did, and soon we were once again locked in a push and pull battle, but try as he may, he couldn't do anything with me.

"COME ON LES!!! The fans persisted, "WHEN ARE WE GOING TO SEE SOME ACTION?!!! I was a villain, the fans were going to boo and jeer what ever I did so I didn't care that they were getting aggravated. Kellett began to growl like a Bear again, but still couldn't do anything with me.

"COME ON LES – WHAT'S WRONG LES?!!!! The audience wanted to know.

Now he was desperate, he bulled in growling louder and louder like a rabid Dog, but I knew he couldn't do anything to me and my confidence soared, and even over his growls he became aware of me singing as I pretended to turn our struggle into a graceful waltz,

"WHO'S AFRAID OF THE BIG BAD WOLF – THE BIG BAD WOLF – THE BIG BAD WOLF?!" I sang, and Kellett because he knew he couldn't do anything else changed his tactics and pretended to laugh. As a result I allowed the contest to improve, but not by much, I didn't trust him one little bit and I wasn't going to give him a chance at revenge. Back in the dressing room after the match was over the Fucking idiot came over to me and asked,

"Why didn't you let me try the gown on tonight?" I replied,

"I bought the gown for myself Les, - not for you." I wore the gown many more times when I wrestled Les Kellett, but he never asked to wear it again. I never got slapped in the face by him again either, on occasion he did try, but I was never home when it arrived and there was fuck all he could do about it.

I had never known Jean to read a book before, but for a while now she had become a rabid reader, amongst her favorite authors was Kyle Onstott who wrote the Mandingo/Falconhurst series. Her sudden interest in that subject fortified my suspicion that 'Guinness-Head' might be paying visits to my home when I was away, for purposes other than getting his hair fixed. Jean herself was also becoming more and more confrontational, so much so that her constant nagging began to remind me of my Father's when I had lived in Wales. I found that the best way to shut her up was to simply ask,

"Seen much of 'Guinness-Head' lately?

The white Singer Vogue finally breathed its last, Linda and I had been on our way to Hamilton in Scotland and I was running late. I had been driving at over 80 miles an hour until we ran out of motorway, I slowed right down as I drove up a ramp to a roundabout and around it. I chose the road I needed and as I began to accelerate the car suddenly seemed to jump about five feet in the air as we almost pole-vaulted on our drive shaft that just dropped down onto the road. After we had been towed into a repair shop in nearby Penrith we were informed that the gear-box was also shattered. We had been extremely lucky, if that had occurred just minutes before when I had been speeding up the motorway there wouldn't have been much left of the car – or us. But there the luck ended, not only were we going to be late arriving at Hamilton, but earlier that day I had ordered a new Volkswagen Caravan and had part exchanged the Singer Vogue as part of the deal. Also there was a waiting list for the particular model I wanted, so to cut a long and frustrating story short I had to hire a car and patiently wait for my new vehicle to be delivered to the dealership.

WINGS ON MY FEET & A SPARK IN THEIR FUSE-BOX

My feud with World-Champion George Kidd had escalated to a whole new level. In a recent match with him, even in his home town of Dundee I had only lost the match on a disqualification, which resulted in my celebrated opponent being carried from the ring covered in blood. In a non-title contest in Paisley Ice-Rink, George had to be carried from the ring to the local infirmary in order to get the gash in his head stitched up, leaving me the triumphant winner. My challenge for a rematch with the title at stake was accepted. The upcoming title match generated an incredible amount of media coverage, here is an example –

1,000 POUNDS AT STAKE IN REVENGE BOUT

Sports Promoter Peter Keenan has booked Kirkcaldy Ice Rink tomorrow night for just about the most attractive wrestling bill ever offered to Scottish enthusiasts.

Dundee's George Kidd is to meet the blond Englishman, Adrian Street in a 1,000 pound needle match – a bout that could prove to be the most controversial and exciting ever seen in Scotland. For when this pair met at Paisley six weeks ago, Street won a tough, bruising fight which ended with Kidd being taken to Paisley Infirmary to get eight stitches inserted in a head wound. This brought the Dundee Star's winning run to a close since then he has been thirsting for revenge. A return match was promptly arranged by the promoter and Kidd wants the 1,000 pounds to be 'a winner takes all purse.'

Street has since aggravated the situation by asking the promoter if there is a Hospital near the Ice-Rink – suggesting that once again Kidd may need treatment at the finish. The Scot, usually a quiet man both inside and outside the ring, was for once angry, and is impatiently awaiting the battle for the biggest wrestling side-stake he has ever fought for. This promotion is also the most expensive ever staged in Scotland with a number of other top stars on the bill. Our photograph shows Kidd after being beaten by Street at Paisley. End.

And then in the Gazette – THE FIGHT OF THE YEAR!

The fight of the season is how wrestling fans have reacted to the news that Adrian Street, the controversial English Star, was to have a re-match with World Champion George Kidd. The top liner in the all star bill should be talked about for a long time and a capacity crowd is expected to see the bout. Since they last met at the Ice-Rink, George has been looking forward to the return. So keen is the Dundee man to win that he has forked out 500 pounds as a side-stake and he has no intention of losing either the cash or the match to his Herculean built opponent. While George is going into special training for the bout Adrian will be building up for the return match with a fight south of the border.

In reply to the challenge of Kidd promoter Keenan has received Street's check for 500 pounds and the money will be held up to the M.C. on the night if the fight.

The fight has caught the imagination of the fans south of the Border and spectators have notified the booking office to keep seats. There is no doubt that the clash will prove to be a no holds barred with both men going flat out for a win. There is that little bit of bite in the match and it is the opinion of the experts that the referee will not be needed for this will be a fight to the finish. George will rely on his skill and experience and will have the fans behind him, but Adrian is not impressed and has let it be known that he intends to score an English victory and leave the Scot a well beaten opponent. END.

GOLDILOCKS

By now I was certain that Guinness-Head was spending time with Jean while I was away that had nothing to do with the care and maintenance of his blond hair, but Jean flatly denied my accusations. There was no way of proving my belief, and the very fact that they both had access to my wrestling schedule made it next to impossible to catch them out.

Linda much preferred it when I was wrestling in the North which meant we were together 24/7. When I wrestled in the South for Dale Martins she would have to stay with her Mother, while I would live in Telford Avenue with my Kids. Also as a result of wanting to spend as much time as possible with my Children, I would often take them to some of the more local matches, which also meant taking Jean too, instead of Linda. As you can well imagine Linda was not at all happy with those arrangements but that was just the way it was. I had been wrestling in the North for a few weeks, and my next match in the South would be a local show in Wembley Town Hall on a Monday night. I told Jean that I would be traveling down from Manchester sometime on the Monday, and if I was early enough I would make a B-line for home and take both her and the Kids to the show. If I am running late I told her, I would have to go straight to the Hall, and wouldn't get back home until after the matches were over.

It was during that few weeks up north that my new Volkswagen Caravan was delivered and proved to be a great investment.

I had never shared my suspicions concerning Jean and Guinness-Head with Linda, so my decision to drive back to London on Saturday night after the show didn't go down too well with her. But it had been my plan all along. After dropping Linda off at her Mother's home, I drove to my own. Jean had obviously never seen my new vehicle, but I still decided to park it around the corner from Telford Avenue well out of sight, even though it was only about 4 am. I walked around the corner, and as I suspected I saw Guinness-Head's car parked right outside my front garden gate. I let myself in as quietly as I could and crept up the stairs in the same manner, gently opened my bedroom door and switched on the light.

Whose been sleeping in my bed? – Surprise, – surprise! There was Goldilocks, in my bed with Jean – there were no three Bears – just two bare arses!

Jean awoke first and leapt out of bed,

"WAKE UP!" She called to Goldilocks, "IT'S ADRIAN – HE'S BACK!!!"

Linda was surprised to see me so soon, and as I was wrestling in the south we spent a lovely week or so living in my mobile Caravan. I popped back to Telford from time to time to see my Kids, but much to Linda's delight we were together most of the time. As soon as I had worked a few things out in my mind, I suggested to Jean, that instead of sneaking about behind my back Guinness-Head should move into Telford with her, and I would move Linda in with me. The children had their own bedrooms and in the daytime they could choose to spend their time in Jean's part of the house, or when I was home, in my part of the house with me. I invited Jean and Guinness-Head to 'The Wine & Kebab' which was one of my new favorite restaurants in order to introduce them to Linda, after which we all went home to Telford Avenue where I hoped we would all live happily ever after. – Some hope!!! Well it worked in 'Goldilocks & the three Bears,' but I guess that was just a Fairy story.

THE SADIST IN SEQUINS WANTS TO RULE WRESTLING - By Clare Colvin. 1971

Welsh-Born Adrian Street is probably the most hated wrestler in the business. He has only to appear in the ring for the audience to start booing. He hands his Ostrich feathered fan to a second, shrugs off his sequined dressing gown and limbers up with a few ballet pirouettes. The audiences are beside themselves with fury by the end of the fight, by which time his opponent has been kicked, battered and ridiculed. Street's image as a sadistic queen has brought him hatred certainly, but success as well. Meeting

Adrian Street outside the ring is something of a shock.

'I ENJOY DRESSING UP.'

One expects to find him lounging in a wall-to-wall fur-lined pad, wearing one of his one thousand pound gowns. In fact he lives in an unassuming and untidy house in Streatham, London, where one trips over children's bicycles in the hall.

Street has a face like a younger Richard Burton and wears a black T-shirt and jeans. The only incongruous thing about him is his hair, it is long and mauve.

But there is no doubt that he puts a lot of himself into his act as the Danny La Rue of the wrestling ring.

"I am vain and conceited and I enjoy dressing up," he admits disarmingly, "I am sadistic too and I like to master my opponent."

'WOMEN JEALOUS.'

Street became interested in physical culture in his teens and left home in Brynmawr at the age of 16 to make his name in London. He soon realized that nice wrestlers went unnoticed.

"I would go and see where I stood on the bill, and I would overhear people saying: 'He's a good little wrestler, but what about that other bastard – what a sod he is.'"

What finally made Street decide to join the bastards was a fight at Dumfries Place Drill Hall in Cardiff against Leon Fortuna.

"It had always been my dream to fight there, and I was very aggressive because I wanted to win in front of my own people. Fortuna got all the sympathy and I was booed. You do your best to please people and then they go for some foreigner who is looking sorry for himself."

Several other wrestlers have tried to climb on to the satin and sequin band-wagon, Street says: "They have neither the ability nor the appearance to follow it up. There's more to it than bleaching your hair and buying fancy gowns. Most of them look like ugly little Ducklings trying to imitate a beautiful Swan."

He is rather pleased with the simile,

"That's good, I like it." He says, looking approvingly at himself in the mirror.

In spite of his exaggeratedly camp appearance, Street has a large following of female fans.

"They are curious about my sex life, they think I am effeminate and they want to convert me. Then there are the women who hate me because they think I am a man going to waste. There are a lot of women who are jealous because I'm better looking than they are, - much more lovely." He is in the process of getting divorced; he says he's definitely against committing himself to marriage again.

THERE'S NO FIXING.

"I have always been the sort of person who likes to get up and go at a moment's notice and do what I want to do. My career was another reason why my marriage broke up. We lived completely different lives; our only interests together are my children."

He has three children, Adrian, aged nine, Vincent, aged seven and Amanda, aged five. Young Adrian's ambition is to be a wrestler, billed as Adrian Street Esq. Jnr.

At the age of 29 Street is earning upwards of 9.000 pounds a year from his wrestling and he thinks he deserves every penny. He is tired of hearing accusations that wrestling is 'fixed'. He has had his nose broken three times, several broken ribs, 15 stitches in one ear and the other one cauliflowered,

"People who say that wrestling is fixed usually haven't watched it," he says, "There is no fixing. In pre-war days there was a certain amount and it became a case of give a dog a bad name,"

In fact many wrestlers have a deep hatred for each other, because of damage inflicted in the ring. He has an intense dislike for the World Lightweight Champion George Kidd, though he admires his skill. Last time they fought they split each other's heads, and George Kidd ended up in hospital.

HURT ME A LOT.

He has challenged Kidd to defend his title, but so far the challenge remains unanswered. "He has hurt me a lot of times, he has done my body a lot of damage – and I believe in paying back with interest."

When they do meet again, it could be one of the cruelest fights in wrestling history, Street is out for blood and he doesn't care who knows it. END.

SAVILLE ROW

My most decisive victory over World Champion George Kidd was a non-title match held in Nottingham Ice Rink when I beat him by two straight leg submissions to nil in three rounds. It was the most decisive and shortest match I was ever to have against The World Champ, after which he was transported to a nearby Hospital in Nottingham to receive treatment for both his badly injured legs. My challenge for a title match was immediately issued and accepted. Although, due to the injuries he sustained during the match that put him in Hospital, he would not be able to wrestle on the next card held in Nottingham Ice Rink. Instead, he intended going into special training, and then facing me on the show after next to ensure that his legs by that time would be sufficiently healed.

I was wrestling on the next show, and I naturally expected a top contender as an opponent over which a good decisive victory would help set the scene for my World Championship quest on the following show. One would think that by now I would be immune to the often ridiculous ideas that many of Joint's promoters came up with, but this one rendered me speechless – and as I'm sure you've gathered by now, that was no easy task. When I saw that night's line up I was completely gob smacked, as in my opinion I would not even be wrestling a wrestler let alone a top contender. My opponent on that night was to be the famous Disc-Jockey, Jimmy Saville! And if you think that was bad – sit down, because it gets worse!

As well as being the best known D.J. in Britain, Jimmy Saville was a rabid publicity Hound, who would do anything and everything for attention. Now if you have been paying attention, you will be aware that I don't have any trouble with that way of thinking whatsoever. But do it in your own field not mine. Jimmy Saville was nationally famous and popular, and for a few of Joint's Promoters that was all that was necessary to put arses on seats. There were wrestlers who had been made to lose to Saville who had eaten, drank and slept wrestling since they had been hardly more than children. Wrestlers who had trained to be wrestlers, had had their arses kicked time and again in rough, tough gyms, where their teachers would attempt over and over again to break their spirit in order to determine if they truly had what it takes. They had done the whole sweat, blood and tears scenario over and over and then some, and then to have to lose to someone like Saville must have been absolutely soul destroying.

You must be wondering what I meant when I said it gets worse?! - Well, as I was getting changed for the match, the promoter, Ted Beresford brought Saville into my dressing room and introduced us to each other, and then told me,

"You and Jimmy are tonight's main event, and I want you to do a draw."

Even though I thought he was joking I didn't laugh as to even think of something so fucking ludicrous was way beyond contempt.

"Yeah – right!" I replied. But as he carried on yapping I suddenly began to suspect that the fucking raving idiot was serious!

"Don't fuck about now Ted," I told him at last, "what do you really want us to do?!"

"I told you, do a draw!" he persisted.

"That is not going to happen," I told him firmly – and then to Jimmy Saville,

"I've got nothing against you personally, but you are not even a wrestler and to be honest I even resent being told to go into the same ring as you."

"Don't underestimate him Street!" Ted Beresford interrupted, "Jimmy may be a lot tougher than you think!" Talk about waving a red flag!!!!!

Saville was always up to tough guy type challenges; he even completed the Royal Marines basic training as a publicity stunt. But, as a result of being brought into wrestling by 'The Grey Rat' Gentleman Jim Lewis, his celebrity had since attracted the attention of the more stupid and greedy promoters who had not only began to employ him, but also awarded him victories over many good and established wrestlers.

"Well we'll find out just how tough he is when we get into the ring won't we?!" I told Beresford.

"Hey Street, I don't want any of that!" he told me firmly.!"

"Listen Ted," I explained, "On the very last show I beat the World Champion in no more than 10 minutes and sent him to Hospital. Now how much sense does it make that I can beat the World Champion, but I can't beat this clown. Do you think the fans are going to believe that a fucking disc-jockey can pin me when the Champion of the World couldn't. How much will the title match mean if the challenger can't even beat Jimmy fucking Saville? What are you trying to do – ruin your own business?!" I wanted to know, and then to Saville I said, "Go away - I'll see you in the ring if you're up to it."

Well he had been warned!

Talk about pouring gasoline on the fucking fire! Being a very flamboyant villain I much preferred my opponent to make his entrance first. It gave the fans a chance to look at him, applaud, cheer and settle down before I made my grand entrance, which was designed to blow the roof off the building.

"Hurry up Street, they're playing your fanfare and your opponent is already in the ring!" announced Beresford as he popped his head around my dressing room door.

I slipped into my fabulous gown and made my way to the stairs that led into the vast, packed arena. At the top of the stairs before I made my descent down to the ring, I struck a similar victory pose to the one I had displayed at the end of my last match in that arena, as the World Champion was carried out of the ring and on his way to Hospital.

'Just a little reminder for the fans.' I thought. It was only then that I looked down at the ring, and discovered that I had been double-crossed; there was no sign of my opponent! It did cross my mind to turn around and walk back to the dressing room, but it was too late, I had been seen by every one of the thousands of fans so I had to go with the flow. I waited impatiently for Saville to make his entrance, but he seemed to be using a tactic that I often used myself of making both my opponent and the fans wait. When the next fanfare began to blare, here comes Britain's premier Disc-Jockey who was wearing what appeared to be a cheap, garish copy of something that I might wear myself – if I was that tasteless. The crowd roared their approval and ogled eagerly to watch for my reaction to what they recognized as a sartorial piss-take of myself. I deprived them of that pleasure by completely ignoring the presence of my opponent who entered the ring with a flourish that could well have been a mirror image of yours-truly. I yawned sleepily and only observed the actions of Saville through the corner of my eye. I would make certain that my opponent disrobed before I did, and then make a huge deal out of parading and posing which I knew would bring the fans attention back to me, where it obviously belonged.

"Okay, take your gown off!" the referee ordered on cue.

"Him first!" I replied stubbornly indicating Saville. I was certain that my opponent would recreate the whole 'Adrian Street' disrobing ceremony for the fans, who no doubt would enjoy my reaction more than the actual ceremony. Once again in order to spoil their enjoyment I turned my back on Saville, and gazed up into the darkness beyond the bright ring lights. When the crowd's roar of approval hit a crescendo and then began to subside, I assumed that Saville had at last stripped for battle, so without further ado I disrobed myself. It was only then that I actually looked at Saville for the first time, and was horrified to see he was wearing a different fancy gown, that he had been wearing underneath the one that he had worn when he had entered the ring. As if that wasn't bad enough, much to the fan's delight after strutting around and performing his most comical Adrian Street impersonation, he removed his gown to reveal yet another fancy robe that he wore underneath the second one. The fans loved it – unfortunately for Saville I didn't!

At last the bell rang to herald the commencement of Saville's 'Last Stand.' I decided to forego building up the tension by slowly and cautiously stalking my opponent as we both circled around each other. Instead I walked directly towards him leapt up and smashed him so hard with a flying dropkick it turned him upside down before he landed on top of his head on the mat. Instead of reacting as though he had been badly stunned by the move, Saville flew off the mat and attempted a flying dropkick of his own. Well the flying part worked – but before his feet found a target I stepped in and threw both his feet high in the air which caused him once again to land on top of his head. Once more he leapt to his feet, and once more I leveled him with a rib crushing dropkick. This time he was down for what I thought would be the full count, so I stood triumphantly and began flexing my chest muscles which made them jump up and down. Then up jumps Saville, and as he didn't have the chest that enabled him to mimic me, he began a jerking hip movement that looked like he was madly humping an invisible Lady from behind. It was really an obscene sight. I was disgusted, and the audience should have been too, but they cheered their encouragement and approval for all they were worth. That was the last time that Saville was given the chance to do anything that the fans might want to cheer! I grabbed a handful of his hair while he was still in mid hump, and ripped him backwards off his feet with so much force that the back of his head smashed onto the mat before the rest of him. And then I was on him, viciously and relentlessly till the end of a very short match, bits of his wispy blond hair was floating in the air as I chased him around the ring and beat on him unmercifully. Linda who was in the audience told me later that Saville looked like a terrified Chicken with a hungry Fox on it's tail, and that the hair flying about looked like the Chicken's feathers.

Although he was no wrestler, I did honor him by treating him in the same fashion that I had treated the best wrestler in the World on the very last show, and beat him with two straight submissions to nil. It may not have sent him to Nottingham Hospital, but it did something much better, and that was put an end to Jimmy Saville's career as a wrestler for good. He did however promote wrestling in a Club that he owned in Bournemouth. I wrestled Main-Event there for him on very many occasions, but on every occasion that I wrestled there, Jimmy Saville was conspicuous by his absence, and I never, ever set eyes on him again.

SANDRA

Linda and I were both watching TV in Telford Avenue when there was a knock on our front door; I opened it to Sandra Muldoon, and another person who at first I thought was a much older looking and bespectacled Mickey. In fact the other person turned out to be Mickey Muldoon's Father, hence the likeness. I invited them both in and asked them what I could do for them; they came straight to the point, and asked me to supply them with photographs as I had Mickey a number of years earlier. They explained that Mickey was still running his pornographic empire from behind bars, with his Father and Sandra at the helm outside in the free World. I explained to them both that I was no longer interested in taking photos, and couldn't afford the time involved even if I was. All the time Sandra was in my house she hardly took her eyes off Linda, speculation like I have never seen surpassed written all over her chops. I would have paid a lot more than a penny for her thoughts. It was while Mickey's Father was using our toilet that Sandra blurted out all the details concerning the brutal death of her ex-lover and co-model that enabled me to gain a more concise picture of what really occurred that day.

Sandra and Mick's Dad left disappointed that day, and I never saw or heard from them again. But I did receive another similar request from a most unexpected source when TV's wrestling commentator Kent Walton, asked me if I was interested in supplying him with models as he had began his new sideline as an Adult movie producer. As I told the Muldoons I also informed Kent that I was no longer in that business. Although I didn't tell either that I still bought and sold movies and still marketed rubber ware.

BARNUM BLUE-BLOOD

Bob Langley, of 'Pebblemill at One,' called me and asked if I could appear on the show the very next day, and I was very happy to tell him that I could. When I arrived there the next afternoon he explained that the day before Sir Athol Oakley had been on the show advertising his new book 'Blue-Blood on the Mat.' During his interview he didn't only pay lavish complements to his own wrestling prowess, and his peers of that period, but claimed that modern wrestling, unlike the sport in his day was fake.

Sir Athol Oakley had been a Wrestler and Promoter from pre-war days until the early-fifties. He suggested that as a result of the new style of wrestling presented by Joint Promotions, his own promotions who only employed 'real' wrestlers, suffered by comparison. It disgusted him to such a degree that he finally gave up promoting. You may recall that during my newspaper interview in 'Sadist in Sequins' when asked if wrestling was fake, and my response was to deny it, but admit that there may have been a certain amount of it in the pre-war period. Well it was with Sir Athol Oakley's promotion in mind that I made that admission. Sir Athol Oakley was wrestling's P.T. Barnum, and judging by the claims he made he must have truly thought 'that there was a sucker born every minute. P.T. Barnum had his Fiji Mermaid, Chang and Eng the Siamese-Twins, Monkey-Man, General Tom Thumb and the 161 year-old Joice Heth, Sir Athol had the tallest, heaviest Giants, weirdoes, beard-oes and freaks from places that no one except Sir Athol had ever heard of.

When Sir Athol promoted in Belle Vue on one occasion he had billed a tag-team of Midgets from America. Their journey was delayed so he replaced them with normal lightweight wrestlers ranging in height from about 5' 4" to 5' 7". When they entered the ring the audience booed for all they were worth until the huckster himself leapt into the ring, grabbed the microphone and indignantly made his speech,

"Ladies and Gentlemen, have I ever let you down – have I not brought you the biggest and strongest athletes from the four corners of the Earth? – And now, not only have I presented you all with the very best Midget Wrestlers in the World, but they are also the World's tallest Midgets!" Believe it or not, everyone cheered the nutty-Knight for all they were worth.

He staged a publicity conference when he brought an American wrestler he had dubbed 'King Kong' over to wrestle for him, and claimed that his latest monster stood over 7' in height. One of the reporters challenged Sir Athol on that point, stating that he himself was 6' 3" and was almost as tall as King Kong.

"Nonsense man," was Sir Athol's response, "you're 6' 8" tall if you're an inch!"

King Kong's last contest for the batty-Blue-Blood was against yet another 'Angel' – not to be confused with the original 'French Angel' Maurice Tillet, who was only about 5' 6" tall, this one was as big as his King Kong.

Well both of these monsters were in the ring battling away and trying their best to look like wrestlers, when The Angel picked up King Kong and slammed him heavily onto the mat. Kong screamed out in pain so loudly, that in panic The Angel dropped down on his knees and as he cradled the monster's head in his lap, King Kong removed his phony fangs and gasped,

"I think ya broke ma leyg Paw!" Out popped the Angels fangs before he replied,

"OH NO SON – WHAT'S YER MAW GONNA SAY?!"

Wrestling's Giant German, Kurt Zehe was enormous, massively built and stood 7' 2" in height. But when he wrestled for Sir Athol he suddenly became 8' 4" tall, with a 110" chest, 42" thighs, 30" biceps, 3 feet across the shoulders and weighed in at 751 pounds. Now if you think that might be a slight exaggeration, what about a claim he made in his book about the time he wrestled a Circus Strongman who stood 9' 3". Sir Athol supposedly wrestled this Giant in front of an audience of 200, and beat him in minutes by leaping up and taking him down with a flying-head-scissors.

If you have ever had the misfortune to see the old film of Kurt Zehe in action – and I use the word 'action' figuratively - against Ed Strangler Bright, I think you will agree that the death of 'pre-war all-in wrestling' was long overdue. I can also imagine where professional wrestling got its phony reputation from. It was also another match involving Kurt Zehe, and not modern wrestling that put the final nail in the coffin of Sir Athol Oakley's style of wrestling, when in 1952 the Giant German was matched against former Boxer, Irish Jack Doyle. The contest proved to be such a chronic fiasco that even P.T. Barnum couldn't have talked his way out of that one.

He also claimed that Joint promotions had filched the 'all-in-wrestling rules' devised by himself decades before. He was forced to write an apology and a retraction in his book after being threatened with legal action from Norman Morrell, who himself claimed authorship of the modern 'Lord Mount-Evans Rules of Professional Wrestling.'

Amongst a number of criticisms made by Sir Athol when he first appeared on Pebblemill was a wrestling throw known as 'The Irish-Whip.' One wrestler would grab the hand or wrist of his opponent and yank it up so forcefully that it would cause him to turn right over in mid air and land flat on his back, and that was the first thing that Bob Langley wanted me to explain. Unfortunately, I secretly held a similar opinion of that particular move, and therefore never ever used it myself. But, thanks to the advanced tuition I was regularly receiving from George Kidd I had learned a method of performing that particular throw in a more believable way.

Bob Langley himself could not have been a more perfect opponent to demonstrate on; he stood at least a couple of inches over six feet, and had large hands with proportionately long fingers. I linked the fingers of my right hand with the fingers of Bob's left, and then instructed the nearest cameraman to take a close-up of our hands. I then moved my thumb from the right side of his hand to the outside of his little finger, squeezed hard and twisted my hand around. Bob yelled out loudly in pain, I held him in that painful position while I explained to him and the camera the possibilities,

"If I yanked your arm up suddenly against the joints of your fingers and wrist, would you try to resist, or would you throw yourself over in an effort to relieve the pain?" I asked as I increased the pressure another few notches.

"I WOULD GO OVER!!!" Replied Bob. I released him immediately, but before he had fully recovered, I told him,

"I never use that throw myself, I much prefer something like this." And with that I dove in taking both of Bob's legs, but not with enough force to take him right off his feet, but with just enough to make him grab me around the waist in order to maintain his balance. Immediately I clamped both my own arms around both of Bob's elbows, and lifted him bodily upside-down on my back. I did not complete the move by throwing myself backwards in my best Bert Assirati impersonation, but I did leave him kicking and yelling for a minute or two in order for him to completely digest the possibilities. I know he was extremely relieved to be placed safely back on good old terrafirma, and even more so after I explained to him and the camera what the completed throw consisted of.

Everyone was very impressed, and very convinced in spite of Sir Athol's claim to the contrary. Modern professional wrestling was real, alive and well, but Sir Athol would have none of it, and in his own Knightly fashion immediately threw down his gauntlet.

"Put on a wrestling match at Pebblemill," he challenged, and he would supply the commentary and refute each and every move made by both of the contestants. His challenge was passed on to me by Bob Langley, and upon my acceptance he asked me if I could also supply an opponent. I chose a comparatively new, but very proficient young wrestler named Stevie Grey, but warned him before hand that under the circumstances our contest would be very rough. There was no way I was going to give Sir Athol the slightest opportunity to cast any doubt concerning any hold or throw that he would witness during our match, as I felt that I would be defending the credibility of myself and modern professional wrestling.

When we arrived at Pebblemill I was quite dismayed after inspecting the setup. The ring had been erected in a small grassy area outside the back of the building, overlooked by Bob Langley and Sir Athol Oakley who would be looking down on us through a window in the studio, one floor above the ring. The ring itself was obviously designed more for Boxing; it was so hard and unyielding that it could have been a 3' high, 20'x20' block of solid concrete with nothing more than a sheet of rough canvas stretched over it. But, maybe worst of all was the fact that Young Stevie and I would be there completely alone, no visible audience, not even a referee. There would be an audience in the studio watching the match on a monitor, and obviously the many thousands of TV viewers would be watching from their homes, but no one to cheer and jeer at our efforts. A lively feedback as any wrestler would tell you was our life's blood, it was very difficult to perform for an unresponsive audience, and we didn't have a visible audience at all. There wasn't even a timekeeper, someone told us when to start, but then that was it, no rounds just begin wrestling and continue – continue – continue!

Well young Stevie Grey and I clashed in the centre of the ring and just beat the living shit out of each other. Everything we did to each other was hard, solid, deliberate, even brutal. How long we battered each other I don't know, when all at once someone called from the corner of the building to take a short break as they were cutting away in order to show a clip of film of Sir Athol in action decades earlier. Unfortunately for me was, that I heard the call and Stevie didn't. I had been struggling to get up from the canvas under the impression that my opponent was aware of a quick rest period and as I was on my way up Stevie was very much on his way down, his knee smashed into the side of my head and I thought he had knocked it right off. There was a loud crack and a tremendous pain shot from the base of my skull all the way down to the base of my spine. I felt as though the solid ring swayed like a rowboat entering the Bay of Biscay on a bad day. I staggered to my feet and a headache from Hell swirled into my head, I could have easily thrown up. I felt a pain that day that I swear never, ever really went away, and even as I write this many decades later, I can still feel a knot in my neck. All too soon a voice told us to continue, and we once again began to savage each other like two rabid Pit-Bulls. By the time time was called I much doubted that Stevie Grey felt any better than I did, I've got to give him full credit for being one tough young kid. The way I felt as I staggered into my dressing room after the match reminded me of the Day I wrestled against Frank Nottingham and Alf Jacobs in the YMCA almost a decade and a half earlier. I was suddenly awoken out of my reverie by a loud knocking on my dressing room door. I opened the door and much to my surprise found the Grand Knight, Sir Athol Oakley himself standing there, beaming all over his face, eyes twinkling with delight, he grabbed my hand and pumped it vigorously as he told me,

"That was the best wrestling contest I have ever seen, wrestling was never that good in my day!" I thanked him as I thought to myself,

'That is probably the first truthful thing I had ever heard of him saying!'

When I spoke to Bob Langley later, he too had been surprised by Sir Athol's complete change of heart,

"I thought he had come for no other reason than to expose modern wrestling as nothing more than a farce," he explained, "but instead he became really excited and paid you complement after complement for your immense wrestling knowledge and ability!"

"Truest thing he ever said in his entire life." I agreed modestly.

CANTERBURY TALES

Italian movie Director Pier Paolo Pasolini and his interpreter were doing a little shopping in Portobello Road Antique-market, when they happened to be passing a television store,

"Who is that wrestling on TV?" Pasolini wanted to know, "I want him for my movie." Pasolini was on location in Britain filming his new movie 'Canterbury Tales' and that was how I got cast in it – as 'The Fighter'.

It had been a decade earlier when I had decided that I wanted to pursue my dream of becoming a full time professional wrestler, and not go to Italy to make movies. It seemed that if Mohamed wouldn't go to the mountain, the mountain would have to come to Mohamed, and here they were, all the way from Italy offering me a part in an Italian movie shot in Britain.

In the opening scene I had a medieval style fight/wrestling match with Heavyweight wrestler 'Judo' Al Hayes. I won, and was presented with the prize of a live Goat which I was to kiss, put down, flex my chest muscles a few times then charge into a huge solid Oak door and smash it off the hinges in order to show off my Herculean power. Well that was what was supposed to happen. What actually happened was that I bounced off that door like a pea blown out of a peashooter would bounce off a Sherman Tank.

"Try it again from the top!" I was told, and once again Al Hayes and I would begin our battle over again. Soon my shoulders were so battered and bruised from smashing into that huge solid, unyielding door that I complained,

"If I am going to kiss this fucking Goat one more time, I'll have to marry it!"

Someone had the bright idea of taking the door off its hinges and just propping it up in position, so that when I charged into it, it would just look as though I had smashed it down. I watched as about a dozen or more stagehands struggled with the huge door, and I realized that even with it off its hinges it would be no mean task to knock it over.

"Okay – once again from the top!" we were ordered again. Al Hayes and I once again began to batter each other; I smashed him to the ground and dived bodily on top of him to win the contest. I leapt up, got handed my prize, kissed the Goat for what seemed the hundredth time, put it down, flexed the chest and charged the door. Even though I was aware that it had been taken off its hinges, I realized that this was no stage prop. We were on location at a real ancient Farm, and that huge Oak door was very, very real. As I hurled myself towards it, just a split second before impact I leapt up and struck the door as high as I could jump in order to ensure that my quest would this time meet with success. I was successful - so successful in fact that with the tremendous force I hit it with, the door collapsed and my impetus turned me upside-down, and I cart-wheeled into the big stone barn in mid air landing feet first in a deep, slimy swamp of Pig shit.

As I said, it was a real farm.

"That's a wrap!" I heard at last, from a director who was holding his nose.

I had made friends with a number of other actors including Hugh Griffith, Geraldine Chaplin, Nicolas Smith, Derek Deadman, a medieval Nun who was prone to flash her tiny frilly pink knickers, and an actor/producer named O.T. None of them would let me anywhere near them once they got a whiff of my new perfume 'Eau de Stinking-Swine'. I eventually managed to remedy my predicament when an extra who happened to be wearing an identical pair of boots to the shit soaked pair that I was wearing, made a derogatory remark concerning my prevailing odor just one too many times. I wrestled him to the ground robbed him of his nice clean boots, gave him my shitty ones in exchange and then accused him of smelling of Pig shit.

Originally, I was offered 5 days work by Pasolini, but for what ever reason the 5 days became several weeks. I told them that if they wanted me for longer than the original 5 days that they would have to pay me cancellation fees for all the wrestling matches I would have to cancel. They would also have to pay all my hotel bills, all my gas bills for the journeys entailed, as I would still have to travel to the wrestling shows that I had been booked on if only to show myself to the wrestling fans before they left the arenas. I also told all the promoters that I was booked to wrestle for, that if I was to honor the dates I had been given by them, they would have to pay all my hotel bills, gas bills, and to put me on last in order to give me more time to get to the venue in time to wrestle for them. Of course, the movie's accountant didn't know where I would be wrestling each night, with the result that my journeys, as far as he was concerned was twice as far as they were in reality. Similarly, the various promoters didn't know what towns the day's location was going to be at, so once again the mileage involved did tend to be a trifle exaggerated – [Sir Athol would have been proud of me.] and as I said, both parties were paying for hotels when in fact Linda and I were both sleeping each night in our Volkswagen-caravan, the money was pouring in!

I was amongst a group who were chosen to be Canterbury Pilgrims, and we were all asked if we were able to ride Horses. I was also the only one who claimed to be very good at it, with the result that I was given a mount with some very serious attitude problems. And – if that wasn't bad enough, I was also required to carry the biggest, most unwieldy set of medieval bagpipes I had ever seen. Every other stride of the horse would jolt the bagpipes out of my grasp, one or more of the pipes would whack the horse between its ears and the bloody animal would rear and then take off at a full gallop, often right in the middle of a shoot. Everyone would then have to wait until I got both the horse and the bagpipes under control and get back into place before they could attempt yet another take. It wasn't only my horse that was guilty of delaying progress; there were two human actors who got a royal bollocking after ruining a number of takes when they realized that they had been wearing modern eye glasses for a medieval period movie. One of them an American actor playing a monk was found to have been wearing his glasses for at least two days. But in his defense, if anyone else had been taking 3 or 4 acid trips a day as he had been, they probably would have made the same mistake. I almost fell off my horse laughing when the disgruntled, but still high Monk shuffled past me, and I heard him grumble to himself,

"Hey man, can't a cat goof?!"

Towards the end of my involvement in the movie we were filming at Battle Abbey School, in the town of Battle near

Hastings. I had been required to learn a couple of pages of lines which I was finding very difficult. I have found since that I am in fact very good at learning lines if I have a speaking part, but in this case they wanted it to be medieval in style and I was finding it really hard to get my mouth around it. My oldest son Adrian jr. helped me and tested me for hours until at last I had it down pat, or at least I thought I did.

The night before I had been wrestling Judo Al Marquette in Derby, as Al was very popular there, and I wasn't we had a very hot contest indeed. I won and the fans were suitably enraged. As I strutted my way back to the dressing room a fan leaned over a rail in front of the bleachers and whacked me with his overcoat. It obviously didn't damage me, but as I didn't see it coming it was a little startling. I warned the perpetrator that his actions could have dire consequences if he ever attempted to do it again. He tried, but I snatched the overcoat out of his hands and took it with me to the dressing room. Minutes later he was hammering on the dressing room door demanding the return of his very expensive overcoat. The promoter Jack Atherton had to fish it out of the toilet with a broom handle before reuniting it with its owner, as I had stuffed it in there and pissed over it after I had torn the lining out of it. A few minutes later there was more hammering on the dressing room door, and this time it was a Policeman with the pissy overcoat fan in tow. He demanded an explanation for the condition of the overcoat,

"I've got a better idea," I told him, "Ask smelly to explain how I came by the overcoat in the first place." With that I closed the door in their faces, and that was that.

It had taken me until the early hours of the next morning to get to Battle from Derby, I parked my van almost outside the school where that days filming was to take place. It hardly seemed that we had closed our eyes to sleep when there was a loud knocking on the side of my van. I opened the door bleary eyed and was asked by the directors gofer what I would normally drink if I wanted to become intoxicated. What a bloody dumb question to ask someone that time of the morning I thought, but replied,

"Wine!" as I slammed the van door closed, glanced at my watch which told me it wasn't yet 6am, and fell back into bed.

No sooner had I fallen asleep when the banging on the van door recommenced. This time when I answered I was handed three liters of Wine, one Rose', one White and one Red,

"Drink all of these and then come to the set," he demanded, then added, "and make sure you drink them all!" Well I did try, but even with some serious help from Linda we couldn't finish it that time of the morning. When with a little difficulty, I found the set, which was in the archway of the school, my Horse, bagpipes and the other actors were all waiting patiently for me. Then began the biggest fiasco of the entire movie.

To begin with I couldn't get on the Horse while holding onto the bagpipes. When at last they hoisted me into the saddle and handed me the bagpipes, the pipes separated and whacked the Horse on the head, and off we went galloping away into the school grounds. I lost count of how many gallops I had to endure before the Horse finally settled down, due probably more to exhaustion rather than my riding skill. Then it was time for my speaking part and I couldn't remember one fucking word.

Later that day with the movie filming behind me, I had about 200 miles to drive to the town I would be wrestling at that night, when I could hardly walk let alone drive. I barely remembered to go to get my final wages from the movie's paymaster. I really got on great with him, he was a huge Mike Marino fan, and as Marino was so easy to tell stories about we got on together like a house on fire. He never questioned the sometimes outrageous expenses I claimed, and would round out every demand in my favor. I remember dashing back to the caravanette with my arms full of cash, dumping the lot into Linda's lap,

"Count that lot and stuff it in your bag!" I told her as we sped to that night's venue. I was offered the title role in another movie playing Hamlet Smith in a film bearing the same name, by actor, producer O.T. I very enthused until I read the script, and all the nude scenes I was going to be playing were explained to me before I decided –

THANKS – BUT NO THANKS!

BELGIUM-HOLLAND

Bob and I took another continental tour this time to Belgium and Holland, it turned out to be a very enjoyable and successful trip. Every night we were main event against fellow British Brothers, Roy and Tony St.Clair. They were both excellent second generation wrestlers, their Father being the great Francis St.Clair Gregory; every time that we stepped into the ring with them was an event that we all looked forward to. We even managed to stay out of jail; if there was a down side to the affair at all it was entirely due to a pair of Arab wrestlers who toured with us. The smaller of the two wore a Judo outfit in the ring, and wrestled in that style. The big one who must have weighed well in excess of 300 pounds, didn't wrestle at all. Instead, he would get introduced to the fans every night as the Champion of what ever Arab country he hailed from, he then leapt into the ring, charged around it waving his arms above his head. As a climax he would yank the bed sheet off his head, shake out his very long, very greasy looking black hair, and then dive out of the ring and march back to the dressing room in triumph. He never actually wrestled once during the whole tour, which is just as well if his wrestling ability didn't surpass the skills of his smaller countryman.

The reason I found the presence of the two Arabs more than a little irritating was that as a result of my wrestling image. The big Arab took my character seriously and really took a fancy to me. I must admit that to begin with his amorous infatuation amused Bob and I, and the St.Clairs, even more so when I sat on his lap one day and stroked his fat greasy head, and occasionally blew him a kiss at breakfast time. We all thought it very funny, but the situation soon began to lose its humorous flavor for me when the love struck Camel-jockey began following me everywhere I went, like an unwelcome shadow. Of course, I was the only one who was no longer amused, Bob, Tony and Roy, as wrestlers do, found my predicament hilarious, and would do whatever it took to throw fat on the fire whenever the opportunity arose. If I went window shopping, he'd follow me like a stray Dog looking for a new home. I knew that Arabs didn't drink alcohol so in the evening time after the matches had ended I'd tour every bar within walking distance of our hotel, but Ali fucking Baba would follow me into every one, and drink coffee instead of alcohol. The climax came, when one evening in our hotel, he presented himself as I came out of the lift on the floor of my room. He had brushed his hair down all around his shoulders and was wearing what looked like a long black negligee. Instead of going to my own room I marched into the St.Clair's room and found them both in bed reading,

"What do you suggest I do about this twat?!" I asked them, indicating the big Arab who entered the room behind me.

"Take him to bed and put him out of his misery." Suggested Roy, Tony added,

"Good idea, after all what's a busted arsehole if he gives you a bucket full of Rubies?!" That was it; I quickly ducked past Ali Baba, flew down the corridor to my own room, entered, slammed the door behind me and locked it tight. Next thing that happened is I heard a scratching at my door, and Ali Baba singing or reciting something that was probably to do with Omar Khayyam – or Homo Khayyam more like it.

I retaliated; I grabbed hold of my steel spring chest expander and held it like a weapon by one handle, 'I'll wrap this fucking thing right around his fucking head if he breaks in here!' I thought, as I sat on the edge of my bed in my purple and mauve suit. The scratching and singing became louder; again I retaliated by singing Hava Nagila in my loudest voice. Soon the occupants of neighboring rooms were banging their walls in protest and the scratching and singing outside my door stopped. I finally fell asleep still fully dressed, still clutching my steel sprung exercise equipment.

Next day we traveled in a private coach to Groningen in the far north of Holland. It was a long journey there and back to Brussels, and for the whole period the only time Ali Baba even looked in my direction was to scowl with disgust.

'Just the way it ought to be!' I thought.

HELL'S ANGELS II

Although Bob and I were probably the first 'Hell's Angels' in Britain we make no claim whatsoever of introducing, or even popularizing the American Motorbike cult in the UK. I can't speak for Bob, but I don't like motorbikes and never did, I don't even know, or want to know how to turn one on. We had very little to do with the motorbike version of the Hell's Angels even after the British version of the cult caught on, but there were two incidents that are worth mentioning.

The first was when Bob and I, billed as 'The Hell's Angels' were wrestling in The Colson Hall, Bristol. After depositing our gear in the dressing room we joined Linda in the cafeteria for a coffee where we were approached by two individuals dressed in black leather decorated with metal studs and pieces of chain. One was a regular size; the other would have stood eye to eye with Ted Cassidy who played 'Lurch' in 'The Adams Family'. He also looked like as though he could have been an 'Adams Family' member.

"Who gave you permission to call yourselves 'Hell's Angels'?! The regular sized one wanted to know.

"I think it may have been The Duke of Edinburgh." I told him.

"If you haven't got permission from the something-something Avon Chapter something-something, you'll have to surrender your colors, and never call yourselves Hell's Angels again!" he told us.

"What colors?" Bob asked,

"My color is Pink!" I injected, but was mostly ignored.

"Your Jackets and ensigns," he replied.

"Not much chance of that." Bob told him.

"You'll both be in big trouble if you don't!" he warned us, and as if to emphasize his partner's ultimatum big Lurch growled, took another swig out of the bottle of Coca-Cola he had been drinking, and smashed it on top of his own head. A mixture of blood and coca-cola ran down and obscured his dopey features.

"Well that will teach us won't it?" I exclaimed, Then I picked up my coffee to prevent Lurch spilling it as he climbed onto the table and went to sleep. We took our coffee to another table as far away from the unconscious giant as possible, followed by his bewildered mate.

"If you don't surrender your colors peacefully we'll be forced to take them by force!" he persisted.

"Do you really think you're up to it?" I inquired.

"Oh, I won't be on my own," he warned, next time I'll have 40 or 50 real Hell's Angels with me!"

"Well I could tell you that we'll have a couple of hundred wrestlers with us," I told him, "but if the rest of your gang is anything like Lurch over there, we'll just bring a couple of crates of coke-cola and let them all do the job for us. – Gotta go now," I told him, 'we've got a proper battle to take care of.'

"We'll make you honoree members of our chapter every time you're in our territory!" he shouted at our backs as we left the café, "then we won't have to take you're your colors, - Waddya say?!"

"Whatever turns you on Petal!" I told him over my shoulder.

The next incident occurred in Plymouth, and at first we thought that Dopey and Lurch had indeed made good on their threats. As we approached the arena we saw that there were literally hundreds of motorbikes parked in the car park, and after entering the building discovered about 400 hundred Hell's Angels filling one whole section of the arena. Our opponents that night were tailor made for us, as far as our regular audience was concerned. And but for the exception of an old Lady who always sat in the front row who always took a swing at me with one of her crutches, they were very vocal, but not overly violent. But, what would happen tonight? Especially as we were wrestling against the Borg twins who were always fan favorites with the regular audience, now that their numbers were swollen with a few hundred thugs of the highway who were born to be wild?! The Borg twins entered the ring first, and the audience erupted with shouts and cheers that shook the building. Bob and I took a deep breath each and stepped out of the safety of the dressing room, and into harm's way as we strode purposefully towards the ring. The fans erupted even louder and more sincerely than they had for the twins, but with a strange mixture of sounds that were somewhat unfamiliar to us. The mystery revealed itself as we were introduced by the M.C. and as we threw our arrogant poses all the Hell's Angels in the building leapt to their feet and their loud cheers all but drowned out the boos, hisses and screams of abuse that we had both expected and craved from our regular audience. As the match began both Bob and I realized that this was not going to be as easy as we would have normally expected. To begin most of my contests I would infuriate the audience by dancing, skipping and prancing gracefully around the ring and easily confounding my opponents efforts to come to grips. This in itself would provoke the audience to voice their protests to the full as they became as frustrated as my opponent who seemed pathetically unequipped to catch me or pin me down. Soon my opponent might appeal to the referee, or make a gesture of helpless apology to the fans. That would be the second I was waiting for to go on the attack and smash my opponent into oblivion, then I would beat on him unmercifully until the fans were hoarse from screaming their disapproval. Tonight my tried, tested, and foolproof formula couldn't possibly work, for as loudly as the regular fans voiced their disapproval The Hell's Angels cheered even louder for us to rag, bag and shag the unfortunate twins. The match for we four wrestlers was becoming hard work, as the real contest began to be waged between the regular fans and the Motorway-Morons who were fast winning the battle for the most volatile vocals. As the match progressed the Hell's Angels became more and more animated, and our regular fans became more and more intimidated by them. Very soon our regular fans seemed to be sitting on their hands while their mouths were taped tightly shut. 'Time to change tactics!' I thought as I dragged the battered twin I had been beating on to his feet and told him,

"Take over its all yours." I imagined that his revenge on me would be extremely brutal after all the torture I had subjected him to, but all he did was to grab me in a simple headlock. That turned out to be more than enough for our motorbike friends, who leapt out of their seats and invaded the ring with twin murder on their minds. The twins were terrified; they had never been subjected to the hostility from the fans that Bob and I merely took for granted. In spite of their terror one of the twins had the presence of mind to dive out of the ring, grab the crutch from the old Lady in the front row. He leaped back into the fray swinging the crutch around his head like a Viking battleaxe. It bought the twins a little time, but it was Bob and I who must take full credit for saving the good guys arses that night as we both began bowling the crazed leather clad hooligans out of the ring telling them to leave the twins to us. And that they would get us disqualified if they didn't get out of the ring and return to their seats at once.

"Okay, but kill them for us!!!" they demanded as they reluctantly departed. I immediately took a submission on one of the twins, and then Bob won the contest for us by submitting the other the moment the match recommenced. The Hell's Angels cheered so loud they must have shaken Valhalla, as our regular fans silently vacated the building as quickly as they were able.

"See you in the pub later!" I called to our leather clad louts, as I pointed vaguely to where there may or not have been a local bar, and we made our way back to the dressing room without further delay. Even in the safety of the dressing room the twins were still trembling and as white as sheets, so white in fact that I suggested that they might change their names to 'The Casper Twins'.

The only Hell's Angels I actually gave a Fig about was Bob and I, and we were doing great for all of Joint Promotions. Until one day Max Crabtree told me that in spite of the fact that he couldn't get enough of me, for all the Scottish shows he promoted, he didn't like Bob and was not going to use him any more. Why he didn't like Bob I don't know, neither Bob nor Max ever gave me a reason.

The next time I was wrestling in Aberdeen, I thought that Max must have changed his mind as when I arrived at The Music Hall where the matches were taking place. There were posters plastered everywhere with Hell's Angels in the main event. The show was to be televised so it really seemed as though Bob had been reinstated. I soon found out that Max had teamed me up with Steve Young, who was the son of veteran wrestler Roy Bull Davies.

"Young Steve will make you a much better tag-partner in The Hell's Angels than Barnes." Max told me. - I was furious,

"Its not going to happen," I told him, "Bob is my partner in the Hell's Angels; I'll wrestle with other tag partners if you won't use Bob, but, not as Hell's Angels!" I added adamantly.

As well as the initial TV match I was billed with Steve Young as one of the Hell's Angels for the rest of my Scottish tour, there was little I could do about that as all the posters in each town advertising the events were already in print. I immediately phoned my attorney, Duncan Straker and told him that I wanted 'The Hell's Angels' name copyrighted. He complied, and I informed Max that the name was now protected and could only be used by myself and a partner of my choice – and that choice was Bobby Barnes and definitely not Steve Young.

In no time flat I had to call Duncan Straker and Joint Promotions, and once again complain that Steve Young and his own 'new partner' were wrestling billed as 'The Hell's Angels', but this time it was not for Max Crabtree but an independent promoter named Orig Williams.

Orig Williams was a flimflam man who could have even given the one and only Sir Athol Oakley a run for his money when it came to total bullshit. He was the sort of person who would rather climb a giant Redwood tree that grew out of the pinnacle of Mount Everest to tell a lie, than to tell the truth standing on the ground. I had only ever heard of him a year or so earlier when it was brought to our attention that he had been billing all of Joint Promotions biggest names on his own shows. I had been billed along with Mick McManus, Jackie Pallo, Big Gwyn Davies and many more. All the big names appeared in huge block letters on his posters advertising his shows, but in tiny letters it stated that these big TV stars had been 'invited' to take part in each night's tournament. All the venues he promoted would be bursting at the seams with fans who all imagined that they were going to witness the show of the century. But they were all sadly disappointed when Orig and his ragtag band of cronies all entered the ring without a single superstar in sight. Then Orig himself would begin his spiel,

"As you all know," he would begin, "all the big name television stars have been 'invited' to take part in tonight's tournament - unfortunately, all these so called superstars – all these TV cowards have ignored our invitation. They were challenged, and were too frightened to accept our challenge, but never mind, we who were brave enough to wrestle here tonight will give you the best night of wrestling you have ever seen. Our main event tonight will be Mat Burns versus Les Bean in a World Heavyweight Championship contest." The crowd would boo and create blue murder, but Orig already had their money, it wasn't his fault, he blamed the TV wrestlers for not attending and that was that.

That was that, until Joint Promotions got wind of his activities, and 'Orrible Orig ended up in court, which promptly put pay to that particular scam. But now Orig had what he claimed to be a legitimate Superstar. He teamed Steve Young up with Dave Shilito, who promptly changed his name to 'Bad Boy' Bobby Baron – can't get much closer to 'Bad Boy' Bobby Barnes can you?! Especially when it's printed under HELL'S ANGELS in huge poster domineering letters on all his advertising posters. When challenged, Orig claimed legitimacy on the grounds that Steve Young had indeed appeared as a member of the Hell's Angels on television, and a number of other matches partnered by Adrian Street. I thought it very fortunate that I had already copyrighted the name, as once again Orig Williams found himself back in a court of law and was prohibited from using The Hell's Angels name on any of his future shows.

WHENEVER A MAN DOES A THOROUGHLY STUPID THING IT IS ALWAYS FROM THE NOBLEST MOTIVE -Oscar Wilde

Before our divorce was even complete Jean was pregnant again, and by the time I was once again a free man, she gave birth to a lovely little dark skinned Girl she named Natasha. It seemed that if there was one thing that Jean could do even better than produce beautiful wrestling gowns, it was to produce beautiful children - three for me, and one for Guinness-Head. One would think that Jean at last would have been happy, but unfortunately for Linda and I she wasn't. The cause of her latest disgruntlement was caused by the holiday that Linda and I had planned to go on to Africa and the Canary Islands.

"You never took me for a holiday like that!" she complained.

"Well maybe you can take one like that with Guinness-Head now instead." I suggested.

"He doesn't earn the same kind of money you do - we can't afford a holiday like that!" she told me irritably.

"Well that's hardly my fault is it?" I replied. She moaned so frequently about our planned vacation that when a little later Guinness-Head announced that he was going to wrestle in Greece I suggested that she might accompany him,

"Linda and I will mind the kids while you're gone," I told her, "even if I'm away wrestling up north they can come with me."

"We can't afford the air fare for me to go to Greece too." Jean told me.

"If you want to go to Greece with Guinness-Head for a holiday I'll pay for your air fare myself." I offered, she seemed to like the idea, and I thought at last we had found an amiable solution. Sadly that was not to be, unbeknown to me at that time Guinness-Head, who had wrestled in Greece before had already written to his Greek girlfriend, and had arranged for her to pick him up from the airport when he arrived there. As you can imagine, having Jean in tow would tend to complicate things a tad, and to cut a long story short, Guinness-Head had no alternative than to cancel what would have been for him a fairly lucrative tour. Although it was a genuine mistake on my part I realized in retrospect that I should have known better.

Guinness-Head's wrestling hero was Johnny Kwango, although it was not for his wrestling prowess that he was idolized, but instead for his dubious boast of fathering 14 illegitimate children both in Britain and on the Continent. It was one of Guinness-Head's greatest ambitions to surpass Kwango's infamous record and he worked on the task diligently. Now that Jean's Greek holiday was no longer in the works she once again began to show her resentment that Linda and my holiday was still scheduled. She obviously discussed her feelings with Guinness-Head who came up with a master plan that was guaranteed to completely sabotage my holiday too.

For whatever reason neither Jean nor Guinness-Head liked Linda at all, they were also well aware that concerning me, Linda was extremely jealous and very possessive. The plan they devised was both treacherous and spiteful.

As you may recall, whenever fans of either sex wanted to contact any wrestler, they could do so by writing to Dale Martin Promotions, and the mail would be placed on a large board so that it could be checked by all the wrestlers whenever they went there. As I also stated, that mail service was not common knowledge as far as the wrestlers family was concerned for obvious reasons. As chance would have it, Linda decided to stay up north in order to put the finishing touches to a flat that we wanted to let in one of our many houses, so the spiteful plan that Jean and Guinness-Head hatched would not have worked for them anyway. But, what was supposed to happen was, that as soon as Linda and I opened the front door to Telford Avenue, when next we returned from up north, the first thing we would see would be the mail addressed to me that Guinness-Head had brought from Dale-Martins' office, and placed on top of the telephone in the hallway. One of the letters in particular was obviously from a Female fan, and was placed in front of all the others. I was furious, even though there was a lot of jealousy in our business there was still rules and boundaries that were not crossed, and wrestlers did not do that to each other. I put my luggage in my lounge then went into the communal kitchen to make myself a meal, and then carried both my food and mail into the communal dinning room so that I could read the mail while I ate. The letter in question turned out to be not only extremely incriminating but downright disgusting. How I could have been so careless as to 'accidentally' leave it on the communal dinning room table after eating, and then retiring to my own lounge to watch TV I don't know?!

I am certain that Jean's loud screams of outrage could have been heard by Linda who was busy working in a flat in Manchester over 200 miles away, I also wondered if Linda could hear me laughing. The letter had been from a sex mad female, just as Jean and Guinness-Head had supposed. But the lady in question explained in minute blow by blow detail of the debauched evening she had just spent with Guinness-Head, and then expressed a very strong desire to do likewise with my good self the very next time I found myself in her vicinity. Thanks – but no thanks! Guinness-Head's infamous promiscuity was known to be as rabid as the most debauched in the wrestling business, and he openly kept company with some real horrors, which prompted my quote that claimed, 'Guinness-Head would happily stick his prick where Hell's Angels fear to tread.'

Although I like this quote by David Bissonette much better -

'When a man steals your wife, there is no better revenge than to let him keep her.'

****

Our trip to The Canary Islands and from there our cruise down the coast of West Africa, visiting Gambia and Senegal was excellent. After our return to the Canaries we also flew over to Aauin in the Spanish Sahara.

It was late January by the time we returned to Britain, I had one of the best suntans I had ever had in my life before, which I thought would contrast beautifully with all my sun starved opponents. Now wouldn't you think that by now I should have known better?! McManus had billed me against the very black Johnny Kwango every single night until my super suntan was history. You've got to give him credit – he never missed a trick!

MARY QUANT

There had been various sport teams cutting records, now it was our turn, - 'from 'The Wrestler' magazine. –

'It had to happen I suppose, after the remarkable success of those teams of singing professional footballers whose fast-selling records have zoomed to the top of the pop charts. Now a dozen of our leading stars have teamed up to burst into song, cutting a disc which they hope will at least make the 'top ten'. The team of singing wrestlers comprises – Mick McManus, Steve Logan, Mike Marino, Adrian Street, Spencer Churchill, Johnny Kwango, Tibor Szakacs, Bruno Elrington, Robby Baron, Steve Veidor and Sean Regan.

Billed as 'The Gladiators' they are featured singing that favorite song of yesterday, 'Tiptoe through the Tulips' and the record is being released immediately on Pye label [Pye 7N45155] I'm sorry to learn that someone hasn't come along with a trendy lyric about wrestling for them to sing, but I wish the melodious-matmen every success, despite having to rely on a musical 'oldie.' Incidentally, prime mover in the project to put wrestlers on the record player is Cyril Black, the music publisher and record producer – who also happens to be a keen wrestling fan.

From the 'Daily Mirror.' –

As Tiptoe through the Tulips is given a sharp new twist.
HOW DOES THIS GRAB YOU?
AND now ladies and gentlemen, in the assorted trunks a group we know you'll fall for – The Gladiators. You will thrill to their high notes, tremble at their low notes and submit to their gentle charm. Mick McManus has collected several hundredweight of top wrestling talent to tear into that lovely old favorite 'Tiptoe through the Tulips'.

This write-up appeared in the newspaper after the 'Eamonn

Andrews Show',

'You could almost hear a pin fall.' Eleven of TV's top wrestlers had gathered in a recording studio – to switch from hate to harmony. The name of the Sunday morning choir with a difference, 'The Gladiators', and the song on which their vocal muscles were flexed: 'Tiptoe through the Tulips.' Whatever would Tiny Tim have to say?

PUNCH.

There was a nasty moment as they lined up behind the microphones. Adrian Street, sporting a velvet coat and feather-fan, took the centre of the stage, Big Bruno Elrington asked if he was going to stay there – and Adrian challenged: "You try to move me." Just when a cross-buttock or double-nelson looked imminent, technicians stepped in to beg for calm. And the singing? Not technically brilliant, but it had plenty of punch.

The Pye record comes out at the weekend; they're hoping it will be a knockout.

By reporter, Elizabeth Harris.

I very much wanted a brand new look for my appearance on 'The Eamonn Andrews Show,' I was going to be one of 11 wrestlers who would be on stage singing 'Tiptoe through the Tulips' and 'When we all go in the Ring' on the flip side, and I wanted to make certain that it would be me and me alone who would be 'seen' while we sang. I had begun using antique Ostrich feather fans that either matched, or contrasted nicely with my dress theme for each night's appearance in the ring. My favorite fan of all was the delightful old Lady who had a fantastic shop in Portobello Antique Market where she sold elegant costumes of yesteryear. Her speciality and passion was the fans, every time I bought one from her she would demonstrate how it was used in her day,

"The fans have a language of their own," she would explain, "if a Lady was interested in a Gentleman who had been paying special attention to her at a ball, she would use the fan like this," and she would demonstrate her seductive technique, "on the other hand if you were not interested in his advances, the fan would be used so." She'd conclude. She really was a treasure and I would have loved to have seen her in her prime.

Although I had already purchased a dozen fans, each to compliment one or more of my favorite costumes, I would never miss the opportunity to pay the elegant old Lady a visit whenever I found myself close by on a Saturday morning. I was always looking for ideas, and my delightful fan Lady handed me a gem when next I paid her a visit,

"Oh, I was hoping you'd come by today," she told me, "look what I have for you." And she presented me with a beautiful Silver-Fox fur stole.

Immediately I began designing a costume in my mind onto which this beautiful stole would put the finishing touch, and with 'The Eamonn Andrews Show' barely a week away I had no time to lose. I designed my new gown, made a pattern, cut it out, then it was poor Linda's turn. The decorations I wanted on it were insane for the very limited time we had before the show. In fact the night before, Linda playing the perfect Fairy Godmother worked all night sewing rhinestones and crystal-cut luster drops all over it, and never slept a wink, just so that Cinderella would go to the ball looking fantastic.

The gown and I were soon to perform an encore TV appearance on 'The Russell Harty Show' where 'Baby Doll' Carol Baker fell in love with the new gown,

"I love Silver-Fox," she told me, "it's my absolute favorite." She also told me after my appearance that 'I was simply charming.' 'Well that's a new one.' I thought.

During my interview with Russell Harty he asked me a number of leading questions concerning the reality, or lack thereof, concerning my profession. Questions I had heard so many times before, questions I was tired of answering. But when he suddenly Pearl Harbored me, by suggesting that he and I wrestle each other on a mat that had already been lain out at the back of the stage for that very purpose, the alarm bells began to ring very loud indeed.

I did not trust Russell Harty at all, he had been asking too many compromising questions. What I feared most was the fact that it might be possible to re-edit the show in such a way that he could challenge me to pin him, or submit him after the wrestling had concluded. And, if I hadn't done either, he could then claim that I wasn't able to, which would strongly suggest that professional wrestling was not real. Let's face it if the show was re-edited in such a way that showed me unable to beat Russell Harty how real could pro wrestling be?!

As we both made our way to the wrestling mat, Harty removed his jacket and struck what he imagined a wrestling pose to be – and I was struck by a dilemma. I did not want to injure this Clown, but at the same time I did not want give him the opportunity to injure my reputation, or the reputation of professional wrestling. As I joined him on the mat I spun him into a very painful 'Chicken-wing', a hold that could cripple him if I chose to apply full pressure. I applied just enough to get the result I desired, a loud squawk from Harty as he collapsed onto the mat, and then to restore the lighthearted mood, I gave him a great smacking kiss on the cheek while he was still tied up and unable to resist. The audience roared with laughter – the mood preserved, as a shaky and disheveled Russell Harty followed me off the mat and back to the interview area, where dear Russell had another battle on his hands – trying to regain his composure.

When I returned to back stage and rejoined Carol, just before she made her entrance Spike Milligan burst out of his dressing room yelling,

"THAT KISS – THAT KISS – HA-HA – THAT WAS AMAZING!!!"

As Carol Baker made her way on stage, Spike dragged me towards the Greenroom where our marathon drinking binge began, where it ended I will never know. After the show was over Spike must have taken me to at least half of his favorite London waterholes. And, knowing Spike he probably visited the other half on his own after he had dropped me off at my home, where I was too legless to exit the hired taxi without the aid of both the taxi driver and Spike.

To match my new long gowns I had wanted to wear long metallic lame' tights, but the gold and silver metallic fabric that my trunks were made of did not have sufficient elasticity to work at all well for making tights. After much frustrating trial and error I found that the only way I could cosmetically achieve the look I wanted was to wear three or four pairs of extra large Mary Quant metallic tights one on top of each other in order to obtain the metallic effect and erase the transparency. The major drawback was that for the purpose I had in mind, the tights were really too fragile and rarely lasted more than one or two contests. For economy sake a new pair of tights that would be worn on top tonight would probably be worn underneath tomorrow's new tights and so on, this usually worked out okay, until one night on TV.

I was wrestling against Scotland's Bill Ross, who I considered to be an excellent opponent for a television contest. He was a good wrestler, with plenty of fire and would prove to be a handful, which I really appreciated for a memorable TV encounter. Thanks to Mary Quant's fragile metallic tights it turned out to be one of the most memorable TV encounters in wrestling's TV history. We must have been halfway through our contest, and I had been punishing the plucky Scot unmercifully. I had him flat on his back and was in the process of twisting his left arm in a way that would make a pretzel look to it's laurels, when to my horror I spied a very large ladder prominently displaying itself in the left knee area of my metallic Gold Tights. I had wrestled hard to get the crowd of angry fans just where I wanted them. But I knew only too well that when the damage to my fancy tights caught the attention of just one of those disgruntled fans, he would not hesitate in blowing the whistle, and then everyone in the audience would be screaming things like,

"OH – SWEETY, YOU'VE LADDERED YOUR TIGHTS – ETC – ETC – ETC!!!" I had to think fast!

I pushed my knee close to my opponents face, while I made a nasty sneering face of my own, so that the fans when they saw me speak, would imagine that I was taunting my helpless victim. What I was really doing was instructing what I wanted him to do in way of retaliation,

"Can you see that hole in my tights?" I asked, then instructed, "I want you to grab hold and tear them to shreds."

Bill blinked and replied, "No, I daren't."

"You dare not!" I assured him, "rip them or I'll smash the crap out of you."

I had made my mind up that one of two scenarios was about to take place. One was – if my opponent refused to take advantage of the damaged tights, I would leap up, point the ladder in the tights out myself to the referee, then blame my opponent for causing the damage, and then attack him in the most vicious way I could devise. Or, and this choice was my favorite, was for Bill to escape from his present predicament by purposely attacking my tights, blatantly taking full blame on himself. This would not only gain himself immense approval from the fans, but would then give me the excuse to completely go insane with fury, and finish the match with even more viciousness than even I had resorted to in the past.

Fortunately, Bill took my threat seriously, and he attacked those tights with more fury than the Valkyries could have managed even in the height their prime. The crowd's response was huge, so much so, that their encouragement drove my opponent to even greater heights of destruction. Soon my tights were in taters, I pulled down my trunks that were worn over the tights. The TV camera wobbled violently so as to avoid showing a possible striptease, but instead I tore what was left of my tights away and replaced my trunks. The crowd whistled and hollered in glee, but not for long, I allowed my temper to explode in a way that would have made the eruption of Mount Vesuvius in 79 AD look like a damp firecracker, and rained havoc on my opponent that would have done credit to that very same volcano.

Did that match of the flimsy Metallic tights cause a lasting impact on the fans?

To answer that question I am going to leap forward in time over two decades.

I was returning to the States from Japan, and had decided to spend a few days in Britain en-route; I traveled on the tube from Heathrow Airport to Victoria Railway Station and became aware of most everyone in my compartment staring at me. I looked at one of the closest oglers and raised my eyebrows inquiringly,

"Didn't you used to be Adrian Street?" he asked me,

"Yes I was - in fact I believe I still am." I responded.

That caused just about everyone in the compartment to respond,

"Yes, I was sure it was you!" and then,

"Oh, I remember that time on television, when you got your gold tights ripped off, WOW – were you mad? – I've never seen anyone so angry!!!" That was the theme all the way to Victoria, I hadn't set foot in Britain for more than a decade – it was more than two decades since the last time I had wrestled on British television - but, not only was I remembered, it was the match of the metallic tights that were responsible for the highlight. I have to say that from the late 60s on I was very grateful to Mary Quant for her invention of Hot-pants and the Mini-skirt, but Mary, Dear Mary, thanks for those flimsy metallic tights, I rated them right up there with your hot-pants and Mini-skirts. They were directly responsible for one of my most memorable TV matches and I couldn't have possibly done it without you!

A DRINK OUT OF THE BOTTLE

Brian Glover, better known in the wrestling business as, 'Leon Arras – The man from Paris,' but actually hailed from Barnsley in Yorkshire. Brian was a second generation wrestler; his Father was a promoter and wrestled under a mask as 'The Red Devil'. Brian was also a school teacher, and it was in this role that he was cast in the movie 'Kes' a couple of years earlier. Although the movie was about a young boy and his pet Kestrel, in my opinion and in many others it was Brian's performance that stole the show and eventually drew him out of wrestling and into movieland.

Amongst his many other accomplishments Brian was a playwright whose play 'A drink out of the bottle' was one of six TV plays in 'The Sporting Tales series.'

The expression 'A drink out of the bottle' was a sarcastic retort used by wrestlers after a match against an opponent who had totally dominated the contest so thoroughly, that they claimed they had even deprived them of a drink of water between rounds. An example would be say, upon entering the dressing room after a match against 'Stiff' Cliff Beaumont, and I was asked by the other wrestlers,

"How did your match go?" my reply would probably have been,

"Fucking awful, I didn't even get a drink out of the bottle!"

I thought the play had a very neat storyline, especially as the only real villain in it was obviously based on my character, and that character could only be played by me. In fact the whole play could have been written for me, and if anything took my character another notch forward when it came to pushing the fan's button. In spite of my very exotic facial make-up, before playing 'Lucky Day' in that movie, I had never worn lipstick, after the movie the fans expected lipstick, and that is what they got.

Of course most of the wrestlers thought it was way over the top, until one night one of them came rushing into the dressing room and shook my hand in gratitude so hard he almost dislocated my shoulder,

"Thank you – thank you!!!!" he told me.

"Thank me for what?" I wanted to know.

When I got home last night my Wife found lipstick on the collar of my shirt, I had to think quickly, and I put the fault on you!" he replied.

After that I became the standard excuse when disgruntled wives found make up on any over garments, or undergarments of their wayward spouses. On many occasions I had been almost set upon by wrestler's wives who have warned me 'to leave their husbands alone'.

At that time there was no VCRs and such, so there was no way of recording the film when it was shown on BBC2, so in order to be able to watch it myself, I did the unthinkable and phoned in sick instead of driving all the way to Lincoln where I would have been wrestling that night. The moment the movie ended, the phone rang and I answered it to Diana Dors, who had also been watching the movie,

"You were fantastic!" she told me, and went on to tell me of her favorite scene.

In the tradition of pro wrestlers it was common practice to 'take the piss' out of each other, especially out of the young wrestlers new to the business. In the movie my character took his character very seriously indeed, his real name was Cyril Jones, but he lived and breathed his professional persona 'Lucky Day' twenty-four hours a day.

Lucky accused the newcomer of being a Mummy's boy, he ridiculed him relentlessly, and nicknamed him 'Christopher Robin'. The newcomer was a second generation wrestler who knew more about the game that his tormentor gave him credit for, and retaliated by calling Lucky Day by his real name Cyril Jones. This really dented Lucky's ego, so much so that he vowed to put the young upstart out of the wrestling business in their upcoming match that was due to take place the very next night in the Fairfield Hall.

"The expression on your face when the new kid called you Cyril," Diana Dors told me, here even she seemed almost lost for words, but then added, "I've seen violence, and been around the most violent characters in the World," she told me, but I've never seen more violence than that expressed on a human beings face before – not ever!"

I was highly flattered, especially as I knew that one of her best friends was Violet Kray, Mother of the notorious Twins, Ronnie and Reggie, both of which were also good friends of Diana's.

That vicious look was not lost on the wrestling audience either, as for many months after the film had been aired I would be greeted by the fans whenever I entered the ring every night with calls of,

"COME ON CYRIL!" As though that would upset me in real life as much as it had appeared to in the movie. On the contrary, once again I was highly flattered – almost as flattered as I was when I read the write-up for the film in 'TV Times' which accompanied a full page photo of me and was headlined with –

'GLITTER-BOY ADRIAN STREET STEALS THE SERIES!'

Possibly as a result of my success in that movie I was contacted by the Sunday newspaper 'The People', who wanted to write my life story that would appear in their paper over a couple of weeks. I received a fairly hefty check for my interview, then another one for performing in a TV advert to publicize it. While at the TV studio I met John Gregson who invited me to dinner, and possibly best of all I was introduced to Dennis Hutchinson. Denis was an alcoholic freelance photographer, who was to take the photos for the newspaper. We became great friends, and his offer to take photos to accompany any scheme or event that occurred, or that I could invent was one that I was destined to take full advantage of.

CLOWN PRINCE OF THE HIGHLANDS

It seemed that the bigger the draw you became, the less your physical size meant to the promoters. One night I may be wrestling against an opponent who was several pounds lighter than myself, the next night I may be wrestling against a very large heavyweight. This often posed a problem, as even when I wrestled against a heavyweight that I was on friendly terms with outside the ring, that big man complex would most always surface inside the ring. This made what could have been a very good contest much harder to achieve. Possibly they may have been embarrassed to allow a much smaller man to take advantage of them, especially, as in my case that man was a villain who relied on arrogance and aggression rather than foul tactics. To allow an opponent to completely domineer me was something that I could not allow to happen, never mind how big my adversary happened to be, and this could often result in a nasty struggle.

The heavyweight idiot of the Highlands, Andy Robbins had his own way of dealing with his embarrassment – if his intelligence, or lack thereof allowed for such an emotion.

Without a doubt, Andy Robbins was a Scottish Idol, worshiped by every living wrestling fan north of the border. In order to expand his super hero status, Scotland's Saint George had been fed a concentrated diet of Giants and Dragons, who to the delight of his fans he would vanquish easily with the help of his own patented Excalibur, which came in the form of an Indian-Deathlock he renamed his 'Powerlock'.

On one occasion Andy was wrestling against the Giant Hawaiian King Curtis Iaukea, who towered almost a foot taller than the Scot, and weighed in the region of 400 pounds. If he thought the match warranted it Curtis liked to spout blood,

"Red makes green." Was his motto. But he made a terrible mistake using the blade for the sake of idiot Andy. The silly Scotsman got so excited as he imagined the effect the blood would have on his adoring fans that he was unable to contain himself, and kicked the Giant Hawaiian in the face just as he was about to cut himself. The force of the kick caused the blade to all but scalp Curtis; blood cascaded out of his head like a fountain, and the 400 pound Polynesian monster was almost carried from the ring with a huge flap of bloody flesh, that resembled a couple of pounds of raw liver hanging right over one eye.

Andy often transported a huge steel wheel off a railway truck that would be carried into the ring by about a half dozen men, and before his wrestling match commenced, then he would challenge his opponent or anyone in the audience to lift the monstrosity to arms length above their head. After it had been attempted by whoever felt up to the task, and they had all failed miserably, Andy would step up to the weight, heave it up to his chest and then jerk it up to arms length while all his admirers cheered themselves dumb. Even if a powerhouse like Gordienko was capable of lifting it, he would most likely pretend he couldn't in order to make the local hero look great. Due to the fact that a very strong weightlifter turned up one night and almost managed to get it up, Andy welded a number of barbell plates to it in the most un-uniformed manner he could devise in order to make it both heavier and unbalanced. He then practiced with it daily until he knew exactly where to grasp it in a way that counterbalanced the vastly lopsided steel wheel, and after that no one ever came close to emulating the Highland Hercules.

After the Scottish fans had witnessed what I was capable of doing to their own Lightweight Champion of the World, George Kidd, one would think that me pitted against their hero Andy Robbins, who outweighed me by about 60 pounds of muscle, would be for them a match made in heaven, but thanks to Andy's ego and stupidity that was not to be. But, in his defense my own ego played a very large part in sabotaging what could have been something spectacular.

As you may recall, it was Andy's lust for the limelight that caused him to mimic, and make fun of George Kidd in order to divert the attention of the wrestlers in the dressing room away from the charismatic Champion and onto himself. His problem with me amounted to the same scenario, but it was the fan's attention he craved to divert from the tremendous response my appearance would always provoke. His response was exactly the same as his response to George Kidd; - he took the piss by mimicking my mannerisms to the very best of his lame-brained ability. This would delight his fans who would explode with laughter at my expense, but as I've said before, I don't do comedy – 'I only laugh when it hurts.'

I could have aided lame-brain's quest tremendously if I had exhibited the distress his impersonating was designed to cause me. But I've been down that road before, and I don't play that game. Instead, I wouldn't even acknowledge his presence, I would remain in my corner, yawning, checking my nails, anything but looking at my opponent who was doing his best silly copycat act. Did my lack of response bring him back to the realm of sensibility? No chance! The bell would ring to start our match, instead of him adopting his own character he would continue his piss taking by skipping gaily around the ring, blowing kisses, and basically doing what I would do myself at the beginning of my matches. I remained immobile, I refused to show that I was even conscious that there was another person in the ring – time was on my side. I knew that the crowd would soon become bored by the complete lack of action. They did become bored, and they booed me for it – but that's okay, I'm a villain they're supposed to boo me. What they needed now was for their hero to attack me and tear me apart.

Eventually, as I knew he would, he tried, but I was not there. Andy may have had the size and power, but not my speed, agility, or – and most importantly, my ability to be able to wrestle.

"COME ON SQUASH THE JESSE, ANDY!" The fans screamed.

Without my assistance Andy couldn't do it.

"COME ON ANDY, SMASH THE COCKY SASANACH!" They'd yell.

Then eventually,

"COME ON ANDY – WHAT'S WRONG TONIGHT ANDY?!!!" Andy's distress would be immense – that's okay, then I would gaily skip around the ring invoking groans of frustration from the crowd. Andy would attempt to grab me, he couldn't do it – and even if he did he was unable to secure me for more than a second, because I could actually wrestle and he couldn't. As I skipped and Andy had no other remedy for stopping me, he would sometimes resort to going back to mimicking my skip. But the most he ever achieved by that tactic may have been a half hearted snigger from a thoroughly bored and disappointed audience. I would punish Andy relentlessly in this manner for the remainder of the contest. Then would come the time for Andy to win with his patented submission hold which he called 'The Power-lock', his own version of an 'Indian Deathlock'. Andy's legs were large and muscular, and just allowing him to secure it properly was often very painful. But I suppose in retaliation for my putting him in his place, the first time he applied it on me I thought he made it much tighter than it needed to be. I knew that I had the ability to wrestle my way out of it just to teach him a lesson, but I thought of a much better method of retribution. Instead of screaming the arena down, as was normal for an opponent to do in order to demonstrate how lethal the Scotsman's 'Power-Lock' was, I merely shifted myself around in an effort to make myself appear a little more comfortable, but without showing the slightest sign of pain or distress.

"DO YOU SUBMIT?!" The referee shouted.

"AH – UM – I'm really not sure?" I replied. Andy partly stood and then threw himself back in order to maximize the effect of his hold.

"DO YOU SUBMIT?!" The referee repeated.

"Okay – why not indeed?" I replied. As was usual, and usually to the crowd's delight, Andy would be loathe to release his opponent even after a submission from his 'Power-lock' had been secured, instead he would stand up and throw himself back again and again. He began to do that with me, but instead of screaming in agony I engaged the referee in a conversational tone and complained,

"Hey referee, I submitted didn't I, isn't he supposed to release me now?"

Andy got back to his feet and threw himself back once more.

"Okay, that's it – if he does that one more time I will revoke my submission and we'll have to go right back to the beginning of the contest and start again!" I told the referee. The referee broke the hold and I leapt back to my feet – which was something that none of Andy's opponents had ever been capable of after suffering the dreaded Power-lock'. I took a half step forward then staggered dramatically, the crowd reacted by roaring their approval of my apparent injury, but that was just my ruse to give them a little false hope. Next, I bent and straightened my leg a few times before dropping down into my hopping squat which I did all around the ring before I exited the ring. Then I skipped back to the dressing room very much in character with my arms raised as though in victory. The crowed was royally pissed off, but not as much as my opponent, who was right in my face the second he followed me into the dressing room.

"Why didn't you sell my Power-lock properly?!" he almost sobbed, "I've had 30 stone Giants stretchered out of the ring after I've beaten them with my Power-lock!"

"Why didn't you stay in character and wrestle like Andy Robbins, instead of trying to take the piss out of Adrian Street?" I countered. Next night much to my dismay I found that I would be wrestling against Andy again,

"Let's talk about our match." I suggested. After explaining to Andy how much more it would mean, and how much more I would be willing to cooperate if we both remained in our own character, we had a very good match, that I felt would become even better now that he had experienced the vast difference. The next night I was wrestling Andy again, and in contrast to the way I felt about ever setting foot in the ring with him again, I found I was looking forward to our match. But once again I found that I had underestimated my opponent, his stupidity held no bounds, and it seemed that he had learned absolutely nothing from the good match we had had the night before. The third match was an exact reply of the first match in every detail, right down to Andy sobbing in the dressing room,

"Why didn't you sell my Power-lock properly?!"

Revenge is sweet even when it's against an idiot, and a perfect opportunity presented itself the night that Andy decided to bring his lopsided steel railway wheel to our next contest. Initially I hadn't planned on upsetting the egotistical git, but even under these new circumstances he was unable to behave himself.

The wheel was carried to the ring by six strong men who

grunted under the strain of carrying, and then lifting it into the ring. Once the steel monstrosity had been rolled to the centre of the ring Andy wasted no time in challenging me to lift it. After disrobing I walked over to the wheel, and after examining it I declared that it was much too dirty. Especially after Andy Robbins' filthy paws had been all over it, and there was no way I could be induced to even touch it until it had been thoroughly cleansed. Andy's second was only too happy to oblige, and he used Andy's own towel to polish the wheel until it almost gleamed.

Well I could write another dozen pages describing how I would approach the wheel, make ready to go for a lift only to walk away with yet another lame excuse. To be perfectly honest I knew for a fact that I would have been unable to even lift the wheel off the ground, let alone jerk it to arms length above my head, even if my very life depended on it. The axle of the wheel was so thick that my hands could not have found purchase even if I had been blessed with an exceptionally strong grip – which I wasn't.

Finally I agreed that I would promise to make an attempt, but only after Andy Robbins had performed the feat first, in order to prove to me that it could be done, and this whole performance was not an elaborate plan to put me at a disadvantage in our upcoming wrestling contest. Now it was Andy who was only too happy to oblige.

He approached the wheel took a few deep breaths, squatted down, gripped the thick bar, and almost effortlessly heaved it up to his chest, another couple of deep breaths and he hurled the heavy steel wheel to arms length above his head. He held it for a few seconds while the Scottish crowed roared their approval as only they could, before hurling back to the canvas with enough force to make the whole ring rattle and shudder under the impact. The crowd cheered and cheered louder and louder, and the noise only began to diminish after I had been once more challenged to emulate the Highland Hercules' feat of pure strength.

Unfortunately for Hercules he decided for whatever reason to punctuate his latest challenge with another of his dancing, skipping and prancing imitations of yours truly – and yours truly took extreme exception to his crap.

While Andy had performed his lift I had paid special attention to exactly where he had placed his hands in order to learn how best to balance it. I waited once more for Andy to issue his challenge before I charged to the middle of the ring and threw myself onto my back sliding right underneath the wheel in the process. I placed my hands in the same area I had seen Andy grip the bar, and pushed the unwieldy piece of junk to arms length for ten easy reps, before allowing it to drop behind me back onto the mat.

Everyone was stunned, most especially Andy. I could have managed more than ten reps with the weight from that position as I was a champion when it came to bench-press. But I wanted my performance to appear to be as effortless as possible, and did not want to be seen to struggle with the wheel just for the sake of a few more reps.

Andy was livid, especially after I took the microphone, and informed every one that anything big Andy could do standing up, I could do ten times better – even laying on my back.

"You've totally fucked me," Andy complained in the dressing room after the match concluded, "I'll never be able to bring my wheel to this arena again!"

"Pity." I replied.

TOO CLOSE FOR COMFORT

I was driving down the M5 motorway from Manchester to Cheltenham in my Volkswagen Caravan. Bob was sitting in the passenger seat while Linda was behind me, but leaning over my left shoulder as we all chatted the miles away. I kept my speed at around 75, and was just getting ready to overtake a very large truck carrying a load of big metal cylinders when one of them fell off the back of the truck and exploded right in front of us as it hit the road. Instantly the space was filled with huge chunks of shrapnel, impact was unavoidable and the whole top of the cylinder which comprised of a big brass wheel fastened to a heavy lump of jagged cast iron literally blasted my windscreen into smithereens. The huge chunk of jagged metal flew right between our three heads with barely inches to spare and embedded itself in one of the back seats. How it missed all of us I don't know, but we were all liberally showered by an avalanche of tiny crystals of glass blown all over us aided by a 75 mile an hour wind that now gushed into our faces. I screeched onto the hard shoulder and slammed on the brakes as the truck sped on oblivious that part of its cargo was now embedded inside the back of my van. After checking each other out for injuries we found that the only wound sustained by any of us was me, who had just one tiny piece of glass embedded in the edge of my little finger of my left hand, it was a tiny wound but very deep and bled profusely.

We could not believe how well we had all fared under the circumstances, if it had struck any one of us it would have taken our heads off as neatly as a Guillotine blade. If it had hit me anywhere while I was driving I'm certain that we would have all copped it.

We had to stop again further down the road and get a temporary plastic windscreen inserted, the tiny wound in my little finger finally stopped bleeding after it must have cost me a pint of the stuff. That was not all the blood I would shed that day either.

We were wrestling against the Royals, Vic and Bert that night and we all bled, from our hands, legs, arms, shoulders and especially our backs. We turned the whole ring into a bloodbath, the reason we found out was that when the windscreen exploded into our faces both Bob's and my long hair got filled with tiny shards of glass that cascaded invisibly all over the canvas as we wrestled. I'm certain that the already packed arena would have been even more packed if the promoters had advertised that the main event was going to be a tag-team contest fought in a ring full of broken glass.

It seemed to me that the Royal Brothers were a jinx; we had been wrestling against them in Dumfries when the little thug broke a Coca-Cola bottle over my head in a café. Also in Lime Grove Baths when I'd got my right ear cut in half by a fan wielding a heavy umbrella. Again in another London venue when a Lady who was sitting in a ringside seat on a stage became so irate that she charged at me with violence in mind and accidentally dived headlong off the stage into the orchestra-pit. She was knocked out cold and everyone in the arena leapt out of their seats claiming that it was me who had picked her up and thrown her off the stage. The time she had performed her spectacular swan dive, I was standing on the ring apron watching Bob wrestling one of the Royals while waiting for a tag and didn't even see the Lady take the bump. But, everyone in the audience claimed to be a potential witness after I had been arrested and charged with attempted murder. It was only after I saw the unconscious woman laying on the floor about 7 or 8 feet below me, and I jumped down, and cradled her head in my lap that she regained consciousness and told the Lynch mob not to be silly it was her own fault for getting over excited and not looking where she was going.

Nevertheless, it made me feel sick to think that there were 700 people in the audience who would have happily perjured themselves in a court of law in order to punish me for something I didn't do, Especially, as I had another court case hanging over my head at that time.

On that occasion we had not been wrestling against the Royals, but against Johnny Kwango and Leon Fortuna and the venue was Weston-Super-Mare.

SADIST IN SEQUINS

Bob was in the ring wrestling with Kwango, I was on the ring apron doing a little cheerleading, when a middle-aged Greek leapt out of his ringside seat and punched me in the back of my knee. The actual punch wasn't devastating, but unexpected, and it almost pitched me backwards off the apron. The attacker ran back to his seat amid huge cheers from the whole audience which must have sent his warrior spirit soaring, and the battle was on. Every time my attention was centered on the events occurring in the ring I got Pearl harbored by Archimedes, I told him time and again to stay in his seat but the applause he was receiving from all the fans was too much for him to resist.

Towards the end of the match the action inside the ring had become hot and heavy and the crowd reaction was immense. My focus was fully on the action when the Gormless Greek grabbed my left ankle and yanked my feet completely off the ring apron. If I had not got a firm grip on the top rope with both hands I would have probably fallen on top of my attacker, but instead I landed with both shins crashing into the hard steel edge of the apron. The Greek still held onto my left ankle and was pulling with all his might while I clung to the top rope and was struggling to get my ankle free. I had been facing away from him but in an effort to break free I spun around to face him and simultaneously lashed out with my right foot. It struck the hopeless Hoplite under the jaw with such force it nearly turned him upside-down, and almost landed him back into his own ringside seat. I had no more bother that night from the Hero of Greece, he was out like a light. As I said, I didn't have any more bother with the aggressive Aegean that night, but I was sure getting some bother now. Apparently, this Greek hotel and restaurant owner was regarded as a highly respected member of the Weston-Super-Mare community, and his lawyers were the best that money could buy. I was told after I had made my statement to the Police that I would be informed when a court day would be scheduled.

Back to the Royals, - the venue, Madley Street Baths, Hull in Yorkshire. Bob and I were wrestling against the Royals in the last match of the evening, and as you might have gathered that would not be 'a send them home happy match', which in a way was unfortunate as we would be following a very controversial contest.

Kendo Nagasaki accompanied by his 'friend' and manager Gorgeous George Gillett was wrestling against the popular young Welsh Giant, Gwyn Davies in a contest that was causing an uproar. After a series of particularly foul tactics, and more than a little help from his 'friend', carried out behind the referee's back, Nagasaki took the win. He then slid out of the ring and back to the dressing room before the result was announced, or the crowd had a chance to react. But react they did! The crowd was angry, but as they were unable to vent their wrath on the cause of their vexation, they did the next best thing and began to attack Bob and myself the moment we began our march from the dressing room towards the ring. We literally had to fight our way to the battleground. Normally we would work to set the scene with attitude and antics designed to antagonize the crowed, tonight they were already antagonized and we found ourselves in a very dangerous climate we had so far done nothing to provoke.

When the bell rang to begin our contest, Bob entered the ring first while I remained on the ring apron. Even before either of the adversaries in the ring came to grips I felt the most agonizing pain on the outside of my right knee as an old lady in the front row swung a folded up umbrella like a Viking would swing a Battle-axe. The crowd exploded their approval as the bloody old Witch waved the umbrella above her head in triumph.

'OH, SHIT, NOT AGAIN!!!' I thought, as you can imagine I had this thing against being whacked with anything – especially umbrellas. But what was I supposed to do about it? I could hardly chin an old lady, even if I did harbor a very strong desire to do just that. Egged on by the screaming fans, and belief that she was protected by age and gender, the vicious old bag did just as the audience wanted and took another swipe at my legs while I was looking straight at her. I attempted to snatch the heavy weapon and missed, but jumped off the ring apron and snatched the umbrella out of her grasp as she waved it in an attempt to illicit another cheer from the fans. The second I gained possession of the bloody brolly I was attacked from all sides by a number of would be heroes who thought they'd like to get into the act. But now I held the weapon and used it to cut a path through the hooligans and dive through the ropes and into the ring. Once I had gained the very temporary refuge of the ring I wasted no time in destroying the offending brolly by sticking it partway down the top of one of the hollow ring posts and bending it into a horseshoe. The whole audience exploded and charged the ring en-masse; it was time to leave,

"LET'S GO!!!" I called to Bob as I threw the remnants of the umbrella at the crowd and dived after it, and right into a mass of hostile bodies. In a split second I found myself flat on my face on the floor alongside the ring being stomped and kicked by everyone who pushed, pulled and struggled to get theirs in. The 6' 5", 250 pound Welsh Giant Gwyn Davies had watched the action and rushed to my aid, but was dragged down along side me as he too was kicked and stomped unmercifully. Only a matter of minutes earlier, this very same audience had been cheering for Gwyn to win, but now they were more than willing to stomp him flat.

Although the predicament I was in was absolutely no fun at all, I was not getting the kicking that the fans thought I was getting. The reason was there were just so many people trying to kick me that they were all getting in each other's way. I had some of them actually standing on me, who were really protecting me more than injuring me, as they were just as likely to get kicked by the mass of assailants as I was.

Big Gwyn was allowed to his feet first, and as he attempted to pacify the crowd I took advantage of the distraction by forcing my way back up and began kicking shins and ankles to enable myself to cut a path right back to the dressing room door. I checked my self in the mirror in my cubicle, and was pleasantly surprised to find no more damage than a few minor scratches on my face, although the whole of the back of my head was just one big mass of lumps and bruises.

My bath had already been filled for me and I sank into it thankfully, willing it to soak away my bruises. I had hardly began to fully relax when I was ripped out of my reverie by a loud shout from the other wrestlers outside my cubicle,

"ADRIAN – COME QUICK – SOMEBODY HAS GOT LINDA!!!!"

I was out of my bath like a shot, and quickly wrapped a towel around my waist as I tore into the wide corridor that separated the rows of cubicles.

There was Linda and a large red headed thug pulling and pushing each other around, both with their fists full of each others hair. I had been upset that I had been attacked, but the fact that the cowardly scumbags would stoop so low as to attack Linda just to get back at me made me way beyond furious. I grabbed the thug's long fuzzy ginger hair and ripped him away from Linda, but he wouldn't let go, and my efforts seemed to add strength to him tearing Linda's hair out by the roots. I brought my fist and then my knee up into his face, but he still held fast. I punched his ribs but he still wouldn't let go of Linda's long hair, nothing I did would dislodge him. Then I had an idea that I knew would work, and I made a grab between his legs from behind and would have ripped his balls out by their roots – if I could find any?!!!! I thought that someone had beaten me to it, until the penny dropped in sympathy with my jaw when I realized that this tough Guy was a tough GIRL!!!

Straight back to the drawing board – and I came up with a new plan to get Linda's hair free with the minimum amount of damage - by undoing her jeans, and I began to pull them down. She let go of Linda's hair immediately, and as soon as she did, Linda who still had hold of the scruffy Amazon kicked her repeatedly in the face with the toe of the thigh high boots she was wearing,

"One more kick – then you let her go!" I told Linda, and she could have scored a field goal with the bitches head. I then grabbed her by her hair and the seat of her jeans and ran her at the swing doors like a human battering ram that she and Linda had crashed through into the dressing room minutes earlier. She fell onto the floor on the other side of the door, but leapt back up and did her very best to sneer at me in contempt. When I went back to check on Linda I found that for once in their lives all the wrestlers were gob smacked and white faced. I managed to lighten the mood and even raise a laugh when I stated, "Thank goodness Linda was here - that Bitch would have killed me if I'd been on my own!"

THE WORM TURNS

It was as a result of chatting about our life's experiences as a way of passing the time on many of our seemingly endless road trips that I learned of Linda's aversion to school as a young Girl. Her overly timid temperament and the chronic bullying she was forced to endure.

"You should have never, ever allowed anyone to bully you," I told her, "if anyone ever hits you, you hit them back twice as hard."

"I was always too afraid." She replied.

"Afraid of what?" I wanted to know.

"Well if I'd tried to hit them back, they would have beaten me up." She told me.

"They were already beating you up," I explained, "so what did you have to lose by getting a few in yourself?"

"I wouldn't have dared." She assured me.

"Listen," I told her, "If you ever make it easy for a bully to hurt you by not retaliating, what incentive do they have to ever stop doing it? Most Bullies are cowards who can only beat on someone smaller, or weaker than themselves, or someone like you who they know won't fight back. If I ever got into a fight with anyone, even if I lost the fight, I would make damn sure that I hurt the other guy, and I won't stop fighting until I do, never mind how long it takes. As I said, they are cowards, and if they discover that you are going to give them a hard time they will leave you alone and go and find easier prey."

My constant nagging paid off. I had just beaten one of the Borg twins in a match in Wolverhampton and as I was getting my arm raised in victory the other twin entered the ring and issued a challenge with the idea of avenging his badly beaten brother. I accepted his challenge on the condition that they made it a little more interesting for me, by wrestling me in an 'Alaskan tag-team match' which was just me against both of them at the same time. The fans loved the idea as although they knew that either of the twins stood no chance against me on their own, the combination would spell my downfall and put a cocky villain in his place. The Match took place on the very next show and much to the disappointment of the crowd I beat them both handily. The fans were livid, especially as after gloating outrageously at their expense. I disappeared back into the dressing room seconds before any of them could take the law into their own hands and try to score a little retribution on behalf of the two pathetic Brothers who I had so soundly trounced.

Unfortunately for Linda, who was standing outside the dressing room, some of the fans had seen her with me earlier, and one vicious woman walked right up to her, and announced to her comrades,

"She's with him!!!" as she drew back her hand and slapped Linda hard right across her face. Did Linda cringe and cower? Like fuck she did – instead she grabbed the nasty bitch by both ears and ripped her earrings right through them. The woman screamed and ran away as all her companions gave Linda all the space she wanted.

Linda had learned a valuable lesson and I couldn't have been more proud of her.

Then Bob and I were wrestling against the Borg Twins in Cleethorpes, it was a wild action packed match and the fans were on fire. Bob and I won a controversial contest and once again had to run a hostile gauntlet back to the dressing room. Bob was just a couple of steps ahead of me when someone stuck their foot out in front of Bob with the idea of tripping him. But Bob spotted the ploy and instead of tripping over the foot he stomped on it. The perpetrator then punched Bob and got punched right back for his trouble. Then all Hell broke loose and somehow even our opponents got involved, and all four of us shoulder to shoulder punched and kicked our way, inch by inch towards the dressing room door. There was a small gang of men a couple of rows back, one of which leaned right over the seats in front of him and caught me with a stinging blow in my left ear. After we broke free of the mêlée I glanced back and saw the sniper demonstrating to his pals the skillful way he had belted me. He was fully involved in his boasting so much so that he was taken completely by surprise when I crept up behind him, leaned over his shoulder and told him,

"That wasn't clever; anyone can land a punch when the other guy isn't looking."

He turned his head to face me – and when he did I put my hand over his face and slammed his head back into one of the metal pillars that helped to support the roof, to emphasis my point.

"BASTARD!!!" He screamed, and leapt out of his seat into the walkway behind the seats where I was standing. As he landed I kicked him in the balls, grabbed his hair and dragged him on his hands and knees towards the dressing room door. That way I prevented him from retaliating, and upon reaching the door, as I figured he'd been punished sufficiently, I released him as I opened the door, stepped in. I slammed it behind me and walked down a few steps inside to a passage that led to my dressing room. By the time I had washed and dressed I had almost forgotten the incident until I was told that the Police wanted to interview me. I related exactly what occurred but they accused me of understating the beating I had given him,

"I didn't give him a beating." I told them truthfully.

"The side of his mouth is badly torn and one of his eyelids is hanging off." they told me.

"I didn't do anything like that to him!" I stated.

"Well his mouth is ripped to pieces and so is his eyelid, and he said that you did it to him." The Policeman insisted.

"Well he's lying because I DIDN'T!" I insisted right back.

"Well what are we supposed to believe – are you saying that he did it to himself just to get you into trouble?" he asked.

"I haven't got a clue how that happened, only that it wasn't me who was responsible for it." I told him. Finally I was told I could leave, but they assured me that I would be hearing from them again in the very near future, -

'Great,' I thought, 'that's all I need with the 'Weston-Super-Mare' incident still hanging over my head.' I must admit I was mystified. Even though I was well aware that some fans could be inventive, and even extreme when it came to getting revenge on me just for doing my best to entertain them, this was a new one on me. As Linda and I walking up the pier from the arena I said to her,

"I can't understand what the Hell happened to that bloody

idiot, I know I didn't damage him like the police said I did. Shit, that's all I need, more of this crap with that Weston-Super-Mare court case hanging over my head!"

"I did it." Linda replied in a little voice.

"YOU DID WHAT?!" I wanted to know – but in a much louder voice.

She then cleared up the mystery.

When Bob and I were exiting the ring and the fracas broke out, Linda had been standing in the corner next to the dressing room door and had witnessed everything that took place. Her warrior blood was aroused and she really felt the urge to join in, but we all managed to break out of the mob before she was able to make a move. Then after I got back at the guy who was boasting about punching me in the ear, and he tried to attack me as a result. Which in turn resulted in my dragging him on his hands and knees to the dressing room door. I just left him there, and quickly opened the door that led to the dressing rooms before the idiot did anything else stupid. As I closed the door Linda pounced, before dumb nuts had a chance to stand up. Linda straddled him as though she was mounting a Horse, and as she didn't have a bridle handy she hooked the fingers of her left hand into the left side of his mouth and the fingers of her right hand into his right eye and began to tear away for all she was worth. For once I couldn't accuse my accuser of perjury in order to get back at me, because he genuinely believed that it was me who had savaged him. It was only his loud screams and the beginning of the crowd's mass exodus from the arena that caused Linda to cease the mutilation and step back into her corner, leaving her victim sobbing on the floor and oblivious of his attacker's true identity. Now what was I supposed to do? The only way I could give the police a barely believable explanation would be to implicate Linda.

When at last I did appear in Weston-Super-Mare's court of law, even though I was fully aware of the fans animosity, I was surprised by the number of would be perjures present. Fortunately for me in a vain effort to make certain that my coffin was nailed good and tight, most of them added so many outlandish embellishments to their evidence that it made easy work for my attorney to outline the discrepancies and emphasis their prejudice. The final nail in the prosecution's coffin was hammered home when they made the mistake of calling their last two witnesses who completely blew their chance of nailing me when they both came up with the novel idea of actually telling the truth. The prosecution's case just disintegrated. The last two witnesses were a married couple named Ken and Beryl Burchall, who I credit with turning the tables in my favor that day. BUT, as they say, 'no good deed goes unpunished' and when they returned to their parked car to drive home after the court case ended, they found that all the tires had been slashed, all the windows smashed and the rest of the car was just a mass of dents and deep scratches. - And who accused me of being a bad looser?!

But back to Linda who had discovered a part of herself that she never dreamed existed. If I was threatened by any male fans with violence – or threatened with anything else by any female fans, Linda would chin them. So whether I was threatened by violence or sex – Linda would be there to make absolutely certain that I didn't enjoy either.

Damn – I really had created a MONSTER!!!

ROYAL VENGENCE

The Royal Albert Hall for me was the site of many memorable Battles. But I wonder what the fans would have thought if they'd known that after a wild and wooly contest that The Hell's Angels fought against The Red Indian team comprising of Billy White Cloud and Mike Thunder Cloud, if they'd seen us all eating together later that night in 'The Wine and Kebab'. Over our meal we talked about the tour that Bob and I were planning in The Redskin's happy scraping ground in the States. Unfortunately the dates got mixed up and Bob was unable to adjust his schedule to enable the trip to take place. I have often wondered since what adventures we would have experienced if the trip had taken place.

Another match at that venue gave me a little cause for speculation prior to entering the ring, as our contest that night would be fought against an opponent who I had last seen laying unconscious on the dressing room floor with a broken jaw after I had punched him in the chops. Speculation also heightened a tad when I saw the monster French Canadian Bodybuilder, 'Monsieur Montreal' that Vassilios 'pour-moiré' Mantopolous, had that night as a tag-team partner. Mantopolous appeared to be very friendly which made me very suspicious indeed, and I wondered if he may make an attempt to avenge what I had done to him when we last met. Especially as he was now partnered by a virtual mountain of muscle. The massive Canadian entered the ring first for his team, so did I for mine. If there was anything dodgy going to occur I wanted to be aware of it right away. I grabbed the muscleman by his head and he lifted me off the ground like a feather just by standing erect and lifting me with brute strength. He had a neck like a telegraph pole, and it was obviously one of his most powerful assets. I let his head go and gestured to the referee in a way that acknowledged the super strength of my opponent's huge neck. I grabbed his head again as though to demonstrate to the referee just how strong his neck was, and once again he obliged me by lifting me bodily with just the strength of his neck. I turned this scenario into a challenge using a number of methods to make myself as heavy as possible, like wedging both elbows against his upper chest and gripping the very top of his head which really increased the leverage. Something that I had learned very early in my quest to become a wrestler was, that never mind how strong your neck is, it really doesn't take a lot of effort for an opponent who knows what he's doing to completely exhaust it. Very soon Monsieur Montreal didn't want to play that game anymore, and only then did I slip him into a painful grovit-hold that he stood no chance of escaping from at all. I gave Mantopolous 'that look' as he stood on the apron watching the action, then let the muscleman free as I tagged Bob in, and myself out of the ring. The match finally ended after going the distance in a no fall draw.

In the third show 'FANFARE FOR EUROPE', I was featured in one of the triple main event matches that was meant to celebrate Britain's entry into the European Common Market. Brian Maxine wearing his King's crown would be wrestling against Tino Salvador of Italy. Les Kellett would be wrestling against Jacky Rickard of France, and I would be wrestling with Frank Dhondt of Belgium.

If you think you may have heard of Frank Dhondt before you might remember that he was the wrestler who George Kidd had refused to wrestle against, and I got to replace him. I could tell by the look on Frank Dhondt's face that night at the Albert Hall that he remembered his demotion too, and I realized that the daggers from his eyes aimed at my throat looked to be as sharp as ever.

Maxine, Kellett and I were asked to enter the ring together so that we could be introduced as the British team. As we made ready to make our entrance, I told the other two, 'that with a hand like we held we couldn't possibly get trumped.' When asked to explain what I meant, I pointed first to Maxine, next to myself and then to Kellett, and told them,

"Well we have the King, the Queen and the Joker – how can they possibly beat that?"

If I remember correctly I believe that both Maxine and Kellett won their matches without much incident. My own match on the other hand had one incident after another. Initially I decided to give my surly Belgian opponent the benefit of the doubt, and take it comparatively easy with him. He soon proved that he didn't deserve that kind of consideration, and as a result I soon reverted to plan B. Or, in Dhondt's case plan B-B which stood for Belgian-Blood.

I gave him a wrestling lesson that would have made George Kidd proud, and towards the end of the match, as he refused to react to the forearm smashes I had aimed at his chest, I aimed one right into his chops that Pasquale Salvo would have been proud of. As Dhondt hit the canvas I swear I could still see a bloody red mist begin to evaporate where his face had been a split second before. I purposely fell on him and struck him a few more brutal blows before collapsing and rolling off his prone form and just laying alongside him. I draped my arm over my eyes, which from the fan's vantage spot must have appeared that I was shading them from the glare of the bright ring-lights. But then as I staggered to my feet and stood shakily above my shattered opponent the crowed screamed and cheered loudly as they saw that my head, face, chest and shoulders were just one mass of red, red blood. By the time my opponent had been counted out, and I had had my hand raised in victory and was leaving the ring I must have looked completely scarlet from head to toe. As I began my march back to the dressing room a man leapt out of his seat and began to help support me,

"I'm a Doctor," he told me, "let me help you." I allowed him to help me back to the dressing room, and after we entered he inquired,

"Where are you cut?"

"I think it's a tooth -----." I began, but couldn't finish as he was now prizing my mouth open.

"I can't see any missing!" he was telling me.

"The tooth is in my elbow, not my mouth." I told him as I showed him the bloody wound in my arm. I had hit Dhondt so hard in the mouth that one of his teeth became embedded in my elbow, and the reason I had draped my arm over my eyes when I lay alongside him wasn't in an effort to shade my eyes from the lights, but to allow the blood to pour from the gash in my elbow all over my own head and face.

Anything at all to get as much reaction as I could from the fans was my motto.

THE GREEN GOWN

The impact on the television audience made by the total destruction of my 'Mary Quant' metallic gold tights was so immense that I was constantly thinking of ways in which I could at least equal, if not surpass the attention it generated.

It didn't take long to devise a plan, but I had to patiently wait until I was pitted against an opponent who I considered worthy enough to be part of it, as I certainly didn't want to waste my idea on one of the many spoilers in our sport.

The perfect opportunity presented itself when I learned that I was going to be wrestling against the 'Darling of Doncaster' Mick McMichael on TV in one of London's Baths Halls. Mick was a great opponent for me, a very good wrestler with the ability to turn up the heat at just the right time. I immediately went to work on my next TV outfit, a mass of Green and Silver glitter with metallic Green 'Mary Quant' tights, metallic silver trunks and multi-color metallic boots. The Gown itself was not only designed to be as flashy as possible, but as brittle as possible also.

As I expected my entrance wearing a brand new look blasted the roof off, and I milked it for all it was worth. Time and again the referee demanded that I disrobe so that the contest could commence, but I needed to draw out the agony to the max in order to aggravate both the fans and my opponent past the point of boiling. I swaggered arrogantly, sneered with contempt at my audience and opponent alike.

At exactly the right time after the audience and Mick could stand no more of my posturing, posing and pouting Mick struck. He tore my new flashy gown right off my back and ripped it to shreds. The fans exploded with delight and disbelief, soon the ringside fans were gathering up the remnants of my gown and draping themselves with them as I protested and screamed my outrage.

And now the scene was set and we had succeeded in jump starting the story and giving me a very legitimate reason to go after my opponent with the most hostile intent imaginable. Although I won the contest, that as I well knew was not what the fans present and watching on TV would remember most, and for a long time to come fans delighted in reminding me of the night I lost my new gown.

I do believe I achieved the desired effect, because even as I write these words almost four decades later they are still showing that contest on British television.

MONEY

There has been very much speculation concerning the reason why, at what many considered the zenith of my career, I would up and leave the promotions that I had dreamed of wrestling for since I was hardly more than a child. Well I'll answer that question right now, no big mystery; it was just a question of Money!

From the time that I had my very first professional wrestling match I had gauged my progress, worth and standing in the business by the amount of money I received for each match. Since I had began wrestling for the 'Big Time' Joint Promotions, I had gradually pushed my wages up from 4 pounds a match to 25 pounds for a non main event contest, and 30 pounds for a main event contest around the regular arenas. For TV and the bigger shows, such as the Ice-Rinks, the Albert Hall and Title matches I would receive a lot more. But it was the regular arenas that I was concerned about, and had been pushing for what seemed an unreasonably long time for another increase. By the time I did get the increase I was already feeling that it was too little too late, plus they were regularly billing me in a semi-main event contests with main event wrestlers, so that they wouldn't have to pay me the extra money. I countered that by giving them a list of names that I considered main event wrestlers, and told them that if I was booked to wrestle any of them I would still expect to be paid my main event fee even if they billed the contest as a semi-main event.

EVENTUALLY I got what I wanted, but again they countered by crossing some of the names I had given them off my list. Two examples was Johnny Kwango, and another was Brian Maxine who they told me they didn't consider to be Main-Event quality. I countered their counter by stating that if they didn't agree that certain wrestlers that were on my list were not main event caliber, then they should never, ever book them to wrestle with me, as I didn't agree with their assessment. They finally agreed, but then told me in no uncertain terms that I was never to make a request for a further increase in wages as long as they employed me, and that I had received the last increase in wages that I would ever get.

So that was how much they estimated I was worth, and according to them I would never be worth more. I had just received my increase to 30 and 35 pounds but under the circumstances I was not happy at all.

I was in a very depressed state of mind when I arrived back at Telford Avenue after leaving Dale Martin's Office, and as I opened my front door and entered the house the phone rang. I answered it and was very surprised to find I was talking to Orig Williams, I was even more surprised to find out what he wanted to talk to me about. - Then I was amazed that after he made me an offer that meant leaving Joint Promotions and join him that instead of telling him to piss off, I accepted his offer.

When I told Joint Promotions of my decision, I was told that Mick McManus said,

"Don't take any notice of him, - he's not going anywhere, - he's only after more money."

Well he sure got the last part right, but as I wasn't going to get 'more money' from Joint Promotions I WAS going somewhere, HOPEFULLY SOMEWHERE WERE I WOULD FIND GREENER PASTURES.

The last show I did for Dale Martins was in a venue just off Bayswater Road in London and a very officious Mike Judd was in charge. After my match Johnny Dale came to speak to me, and asked me if I really thought I was making a wise decision. He also hinted at a lack of appreciation on my part after Dale Martins was not only responsible for making me a Star, but had also created my image and persona!

Can you imagine that shit?!

He was then joined by Mike Judd who more or less echoed Johnny Dale, and then as a parting shot he said,

"Well, goodbye and good luck in the Welsh Hills – I'm sure we'll be seeing you back here in the very near future."

"Thanks Mike," I replied, "but, I'm not so sure you're right."

I have often been named an innovator in my approach to professional wrestling after I had began wrestling for Joint Promotions, but it seemed now that I was also an innovator in my departure from Joint Promotions, as right on my heels on the pathway that I had blazed came first Mr. TV Jackie Pallo, Then the Best masked man since Dr. Death, Kendo Nagasaki, and last but not least the hard-man Les Kellett. Collectively we proved that not only was there life for a professional wrestler after Joint Promotions, there was also a life with much richer rewards.

****

For most of my young life my dream had been to wrestle full time for Joint Promotions, I had achieved my dream with flying colors. Not only a Joint Promotions wrestler, but a MAIN EVENT Joint Promotions wrestler. I was at the pinnacle of my game and after twelve and a half years I was giving it up to Join with Orig Williams - the biggest huckster in professional wrestling since Sir Athol Oakley. I was told I would not be successful - Where have I heard that one before?!

I would be leaving Joint Promotions for the independents where anything and everything was acceptable including the Wild, Wild Women of British Pro Wrestling! Learn all about it when you join me for BOOK 5 - **'IMAGINE WHAT I COULD DO TO YOU.'**

PHOTOS

Linda at Battersea Park Zoo, 1964.

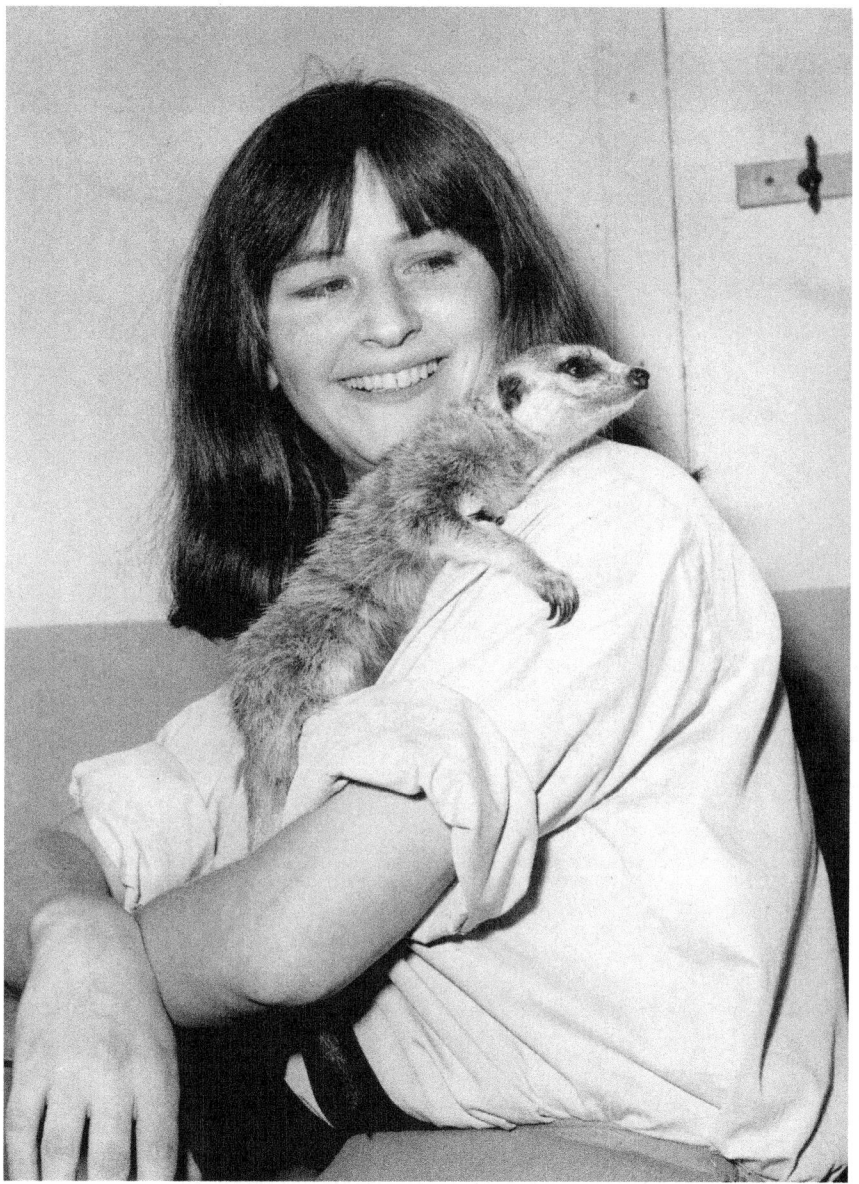

SADIST IN SEQUINS

Linda at Battersea Park Zoo, 1965.

Linda at Battersea Park Zoo, 1965.

Homework for Tradition, 1965.

Amanda and Jean, 1967.

Dale Martin's Gym, 1967.

My beautiful baby, Amanda, 1968.

Sons, Vincent and Adrian, 1968.

Hell's Angels in white satin, 1969.

Me in Manchester, 1969.

SADIST IN SEQUINS

Mick McManus, Me, and others pulling down a wall, 1969.

Me with my biggest fan, 1970.

SADIST IN SEQUINS

Me and Linda in Edinborough, 1970.

Hell's Angels in black leather, 1970.

Hell's Angels in silver leather, 1970.

Linda, 1970.

Have bed, Will travel, 1971.

Linda, 1971.

Wrestlers on strike, 1971.

Wrestlers on strike at Fairfield Hall, 1971.

Training the trainers in Perth, Scotland, 1971.

Me in the movie *Canterbury Tales*, 1971.

Me, The Fighter, in *Canterbury Tales*, 1971.

Me with Derek Dedman from *Canterbury Tales*, 1971.

Me vs. Les Kellett, 1971.

Winning submission on world champion, George Kidd, 1971.

SADIST IN SEQUINS

Kings Road, Chelsea, 1972.

The Gladiators recording of "Tip Toe through the Tulips," 1972.

"Mad Fred the Ear Biter"

Printed in Great Britain
by Amazon